KOREA

KOREA

JAPAN

G000069652

NORTHERN
MARIANA
ISLANDS

GUAM

MICRONESIA

MARSHALL ISLANDS

NAURU

KIRIBATI

PAPUA NEW
GUINEA

SOLOMON
ISLANDS

TUVALU

FRENCH
POLYNESIA

VANUATU

FIJI

WESTERN
SAMOA

AMERICAN
SAMOA

NIUE

NEW CALEDONIA

TONGA

AUSTRALIA

NEW
ZEALAND

The
Economist

POCKET ASIA

The Economist

— POCKET —

ASIA

John Andrews

Fourth Edition

THE ECONOMIST IN ASSOCIATION WITH
PROFILE BOOKS LTD

Published by Profile Books Ltd,
62 Queen Anne Street, London W1M 9LA

First published by The Economist Books Ltd 1993

This fourth edition published by Profile Books Ltd
in association with The Economist 1998

Printed by
LEGO. S.p.a – Vicenza – Italy

A CIP catalogue record for this book is available
from the British Library

ISBN 1 86197 076 5

Contents

INTRODUCTION

Asia is a continent of contrasts: extremes of geography; myriad languages and ethnic groups; philosophies and religions both ancient and modern. There are rich Asians, such as the Japanese, and desperately poor Asians, such as the Afghans. But what defines Asia, east of the Arab world and Iran, for most outsiders is its collective sense of dynamic change. By the growing weight of its population and the pace of its economic development Asia is bidding to be the centre of the world. The process will involve political challenges going well beyond Asia's frontiers.

People power

By the end of this century, more than 60% of humanity will live on the landmass of Asia. Out of some 3.75 billion Asians most will still be relatively poor: one in every three will be Chinese and one in every four Indian.

By contrast, the rich will be relatively few: perhaps 130m Japanese; 80m Koreans (assuming the potential reunification of the peninsula's North and South); 3m in Singapore; 25m Chinese in Taiwan; and 6m Chinese (barring any influx of migrants from China) in Hong Kong. Their quality of life will be matched or exceeded in the region only by the Australians and New Zealanders, whose claims to be part of Asia are recent and often disputed.

Discrepancies of wealth tend to breed conflict. But if history is a guide, it is Asia's poor who will suffer most. In the 1990s poverty was the common denominator in all the region's areas of conflict, be they in Afghanistan, Sri Lanka, Myanmar or Tajikistan. The same was true of the stubborn, but ineffectual, communist insurgency in the Philippines. Meanwhile, Asia's various secessionist movements are invariably connected with underdeveloped economies, whether they be the Papuans in Indonesia's Irian Jaya or the Sikhs in India's Punjab.

One general lesson is that any country that fails to increase living standards risks violent unrest. A second lesson is that fast-growing populations and fast-rising living standards are incompatible. The typical Singaporean woman during her child-bearing years will have two children (indeed, statistically slightly under two); her Filipina counterpart will have four; and a Laotian or Bangladeshi perhaps six. Yet when their wealth is compared, the differences are multiplied: per head economic output in Singapore is roughly 75 times the rate in Laos.

To put the same point another way: as "total fertility rates" – the number of children a woman will bear in her fertile years – decline, so prosperity increases. Singapore's rate has dropped steeply from 4.7 in 1965; Bangladesh's rate has fallen only slightly from 6.8.

Such demographic calculations have had a tremendous impact in Asia, and will continue to do so. In 1960 the Philippine population, for example, was almost 30m; by 1990 it had doubled; and by 2010 it is estimated that it will almost have trebled.

For political leaders such exponential growth in population poses near-impossible challenges to provide adequate employment, housing, education and health care. If they fail, the consequence is likely to be social instability.

Changing the figures

The country most aware of this is the People's Republic of China. Although Mao Zedong once preached that "people are the most valuable resource" – so the more the better – since 1979 China has pursued a "one-child" policy, often with Draconian strictness. One consequence has been a huge drop in the fertility rate; another has been a generation of spoilt single children (especially boys, because of female infanticide); a third is likely, in the future, to be a society demographically distorted, with too few young to provide economically for the elderly.

No country, whether for cultural, religious or political reasons, is likely to imitate China's dictatorial approach to family planning. Some, like Singapore (which in the mid-1990s was trying to increase its population growth, so effective were past efforts to decrease it), will use financial incentives. Most will hope that better education will lead to declining birth rates (the evidence is that when women become literate they have fewer children). But better education cannot come without economic development. The challenge, therefore, is for the poor countries of Asia to emulate the economic success of rich Asia.

Economic miracles

In the early 1980s Asia's share of the world economy was roughly one-fifth; by the end of the century it will be around one-third. By almost every yardstick, and despite the revelation in the late 1990s of serious flaws in many banking systems, Asia has been home to the most impressive economic growth in history: Japan, China and the "Asian dragons" of Hong Kong, South Korea, Singapore and Taiwan have all managed, since the end of the second world war, to double their economic output within a single decade, and have done so more than once. By contrast, no country – not even America in the last century – had managed it even once before.

And the high levels of saving and relatively low levels of foreign debt-service enjoyed by most of the East Asian countries should help them recover from the economic crisis that broke in late 1997.

The Confucian edge

One feature of Asia's economic success after 1945 is that the miracles have occurred mainly in East and South-East Asia. The reasons are several. Japan was already an advanced and highly industrialised country, and its recovery was helped by the restructuring carried out under the aegis of the American occupation. In addition, development was given a boost by land-reform programmes imposed in South Korea by the Americans and in Taiwan by the incoming Kuomintang. But probably the most important reasons are Confucianist culture – with its stress on consensus and obedience to authority – and the propensity to save. This combination helped China's economy, even during the doctrinaire era of Mao Zedong, to grow almost twice as fast as India's.

Confucianism, however, has no hold beyond East Asia and the Chinese diaspora (whose influence runs from Myanmar across to the Philippines). Is non-Confucianist Asia therefore doomed to lag in relative poverty? Rationally there is no reason why it should, or else how would non-Confucianist Europe and America have advanced? What is needed, however, is the freedom for market forces to reward the efficient. Probably the single biggest reason for India's slow economic progress (sometimes derided as the "Hindu rate of growth") was the post-colonial, Fabian socialist obsession with protectionism and state control of the economy. Only when India was in dire straits did Narasimha Rao's new government in 1991 have the political courage to begin economic and financial deregulation.

Helping yourself, helping others

Fortunately, such efforts do not have to be made in isolation. In the 1980s Japan was a huge direct investor in South-East Asia, investing in car factories in Thailand, electronics businesses in Singapore and petrochemical plants in Indonesia. The process has been imitated in the 1990s by Asia's other capital-rich economies, notably Taiwan, Hong Kong and Singapore. Inevitably, the investment will spread to wherever it is most welcome, including previously autarkic countries such as India. With the investment will come new technologies and methods of work. To use a Japanese analogy, economic development is like the formation of geese in flight: Japan will be at the head, and in its wake will be those countries that learn to fly.

However, economic development will involve political change. Political stability is a pre-requisite for rapid economic development, but such development inevitably brings political strains – as in the pro-democracy demonstrations in China's Tiananmen Square in 1989. Moreover, when economic success is achieved, it brings strains of a different form, witness western – especially American – complaints over the persistent trade surpluses of Japan.

Political evolution

The most important political feature of modern Asia has been the discrediting of communism. Only North Korea still appears to take the doctrine seriously (although the reality has been a straightforward dictatorship and personality cult). In China and Indochina, Marxism has more or less given way to a crude form of capitalism, and communist insurgencies elsewhere in Asia are all weak.

Yet in 1975, when South Vietnam fell to the communist North, it seemed as though a communist tide might flow inexorably through South-East Asia. That it was stopped was due in part to capitalism's ability, in glaring contrast to Vietnamese communism, to deliver prosperity; it was due also to America's determination that "the dominoes should not fall". Through the 1970s and much of the 1980s countries from Thailand to the Philippines received American economic aid and military assistance. By the end of the 1980s even the poorest capitalist country east of India was better off than the richest communist country. Add the collapse of the Soviet Union in 1991 and communism has surely disappeared as a political choice for Asia.

But the process of defeating communism has aroused different problems. The most obvious is that economic growth has produced an Asian middle class which increasingly demands political liberalism. In 1987 the impatience of South Korea's middle class helped topple the dictatorship of Chun Doo Hwan; in 1992 demonstrations by the Bangkok middle class forced General Suchinda to step down as prime minister. Even the "people power" that in 1986 ousted the corrupt Ferdinand Marcos from power in the Philippines had a large middle-class component. In short, the authoritarian "strongmen" of the present and recent past – men such as Suharto in Indonesia, Ershad in Bangladesh, Zia in Pakistan, Ne Win in Myanmar or, indeed, Lee Kuan Yew in Singapore – have become anachronisms.

What comes next?

What will replace them is not entirely clear. Although the Indian subcontinent has a cultural affinity to the adversarial democracy of the West (indeed, India boasts of being the world's biggest democracy), South-East and East Asia have the habits of consensus and hierarchy. The consequence so far has been one-party rule even in the context of democracy: the Liberal Democratic Party, until 1993, in Japan; the People's Action Party in Singapore; the Kuomintang in Taiwan. The danger is that when a ruling party is electorally impregnable its policies will be neither properly challenged nor debated.

Conceivably, opposition parties will become less puny over time, especially if (as happened to Japan's LDP) ruling parties become excessively corrupt. A more likely channel for dissent, however, will be (again as was true in Japan) factionalism within the ruling party. This is one way, indeed, in which China could become a politically plural society without first passing through destabilising turmoil.

Foreign dealings in the new world order

Paradoxically, Asia is as much disturbed as pleased by the discrediting of communism, the demise of the Soviet Union and the consequent end of the Cold War. The reason is that without a rival superpower to keep in check, America is becoming ever less willing, and certainly less financially able, to act as the policeman of the Asia-Pacific region. Although American officials have promised to maintain a security presence in the region, the fact is that as long ago as 1990 the Department of Defense announced that American forces in Asia would be cut by 15,000, more than a tenth of the total, within two years, and this was before America lost its military bases in the Philippines. True, Japan and South Korea have picked up more of America's costs and Singapore has provided military facilities to keep America engaged in the area, but the *pax Americana* – in place since the fall of South Vietnam – no longer looks quite as permanent as before.

Others will therefore strive to keep the peace on their own terms. The three obvious candidates are Japan, because of its wealth, and China and India because of their populations. Their ambitions, however, are unlikely to coincide. China fears Japan's "hegemony" just as much as America's, and in any case – like many in Asia – harbours deep resentment over Japan's brutal behaviour during and before the second world war. China and India are likewise ill at ease with each other, having fought a war in 1962 over their still-unresolved border dispute.

Flash-points

Meanwhile, Asia is dotted with flash-points, both actual and potential, from Kashmir, the spur for two wars between Pakistan and India, to the Spratly Islands, variously claimed by China, Taiwan, Vietnam, Brunei, Malaysia and the Philippines. Some long-standing conflicts may well be resolved. For example, a peace agreement for Cambodia was signed in October 1991, and in December 1991 North and South Korea signed a pact of non-aggression. But other tensions will doubtless arise, perhaps in the states of ex-Soviet Central Asia or, notwithstanding the summit in 1989 between the Soviet Union's President Gorbachev and China's Deng Xiaoping, again between Russia and China.

Security questions ... and answers

What will add to the risks is Asia's proliferation of nuclear weapons. China and Russia are admitted nuclear powers; Pakistan, India and possibly North Korea are within a screwdriver or so of possessing nuclear arms. Although Pakistan in 1991 proposed talks with India, China, Russia and America to make the subcontinent nuclear-free, India's fear of China (and its desire to be a regional power) means it is unlikely to step back from the nuclear threshold.

Will a weakening of America's role automatically lead, therefore, to conflict? Not necessarily. With luck, Asia will enjoy enough sustained and collective economic progress to smooth away bilateral tensions. If so, the economic motor will be Japan.

Although the Japanese are constrained by their post-war constitution from projecting military force, and although the impetus for Japan to play a larger security role comes from America and Europe, rather than from Japan's mistrustful neighbours, there are signs that Japan is trying to be more internationally active, not least to protect its investments overseas. At the start of the 1990s Japan took a leading diplomatic role in the Cambodian issue, and in 1992 the Japanese parliament voted to allow Japanese troops to serve (albeit with restrictions) in United Nations peace-keeping operations. Indeed, Japan is quietly hoping that quite soon it will become a permanent member of the UN Security Council.

If Asia were then able to form an equivalent of the Organisation for Security and Co-operation in Europe (OSCE), Asian countries as they enter the 21st century would be characterised by multilateral confidence rather than bilateral distrust. Meanwhile, however insurmountable Asia's problems sometimes seem, at least some of its countries have mustered the will and economic energy to confront them.

=== Part I ===

COUNTRY RANKINGS

Size and society

Area *'000 sq km*

1	China	9,561.0	18	New Zealand	268.7
2	Australia	7,686.8	19	Laos	236.8
3	India	3,287.6	20	Kirgizstan	199.0
4	Kazakhstan	2,717.0	21	Cambodia	181.0
5	Indonesia	1,904.6	22	Bangladesh	144.0
6	Mongolia	1,565.0	23	Tajikistan	143.0
7	Pakistan	746.0	24	Nepal	140.8
8	Myanmar	676.6	25	North Korea	120.5
9	Afghanistan	625.2	26	South Korea	99.2
10	Thailand	514.0	27	Sri Lanka	65.6
11	Turkmenistan	488.0	28	Bhutan	46.5
12	Papua New Guinea	461.7	29	Taiwan	36.0
13	Uzbekistan	447.0	30	Solomon Islands	27.6
14	Japan	377.7	31	New Caledonia	19.1
15	Malaysia	329.7	32	Fiji	18.3
16	Vietnam	329.6	33	Vanuatu	12.2
17	Philippines	300.0	34	Brunei	5.8

Population *millions, 1995 estimates*

1	China	1,217.6	18	Sri Lanka	18.4
2	India	935.7	19	Australia	18.3
3	Indonesia	193.8	20	Kazakhstan	16.4
4	Pakistan	129.8	21	Cambodia	9.8
5	Japan	125.8	22	Hong Kong	6.0
6	Bangladesh	120.4		Tajikistan	6.0
7	Vietnam	73.0	24	Kirgizstan	5.0
8	Philippines	70.3		Turkmenistan	5.0
9	Thailand	59.4	26	Laos	4.7
10	South Korea	45.5	27	Papua New Guinea	4.1
11	Myanmar	45.0	28	New Zealand	3.6
12	North Korea	24.0	29	Singapore	3.0
13	Uzbekistan	23.0	30	Mongolia	2.0
14	Nepal	21.9	31	Bhutan	1.6
15	Taiwan	21.1	32	Fiji	0.8
16	Malaysia	20.7	33	Macau	0.4
17	Afghanistan	18.9	34	Solomon Islands	0.4

Population growth *average annual growth 1980–95, %*

1	Afghanistan	4.0		Papua New Guinea	2.2
2	Pakistan	3.0	14	Vietnam	2.1
3	Turkmenistan	3.0	15	India	2.0
4	Cambodia	2.9	16	Myanmar	1.9
5	Laos	2.8	17	Indonesia	1.8
6	Bhutan	2.6		North Korea	1.8
	Tajikistan	2.6		Singapore	1.8
8	Malaysia	2.5	20	Kirgizstan	1.5
	Nepal	2.5		Thailand	1.5
10	Uzbekistan	2.4	22	Australia	1.4
11	Philippines	2.3		Hong Kong	1.4
12	Bangladesh	2.2		Sri Lanka	1.4

Population density *population per sq km, 1995*

1	Macau	20,750	18	North Korea	198
2	Hong Kong	6,252	19	Pakistan	169
3	Singapore	4,896	20	Nepal	157
4	Bangladesh	920	21	Micronesia	143
5	Maldives	850	22	Tonga	134
6	Taiwan	571	23	China	129
7	South Korea	454	24	Thailand	114
8	Nauru	439	25	Kiribati	109
9	Japan	333	26	Indonesia	107
10	Tuvalu	317	27	Northern Mariana Islands	95
11	India	313	28	Cook Islands	80
12	Sri Lanka	280	29	Myanmar	69
13	Guam	242	30	Malaysia	61
14	Marshall Islands	241	31	Cambodia	57
15	American Samoa	240	32	Uzbekistan	55
16	Philippines	230	33	Brunei	54
17	Vietnam	226	34	French Polynesia	48

Oldest populations *% aged over 60, 1995*

1	Japan	20		North Korea	7
2	Australia	15		Papua New Guinea	7
	New Zealand	15		Tajikistan	7
4	Hong Kong	14		Thailand	7
5	Kazakhstan	11		Uzbekistan	7
6	China	10		Vietnam	7
7	Kirgizstan	9		Macau	7
	Solomon Islands	9	22	Bangladesh	6
	South Korea	9		Malaysia	6
10	India	8		Mongolia	6
	Sri Lanka	8	25	Laos	5
	Taiwan	8		Nepal	5
13	Indonesia	7		Philippines	5
	Myanmar	7			

Human development index[a] *1994*

1	Japan	94.0	15	Western Samoa	68.4
2	New Zealand	93.7	16	Philippines	67.2
3	Australia	93.1	17	Indonesia	66.8
4	Hong Kong	91.4	18	Uzbekistan	66.2
5	Singapore	90.0	19	Mongolia	66.1
6	South Korea	89.0	20	Kirgizstan	63.5
7	Brunei	88.2	21	China	62.6
8	Fiji	86.3	22	Maldives	61.1
9	Thailand	83.3	23	Tajikistan	58.0
10	Malaysia	83.2	24	Vietnam	55.7
11	North Korea	76.5	25	Vanuatu	54.7
12	Turkmenistan	72.3	26	Papua New Guinea	52.5
13	Sri Lanka	71.1	27	Myanmar	47.5
14	Kazakhstan	70.9	28	Laos	45.9

a See Notes on data, page 224.

Living standards

Life expectancy: men *age in years, 1995*

1	Japan	77	13	China	68
2	Hong Kong	76		South Korea	68
3	Macau	75	15	North Korea	67
4	Australia	74		Thailand	67
	Singapore	74		Western Samoa	67
6	Brunei	73	18	Tajikistan	66
	New Zealand	73		Uzbekistan	66
8	Taiwan	72	20	Vietnam	65
9	New Caledonia	71	21	Kazakhstan	64
10	Fiji	70		Maldives	64
	Sri Lanka	70		Mongolia	64
12	Malaysia	69		Philippines	64

Life expectancy: women *age in years, 1995*

1	Japan	83		Kazakhstan	74
2	Hong Kong	81		Malaysia	74
3	Australia	80		North Korea	74
	Macau	80	16	Kirgizstan	72
5	New Zealand	79		Thailand	72
	Singapore	79		Uzbekistan	72
7	Brunei	78	19	China	71
8	Taiwan	77		Western Samoa	71
9	South Korea	76	21	Vietnam	70
10	New Caledonia	75	22	Mongolia	68
	Sri Lanka	75		Philippines	68
12	Fiji	74		Turkmenistan	68

Infant mortality *number of deaths per 1,000 live births, 1995*

1	Afghanistan	163	12	Maldives	52
2	Cambodia	108	13	Indonesia	51
3	Nepal	91	14	Turkmenistan	46
4	Laos	90	15	Tajikistan	42
	Pakistan	90	16	Solomon Islands	41
6	Myanmar	83		Vanuatu	41
7	Bangladesh	79		Vietnam	41
8	India	68	19	Philippines	39
9	Papua New Guinea	64	20	Thailand	35
10	Kiribati	55	21	China	34
	Mongolia	55			

Education spending *% of GDP, 1995*

1	Taiwan	6.5	10	India	2.9
2	Malaysia	5.3	11	Pakistan	2.7
3	Japan	5.0	12	China	2.6
4	South Korea	4.5	13	Hong Kong	2.5
5	Australia	4.4	14	Philippines	2.4
	New Zealand	4.4	15	Afghanistan	1.8
7	Thailand	3.8	16	Bangladesh	1.7
8	Singapore	3.3	17	Laos	1.6
9	Sri Lanka	3.2	18	Indonesia	1.3

Doctors and patients *number of people per doctor, 1995*

1	Kirgizstan	303	16	Vietnam	2,279
2	Turkmenistan	306	17	Malaysia	2,441
3	Mongolia	371	18	India	2,459
4	North Korea	419	19	Thailand	4,416
5	Tajikistan	424	20	Laos	4,446
6	Uzbekistan	501	21	Afghanistan	4,797
7	New Zealand	518	22	Sri Lanka	6,843
8	Australia	559	23	Indonesia	7,028
9	Japan	608	24	Philippines	8,273
10	Singapore	714	25	Cambodia	11,996
11	South Korea	951	26	Myanmar	12,528
12	Taiwan	961	27	Bangladesh	12,884
13	China	1,063	28	Nepal	13,634
14	Hong Kong	1,211	29	Kazakhstan	21,970
15	Pakistan	1,923			

Television *number of televisions per 1,000 people*

1	Australia	641	16	Indonesia	147
2	Japan	619	17	Afghanistan	125
3	New Zealand	508	18	Philippines	121
4	Singapore	362	19	South Korea	115
5	Hong Kong	359	20	Vietnam	110
6	North Korea	323	21	Myanmar	76
7	Taiwan	312	22	Sri Lanka	66
8	Kazakhstan	266	23	India	61
9	Tajikistan	258	24	Mongolia	59
10	China	250	25	Pakistan	22
11	Malaysia	231	26	Cambodia	8
12	Thailand	221	27	Bangladesh	7
13	Turkmenistan	217	28	Laos	7
14	Uzbekistan	183	29	Nepal	3
15	Papua New Guinea	166	30	Kirgizstan	3

Computers *number of personal computers per 1,000 people*

1	Australia	275.8	8	Thailand	15.3
2	New Zealand	222.7	9	Philippines	11.4
3	Singapore	172.4	10	Indonesia	3.7
4	Japan	152.5	11	China	2.2
5	South Korea	120.8	12	India	1.3
6	Hong Kong	116.0	13	Pakistan	1.2
7	Malaysia	39.7	14	Sri Lanka	1.1

The economy

GDP[a] *$bn, 1996*

1	Japan	4,599.7	10	Philippines	83.8
2	China	824.0	11	New Zealand	65.9
3	South Korea	484.8	12	Pakistan	60.2
4	Australia	391.1	13	Bangladesh	30.7
5	Taiwan	272.3	14	Sri Lanka	13.9
6	Indonesia	227.4	15	Nepal	4.4
7	Hong Kong	154.3	16	Laos	1.9
8	Malaysia	99.3	17	Mongolia	1.0
9	Singapore	94.1	18	Bhutan	0.3

Economic growth *average annual GDP growth, 1991–96, %*

1	China	12.1	10	Nepal	4.9
2	Malaysia	8.7	11	Pakistan	4.8
3	Singapore	8.6	12	Bangladesh	4.5
4	Indonesia	7.3	13	Australia	3.8
5	South Korea	7.1	14	Philippines	3.4
6	Taiwan	6.3	15	New Zealand	3.2
7	Bhutan	6.2	16	Laos	2.6
8	Hong Kong	5.3	17	Japan	1.4
9	Sri Lanka	5.2			

Inflation *%, 1996*

1	Japan	0.2	13	China	8.3
2	Singapore	1.3	14	Philippines	8.4
3	New Zealand	2.3	15	India	8.9
4	Australia	2.6	16	Pakistan	10.4
5	Bangladesh	2.7	17	Cambodia	10.6
6	Taiwan	3.0	18	Laos	13.1
7	Malaysia	3.6	19	Sri Lanka	15.9
8	South Korea	5.0	20	Kirgizstan	30.3
9	Thailand	5.9	21	Kazakhstan	39.2
10	Hong Kong	6.0	22	Uzbekistan	64.0
11	Vietnam	6.5	23	Tajikistan	443.0
12	Indonesia	8.0	24	Turkmenistan	992.0

Debt service ratio[a] *%, 1996*

1	Cambodia	0.6	8	Thailand	10.2
2	Hong Kong	0.8	9	Bangladesh	13.3
3	Vietnam	5.2	10	Philippines	16.0
4	Laos	5.8	11	India	27.9
5	Sri Lanka	7.3	12	Indonesia	30.9
6	Malaysia	7.8	13	Pakistan	35.3
7	China	9.9			

GDP per head $, 1996

1	Japan	36,575	10	Indonesia	1,175
2	Singapore	30,940	11	Sri Lanka	760
3	Hong Kong	24,440	12	China	680
4	Australia	21,385	13	Pakistan	465
5	New Zealand	18,455	14	Mongolia	405
6	Taiwan	12,740	15	Laos	390
7	South Korea	10,645	16	Bangladesh	255
8	Malaysia	4,800	17	Bhutan	200
9	Philippines	1,190		Nepal	200

Purchasing power GDP per head in PPP[a], $, 1995

1	Hong Kong	23,290	17	Papua New Guinea	2,420
2	Singapore	22,770	18	Uzbekistan	2,370
3	Japan	22,110	19	Vanuatu	2,290
4	Australia	18,940	20	Pakistan	2,230
5	Taiwan	16,520	21	Solomon Islands	2,190
6	New Zealand	16,360	22	Western Samoa	2,030
7	South Korea	11,450	23	Mongolia	1,950
8	Malaysia	9,020	24	Kirgizstan	1,800
9	Thailand	7,540	25	India	1,400
10	Fiji	5,780	26	Bangladesh	1,380
11	Indonesia	3,800	27	Bhutan	1,260
12	Sri Lanka	3,250	28	Brunei	1,260
13	China	3,120	29	Nepal	1,170
14	Maldives	3,080	30	Tajikistan	920
15	Kazakhstan	3,010	31	Afghanistan	800
16	Philippines	2,850			

Agriculture's contribution to GDP %, 1995

1	Myanmar	63	17	China	21
2	Afghanistan	53	18	Fiji	20
3	Laos	52	19	Indonesia	17
4	Cambodia	51	20	Malaysia	13
5	Kirgizstan	44	21	Kazakhstan	12
6	Bhutan	42	22	New Zealand	11
7	Nepal	42		Thailand	11
8	Bangladesh	31	24	South Korea	7
9	Niue	30	25	Australia	3
	North Korea	30		Taiwan	3
11	India	29	27	Brunei	2
12	Vietnam	28		Japan	2
13	Pakistan	26	29	Hong Kong	1
	Papua New Guinea	26	30	Macau	0
15	Sri Lanka	23		Singapore	0
16	Philippines	22			

a See Notes on data, page 222–224.

Arms, energy and tourism

Regular armed forces[a] *total number, '000, 1996*

1	China	2,930.0	16	Australia	56.0
2	India	1,145.0	17	Singapore	53.9
3	North Korea	1,128.0	18	Kazakhstan	40.0
4	South Korea	633.0	19	Laos	37.0
5	Pakistan	587.0	20	Nepal	35.0
6	Vietnam	572.0	21	Uzbekistan	25.0
7	Myanmar	286.0	22	Mongolia	21.1
8	Indonesia	274.5	23	Turkmenistan	11.0
9	Thailand	259.0	24	New Zealand	10.0
10	Japan	240.0	25	Kirgizstan	7.0
11	Sri Lanka	125.3	26	Brunei	4.9
12	Bangladesh	115.5	27	Fiji	3.9
13	Malaysia	114.5	28	Papua New Guinea	3.8
14	Philippines	106.5	29	Tajikistan	3.0
15	Cambodia	88.5			

Energy use *kg per person, oil equivalent, 1994*

1	Singapore	6,556	13	China	647
2	Australia	5,173	14	Tajikistan	642
3	Japan	3,825	15	Indonesia	393
4	Kazakhstan	3,710	16	Philippines	364
5	Turkmenistan	3,198	17	Pakistan	255
6	South Korea	3,000	18	India	243
7	Hong Kong	2,280	19	Papua New Guinea	236
8	Uzbekistan	1,886	20	Sri Lanka	111
9	Malaysia	1,711	21	Vietnam	105
10	Mongolia	1,079	22	Bangladesh	65
11	Thailand	770	23	Laos	38
12	Kirgizstan	715	24	Nepal	23

Tourism receipts *$bn, 1996*

1	Hong Kong	10.80	17	Fiji	0.32
2	China	10.20	18	French Polynesia	0.28
3	Australia	8.70	19	Maldives	0.26
4	Thailand	8.50	20	Sri Lanka	0.17
5	Singapore	7.90	21	Nepal	0.13
6	Indonesia	6.10	22	Cambodia	0.12
7	South Korea	5.40	23	Pakistan	0.11
8	Japan	4.10		New Caledonia	0.11
9	Malaysia	3.90	25	Vietnam	0.09
10	Macau	3.50	26	Papua New Guinea	0.06
11	Taiwan	3.10		Myanmar	0.06
12	India	3.03	28	Laos	0.05
13	Philippines	2.80		Cook Islands	0.05
14	New Zealand	2.40	30	Bangladesh	0.04
15	Guam	1.40		Brunei	0.04
16	Northern Mariana Islands	0.67	32	Mongolia	0.02

a All service men and women on full-time duty (including conscripts and long-term assignments from the reserves).

═══ Part II ═══
COUNTRY PROFILES

AFGHANISTAN

Total area	625,225 sq km	Population	18.9m
GDP	$2.4bn	GDP per head	$150
Capital	Kabul	Other cities	Qandahar, Herat, Mazar-i-Sharif

Afghanistan has been doomed by geography and ethnic differences to constant warfare. It is a landlocked country surrounded by instability from Iran in the west through the Muslim republics of what was the Soviet Union to the north. Without political stability, the economic prospects of one of the world's poorest nations remain grim.

History: the "great game"

Afghanistan has always been the arena for the "great game" of outside powers. The list of invaders runs from Cyrus II in the 6th century BC and Alexander the Great in the 4th century BC to the Russians in the late 20th century AD.

Afghanistan finally emerged as a united country in the 18th century, under Ahmad Shah Durrani. However, when Durrani died in 1773, the country was riven by tribal rivalries and by the competing ambitions of Russia and Britain. In the 19th century the British invaded twice in order to maintain Afghanistan as a buffer between British India and the expanding Russian empire. In 1919, after the third Anglo-Afghan war, Britain signed the treaty of Rawalpindi, giving Afghanistan the right to conduct its own foreign policy. Before signing the treaty's final document in 1921, the Afghans also concluded a treaty of friendship with the Bolshevik regime in Russia, thus becoming the first nation to recognise the Soviet government.

Politics: the Russian connection

From the 1920s, when the anti-British Amanullah instituted social reforms (such as founding co-educational schools and advocating the unveiling of women), there has been a tension between Muslim conservatism and a Russian-influenced radicalism. This was true even during the long reign, beginning in 1933, of King Muhammad Zahir Shah. The king pursued a policy of non-alignment; his cousin, Muhammad Daud Khan, prime minister from 1953 to 1963, was intent on using Soviet aid to modernise the country.

In 1973 Zahir was deposed and Afghanistan was declared a republic with Daud, who renounced his royal titles, as head of state, prime minister and minister of foreign affairs and defence. In April 1978 Daud was killed in a

Soviet-backed coup and was succeeded as president by Nur Muhammad Taraki, the head of the Khalq ("Masses") faction of the communist People's Democratic Party of Afghanistan (PDPA), which became the sole legal party. In September 1979 a new coup brought Hafizullah Amin to power with a programme of uncompromising communism. This ended in December with the invasion of the Soviet army, which installed Babrak Karmal, the leader of the moderate Parcham ("Flag") wing of the PDPA, as president.

Paradoxically, the presence of 115,000 Soviet troops proved the eventual undoing of the regime, which was seen as un-Islamic by *mujahideen* ("holy warriors") tribesmen.

In the ensuing civil war as many as 1m Afghans were killed; about 3m fled to Pakistan and 2m to Iran. In 1986 Najibullah Ahmadzai, formerly head of the secret police, deposed Mr Karmal.

The deadlock was broken by the determination of the Soviet Union under Mikhail Gorbachev to leave what had become a political and military quagmire. After an agreement in Geneva in March 1988 all Soviet troops were withdrawn by February 1989. Then in September 1991 America and the Soviet Union agreed that they would cut off all military aid to their Afghan clients by January 1st 1992. In April the Najibullah regime collapsed and the *mujahideen* entered Kabul, but their victory dissolved into internecine fighting, with the fundamentalist – indeed, fanatical – *Taliban* ("student") militia seizing Kabul in 1996.

Society: an ethnic mosaic

Although some 87% of the population is Sunni Muslim (almost all the rest are Shiites), there are many ethnic and tribal differences. About half of the population are Pathans (Pushtun); a quarter are Tajiks. The rest are Uzbek, Turkmen, Baluchi or Hazara. There is a real danger that Afghanistan could yet splinter into its ethnic components.

The economy: foundations of war and drugs

Agriculture is the main economic activity, employing three-fifths of the workforce. There are exports of fruit, nuts, wool, animal skins, carpets and cotton, and natural gas is exported to what was the Soviet Union.

Such exports can do little to reduce the dependence on foreign aid, most of which came from the Soviet Union until its collapse in 1991. *Mujahideen* groups have bought many of their arms by selling hashish and heroin.

Total area	625,225 sq km	% agricultural area	58
Capital	Kabul	Highest point metres	Kommuizma
Other cities	Qandahar, Herat		7,495
	Mazar-i-Sharif	Main rivers	Helmand, Kabul

The economy[a]

GDP $bn	2.4	GDP per head $	150
% av. ann. growth in		GDP per head in purchasing	
real GDP 1991–96	...	power parity $	800

Origins of GDP[a]	% of total	Components of GDP[a]	% of total
Agriculture	53	Private consumption	71
Industry	29	Public consumption	35
of which:		Investment	17
manufacturing	...	Exports	20
Services	2	Imports	50

Structure of manufacturing

% of total

Agric. & food processing	...	Other	...
Textiles & clothing	...	Av. ann. increase in industrial	
Machinery & transport	...	output 1991–96	...

Inflation and exchange rates

Consumer price 1996 av. ann. incr.	...	Afghanis per $ 1997 average	50.6
Av. ann. rate 1991–96	...	Afghanis per $ end-1997	...

Balance of payments, reserves and debt

$m

Exports, goods & services	...	Net capital account	...
Imports, goods & services	...	Net current account	...
Net income	...	Other net investment	...
Net current transfers	...	Net errors & omissions	...
Current-account balance	...	Net change in reserves	...
as % of GDP	...	Level of reserves, end-Dec.	...
Foreign debt	...	Debt service	...
as % of GDP	...	as % of export earnings	...

Principal exports	$m fob	Principal imports	$m fob
Fruit & nuts	93.0	Capital goods	293.0
Carpets	44.0	Food	150.0
Wool	10.0	Textiles	117.0
Karakul skins	3.0	Petroleum products	99.0
Cotton	3.0	Sugar & vegetable oil	53.0
		Tyres	50.0

Main export destinations	% of total	Main origins of imports	% of total
Soviet Union	72.4	Soviet Union	56.3
Germany	3.1	Japan	9.4
India	3.1	Singapore	5.6
Belgium-Luxembourg	2.3	India	2.9
UK	1.9	South Korea	2.2
Ex-Czechoslovakia	1.2	Germany	1.0

Government
System Islamic Taliban movement seized power in September 1996. A six-member ruling council has power until a government is formed.

Climate and topography
Extreme temperatures, especially at high altitudes. Kabul average monthly temperature range is -3°C–25°C. South of country is a desert plateau, north is fertile plains and mountainous.

People and society

Population m	18.9	% under 15	44.0
Pop. per sq km	28.0	% over 60	2.5
% urban	20.0	No. women per 100 men	96.0
% av. ann. growth 1980–95	4.0	Human Development Index	...
No. households m	...		

Life expectancy	yrs	Education	
Men	44	Spending as % of GDP	1.8
Women	45	Years of compulsory education	8
Crude birth rate	5	Adult literacy %	28.9
Crude death rate	22	Primary school enrolment %	24
Infant mortality		Secondary school enrolment %	8
per 1,000 live births	163	Tertiary education enrolment %	1

Workforce	% of total	Consumer goods ownership	
Services	25		per 1,000 people
Industry	14	Cars	2
Agriculture	61	Televisions	125
% of pop. over 15 in workforce	...	Telephones	...
		Personal computers	...

Ethnic groups	% of total	Religious groups	% of total
Pushtun	50	Muslim (Sunni 87, Shia 12)	99
Tajik	25		
Uzbek	9		
Hazarah	3		

Tourism		Health	
Tourist arrivals m	...	Spending as % of GDP	...
Tourism receipts $bn	...	People per doctor	4,797

a 1995.

AUSTRALIA

Total area	7,686,848 sq km	Population	18.3m
GDP	$391.1bn	GDP per head	$21,385
Capital	Canberra	Other cities	Sydney, Melbourne, Brisbane, Perth, Adelaide

Australia – vast, beautiful and sparsely populated – faces a difficult challenge: how to preserve a quality of life that is virtually without equal. To answer that challenge, Australia is attempting to move away from its European roots to seek its future in Asia. But if it is to be more than Asia's "beach, farm and quarry", resource-rich Australia will have to make its society better-educated and harder-working.

History: after Dreamtime

The first Australians were the aborigines, arriving from Asia about 40,000 years before Christ. The first Europeans were the Portuguese in the 16th century, followed by Dutch explorers Wilhelm Janszoon and Abel Tasman in the 17th century. In 1770 Captain James Cook claimed the land for the British Crown. Finally, in 1788 the "First Fleet" arrived in Botany Bay from England with 568 male and 191 female convicts, plus 13 children. The Dreamtime of the 300,000 or so aborigines had been shattered.

Those convicts formed the nucleus for New South Wales, the first British colony. In 1825 Tasmania was made a separate colony. In 1829 Britain formally claimed the whole continent and founded Perth, in the far west. Eventually, there were six British colonies, whose population grew as a result of discovering gold in New South Wales and Victoria. Only South Australia was settled entirely by free men rather than convicts. In 1901 the colonies joined to form a federation of states, independent of Britain, and known as the Commonwealth of Australia.

The British connection

In 1914, at the outbreak of the first world war, Australia promised its support for Britain "to the last shilling". The same attitude held in the second world war, when Australian troops again went to Europe and North Africa (Australia's own war damage was confined to the bombing of Darwin by the Japanese in 1942).

In recent years, however, the ties to the Crown have weakened. Indeed, in 1992 Australia's prime minister, Paul Keating, accused Britain of having "betrayed" Australia, first by exploiting Australia's troops during the second world war, and then by joining the European Community – to the detriment of Australia's agricultural exports – in the 1970s. A further weakening of the ties to the "mother country" is the changing pattern of immigration away from the British Isles.

Politics: a plethora of politicians

The head of state is the British monarch, represented by a governor-general. The federal legislature consists of a 76-member Senate (12 for each state, and 2 each for the Australian Capital Territory of Canberra and its environs and for the Northern Territory) and a 148-member House of Representatives. Elections are held every three years for all of the House of Representatives and for half of the Senate (whose members have six-year terms).

This system of governor and bicameral legislature is replicated at the state level, except in Queensland, which has a one-chamber Legislative Assembly. Add to the system the elected officials at the city, town, municipal and shire level, and Australians – for whom voting is compulsory – may well feel over-represented. However, initiatives to lengthen parliamentary terms have failed: the constitution may be changed only by referendum, and then only if a majority of voters in at least four states are in favour. The states administer areas such as education, agriculture, law enforcement, health and transport; the federal government is responsible for the Australian Capital Territory; the Northern Territory, although not a full state, was given considerable self-government on July 1st 1978. One indication of Australia's democratic instincts is that as early as 1894 South Australia gave women the vote.

Party games

Australia's vibrant, sometimes abrasive, democracy is dominated by four parties: the Australian Labor Party (ALP), the Liberal Party, the National Party of Australia (originally called the Country Party) and the Australian Democrats (who hold the balance of power in the Senate).

The first federal government after the second world war was Labor, but in 1949 a Liberal-Country Party coalition came to power under Robert Menzies. He resigned in 1966 and was succeeded by Harold Holt, who drowned in a swimming accident the following year, then by John Gorton and finally, in 1971, by William McMahon.

The ALP, led by Gough Whitlam, ended the coalition's 23-year supremacy in December 1972, winning 67 of the then 125 seats in the House of Representatives. However, the government did not have a majority in the Senate, which in October 1975 blocked budget legislation. Mr Whit-lam would not resolve the issue by calling a general election, and so the Governor-General, Sir John Kerr, in November dismissed the government, a move which caused widespread outrage. A caretaker Liberal-Country government was then formed under the Liberal leader, Malcolm Fraser; this won large majorities in both houses of parliament in a general election in December 1975.

Labor's turn – and then the Liberals'

In March 1983, nine months earlier than necessary, Mr Fraser called an election, only to be defeated by the ALP under its new leader, Robert ("Bob") Hawke, an Oxford graduate and former leader of Australia's trade unions. Mr Hawke called a meeting of government, trade unions and employers to reach an "Accord" on a prices and incomes policy to foster economic recovery.

Adopting almost Thatcherite policies of market reform, the Hawke government won elections in December 1984, July 1987 and March 1990. The sequence demoralised the opposition: in April 1987 part of the National Party (formerly Country Party) defected to form the New National Party under the right-wing premier of Queensland, Sir Johannes Bjelke-Petersen; in May 1989 the Liberal Party leader, John Howard, stepped down in favour of Andrew Peacock, who resigned after the 1990 defeat in favour of John Hewson.

But as the austerity programme of the Treasurer (chief finance minister), Paul Keating, continued, so the electorate became increasingly disenchanted. In June 1991 Mr Hawke narrowly defeated a challenge for the leadership by Mr Keating, who resigned as treasurer, only to take the leadership, and with it the post of prime minister, in another ALP election in December 1991. Against all the odds Mr Keating in March 1993 led the ALP to yet another federal election win. That triumph, however, was Mr Keating's last. The Liberal/National coalition, again led by John Howard, swept the polls in the federal election of March 1996.

Foreign policy: looking more to Asia

Australia has always felt itself part of the western alliance. In 1951 it signed the ANZUS pact with New Zealand and America for mutual defence in the Pacific, and the prime minister, Mr Menzies (who tried unsuccessfully to outlaw the Communist Party), sent troops to the Korean War. In 1965 Menzies also committed Australia's troops to fight alongside the Americans in Vietnam. When New Zealand in 1984 strained relations with America by refusing to allow nuclear-powered or nuclear-armed ships to dock, Mr Hawke took America's side of the issue.

But Australia has increasingly tried to be part of Asia, rather than an outpost of the Anglo-Saxon world. The effort has had its problems: relations with Indonesia were soured by Indonesia's occupation of East Timor in 1975 and then, in April 1976, by an Australian newspaper story detailing the business activities of President Suharto's family. These problems seemed to have been pushed aside by the signing in December 1989 of an agreement for the joint exploration of the petroleum reserves in the Timor Gap, the site of a disputed sea-border between the two countries.

Australia has also won diplomatic kudos for successfully proposing in January 1989 the Asia-Pacific Economic Co-operation (APEC) council to facilitate economic – and perhaps eventually political – dealing with countries on both sides of the Pacific (the initial membership was Australia, New Zealand, America, Canada, South Korea, Japan and the six members of ASEAN). At the same time, the initiative that led to the Cambodian peace accord in Paris in 1991 was begun by Mr Hawke's foreign minister, Gareth Evans.

Within the Pacific region, Australia is a well-intentioned big brother and provider of economic assistance. In 1946 it was given the UN trusteeship over New Guinea (which ended with Papua New Guinea's independence in 1975). It is also a founder-member of the South Pacific Commission and the South Pacific Forum. In December 1986 it ratified a treaty declaring the South Pacific a nuclear-free zone.

Australia is an energetic member of the "Cairns Group" of agricultural exporters, who lobby against protectionist policies in Europe and America. A fellow member is New Zealand, with whom in 1966 Australia signed a free trade agreement, updated in 1983 by a Closer Economic Relations agreement which culminated in July 1990 in the removal of all bilateral trade barriers.

Society: increasingly mixed

The average Australian is Protestant and Anglo-Saxon, reflecting the country's colonial origins and a "White Australia" immigration policy that lasted until 1973. About a fifth of the population – including New Zealanders, who enjoy free access to Australia – were not born in Australia.

Now, however, immigration is based on skills, rather than on geographical and ethnic origin. The result is that

Asia and the Middle East have supplanted Europe as the greatest source of immigrants. By 1990 two out of every three migrants entering Australia were Asians, compared with one in every three in 1988.

The trend has provoked a debate on immigration which is sometimes racist, but which is also economic and ecological. One argument is that Australia, whose population has doubled since the second world war, needs more people in order to create a market for its own industry. A counter-argument is that Australia's soil and water resources are too poor to support a much bigger population, which is why half the population is concentrated in the south-eastern states of New South Wales and Victoria. The view accepted by most politicians and academics, however, is that Australia is underpopulated and that high immigration levels – running, according to economic circumstances, at up to 140,000 a year – produce a net economic gain.

Meanwhile, the first Australians now number about 230,000 aborigines and Torres Straits islanders; this 1.5% of the population accounts for 20% of the prison population. In 1992 the High Court ruled that, in the absence of proper title to other parties, aborigines had rights to their traditional land. In 1993 the government legislated for improved land registration. Mining companies remained worried, having been refused permission to develop various areas considered holy by the aborigines.

The economy: she'll be right

At the beginning of the 20th century Australia was the world's richest country in terms of income per person; today, it struggles to stay in the top 30. The reason is simple. Australia is immensely rich in natural resources: it has, for example, coal, bauxite, copper, uranium, gold, oil and gas; its agricultural sector produces beef, mutton, wool, wheat, butter, milk, sugar, and so on. However, despite the establishment of a manufacturing base (behind protectionist tariffs) in the 1950s and 1960s, the country has done relatively little to add value to its resources, while, at the same time, the emphasis on primary production has allowed the economy to be vulnerable to the swings of commodity prices and the vagaries of the world economy. In 1996 Australia's net foreign debt was around $188 billion, one of the highest burdens in the world in both absolute and per person terms, and evidence of a country which for decades had lived beyond its means.

Labor's accord

It was the economic malaise of the early 1980s which toppled the Liberal-National government, and gave the ALP a mandate to introduce radical economic reform. The key to this programme was the Accord, in which the government, employers and unions set centrally agreed wage increases.

The Accord allowed a period in which real wages have fallen and government austerity has become the norm. Strict controls on government spending and a broader tax base combined to change a federal budget deficit in 1984–85 of A$6.7 billion into a surplus of A$8 billion by 1989–90. Meanwhile, the prime minister and treasurer were determined to make Australia's services and manufacturing industries internationally competitive: in 1984–85 they deregulated the financial system, including an invitation to 16 foreign banks to operate in Australia; in 1988 they announced a four-year programme to reduce tariffs and eliminate import quotas; and in 1990 they proclaimed structural reforms which included the privatisation of aviation and telecommunications.

Stubborn problems

The success of a decade of reform has been mixed. The ALP's critics said the Accord hampered the economy by not allowing wage bargaining at the "enterprise", or local level; they accused the ALP of ducking the need to follow up macroeconomic measures with micro ones. All this, Mr Howard has promised to correct.

Meanwhile, there have been other problems: the propensity of economic recovery to be marked by a surge in imports; the proliferation of larger-than-life businessmen, whose speculative activities helped increase the foreign debt despite the government's austerity.

Future fears, future hopes

The risk in a country with a three-year election cycle is that politicians – and voters – will think only of the short term. The ALP resisted this temptation during the 1980s, and was cheered by four consecutive election victories. Such steadfastness, however, may not be permanent. A second danger for Australia is its vulnerability to external factors: a fall in energy prices or (as in 1990–91) in wool demand; protectionist measures by the European Union or America.

Australia's aim is to lessen these risks by becoming a "niche player" in Asia, offering sophisticated technology, educational services, tourism, and so on. If it succeeds, it may still afford the easy life it has been accustomed to for so long.

Total area	7,686,848 sq km	% agricultural area	61
Capital	Canberra	Highest point metres	Mt. Kosciusko
Other cities	Sydney, Melbourne,		2,228
	Brisbane, Perth, Adelaide	Main rivers	Darling-Murray,
			Lachlan, Ord

The economy

GDP $bn	391.1	GDP per head $	21,385
% av. ann. growth in		GDP per head in purchasing	
real GDP 1991–96	3.8	power parity $	18,940

Origins of GDP	% of total	Components of GDP	% of total
Agriculture	3	Private consumption	60
Industry	28	Public consumption	17
of which:		Investment	23
manufacturing	15	Exports	20
Services	70	Imports	20

Structure of manufacturing

			% of total
Agric. & food processing	18	Other	56
Textiles & clothing	6	Av. ann. increase in industrial	
Machinery & transport	20	output 1991–96	3

Inflation and exchange rates

Consumer price 1996 av. ann. incr.	2.6%	A$ per $ 1997 average	1.38
Av. ann. rate 1991–96	2.4%	A$ per $ end-1997	1.11

Balance of payments, reserves, aid and debt

			$bn
Exports, goods & services	68.7	Net capital account	0.6
Imports, goods & services	74.8	Net current account	4.7
Net income	-13.0	Other net investment	8.4
Net current transfers	-0.1	Net errors & omissions	5.8
Current-account balance	-19.2	Net change in reserves	-0.4
as % of GDP	-5.7	Level of reserves, end-Dec.	15.0
Foreign debt	…	Debt service	…
as % of GDP	…	as % of export earnings	…

Principal exports	$bn fob	Principal imports	$bn fob
Metal ores, minerals & metals	14.2	Machinery	19.3
Coal, coke & petroleum	9.4	Consumer goods	14.2
Machinery	7.6	Transport equipment	9.1
Gold	4.9	Fuels & lubricants	3.3
Cereals & preparations	3.7	Chemicals	2.3

Main export destinations	% of total	Main origins of imports	% of total
Developing countries	45.7	Developing countries	29.2
Japan	21.6	EU	24.9
ASEAN	15.5	United States	22.6
EU	11.1	Japan	13.9
United States	6.1	ASEAN	9.4

Government

System Parliamentary monarchy, but plans to hold a referendum on becoming a republic. Head of state is the British monarch, represented by a governor-general. The six states and two territories are largely autonomous. The bicameral federal parliament comprises a 76-member senate (12 from each state and 2 from each territory), and a house of representatives with 148 members elected for a 3-year term.

Main political parties Labor Party, Liberal Party, National Party, Australian Democrats

Climate and topography

Tropical and subtropical, wet summers in north; temperate with wet winters in south and east. Dry and barren uninhabited interior which gives, in the south, straight on to the sea; elsewhere it is bordered by coastal mountain ranges.

People and society

Population m	18.3	% under 15	21.9
Pop. per sq km	2	% over 60	15.0
% urban	85	No. women per 100 men	99.0
% av. ann. growth 1980–95	1.4	Human Development Index	93.1
No. households m	5.7		

Life expectancy	yrs	Education	
Men	74	Spending as % of GDP	4.4
Women	80	Years of compulsory education	10
Crude birth rate	15	Adult literacy %	99
Crude death rate	7	Primary school enrolment %	108
Infant mortality		Secondary school enrolment %	84
per 1,000 live births	6	Tertiary education enrolment %	42

Workforce	% of total	Consumer goods ownership	
Services	68		per 1,000 people
Industry	26	Cars	435.0
Agriculture	6	Televisions	641.0
% of pop. over 15 in workforce	50	Mobile telephones	127.7
		Personal computers	275.8

Ethnic groups	% of total	Religious groups	% of total
European	95	Anglican Church of Australia	26
Asian	4	Roman Catholic	26
Aborigine	1.5	Uniting Church	5
		Presbyterian	4
		Methodist	3

Tourism		Health	
Tourist arrivals m	3.7	Spending as % of GDP	8.4
Tourism receipts $bn	8.7	People per doctor	559.0

BANGLADESH

Total area	143,998 sq km	Population	120.4m
GDP	$30.7bn	GDP per head	$255
Capital	Dhaka	Other cities Chittagong, Khulna, Rajshahi	

The People's Republic of Bangladesh is one of the world's most densely populated, yet least urbanised, nations. Its challenge is to keep abreast of population growth, and to cope with regular, catastrophic floods and cyclones.

History: from Bengal to Bangladesh

The origins of Bangladesh can be traced back 3,000 years to the Banga (Bengal) kingdom on the delta of the Ganges, Brahmaputra and Meghna rivers. But independent Bangladesh (the Bengal Nation) began only on March 26th 1971. It had previously been East Pakistan, formed by the partition of British India, but separated from dominant West Pakistan by culture, language and 1,000 miles.

In Pakistan's election of December 1970 Sheikh Mujibur Rahman's Awami League won such an overwhelming victory in East Pakistan that it would have had a majority in Pakistan's National Assembly, with Sheikh Mujib as prime minister. This was unacceptable to Pakistan's president, General Yahya Khan, who postponed indefinitely the convening of the assembly and precipitated Mujib's March declaration of independence. This led to civil war. On December 4th 1971 India entered the war in support of the East; on December 16th Pakistan surrendered and Bangladesh's independence became a reality (although not accepted by Pakistan until 1974).

Politics: growing pains

Amid growing chaos, in January 1975 Sheikh Mujib abolished the parliamentary system and made himself president with dictatorial powers. The following month he declared Bangladesh a one-party state under the Bangladesh Peasants' and Workers' Awami League.

Mujib's power was short-lived. In August 1975 he and his family were assassinated in a right-wing military coup which installed Khandakar Mushtaq Ahmed as president. A counter-coup on November 3rd brought the pro-Indian Khalid Musharaf to power, but four days later he was deposed by the armed forces chiefs. Major-General Ziaur Rahman emerged first as the Chief Martial Law Administrator and then, in April 1977, as president. One of his first acts was to make Islam the basis of the constitution.

From husband to widow

Zia was autocratic, but also charismatic and incorruptible. He improved the economy and law and order, restored many democratic rights and helped his Bangladesh National Party (BNP) to victory in the general election of February 1979.

But on May 30th 1981 Zia was assassinated by Major-General Abdul Manzur, who was then killed by loyal troops. The vice-president, Abdus Sattar, became acting president and won a landslide victory in the presidential election in November. But his regime was ineffectual and corrupt. In March 1982 Lieutenant-General Hossain Mohammad Ershad took power in a bloodless coup.

Ershad, although capable, was both dictatorial and corrupt. His main opponents (frequently under house arrest) were Sheikh Hasina Wajid and Begum Khalida Zia. Sheikh Hasina was the daughter of Mujibur Rahman and leader of the Awami League; Khalida Zia was the widow of Ziaur Rahman and leader of the BNP.

From the mid-1980s there was widespread unrest. Eventually, in 1990, Ershad resigned as president and was promptly arrested on charges of corruption and other offences (he was jailed for ten years). In the parliamentary elections of February 27th 1991, the first truly democratic ones in Bangladesh's history, the BNP secured 168 seats in the 330-member parliament and Khalida Zia became prime minister. A parliamentary vote in August 1991, ratified by a referendum in September, established a parliamentary system of government in place of the presidential one. After much civil unrest, Sheikh Hasina's Awami League came to power in 1996 (the BNP predictably reacted with violent street protests).

Society: too many mouths

The typical Bangladeshi woman will have four or five children. Perhaps 60m peasants are effectively landless, living at the subsistence level through sharecropping. The pressure from Muslim Bengali settlers has helped fuel a lengthy campaign by the Shanti Bahini guerrillas on behalf of the Buddhist tribes in the Chittagong Hill Tracts near Burma.

The economy: vulnerable

Four-fifths of the population depend on farming and fishing, which make up one-third of the economy's output. Exports consist mainly of garments and jute, so the economy must rely on the props of foreign aid and remittances from Bangladeshi workers in the Gulf oil states.

Total area	143,998 sq km	% agricultural area	73
Capital	Dhaka	Highest point metres	Keokradong 1,230
Other cities	Chittagong, Khulna, Rajshahi	Main rivers	Ganges, Brahmaputra, Meghna

The economy

GDP $bn	30.7	GDP per head $	255.0
% av. ann. growth in real GDP 1991–96	4.5	GDP per head in purchasing power parity $	1,380

Origins of GDP	% of total	Components of GDP	% of total
Agriculture	31	Private consumption	78
Industry	18	Public consumption	14
of which:		Investment	17
manufacturing	10	Exports	14
Services	52	Imports	22

Structure of manufacturing[a]

	% of total		% of total
Agric. & food processing	24	Other	30
Textiles & clothing	43	Av. ann. increase in industrial	
Machinery & transport	4	output 1991–96	9.7

Inflation and exchange rates

Consumer price 1996 av. ann. incr.	2.7%	Taka per $ 1997 average	44.21
Av. ann. rate 1991–96	3.3%	Taka per $ end-1997	45.04

Balance of payments, reserves and debt

			$bn
Exports, goods & services	4.1	Net capital account	0.9
Imports, goods & services	6.5	Net direct & portfolio investment	0.1
Net income	-0.0	Other net investment	0.2
Net current transfers	1.4	Net errors & omissions	-0.6
Current-account balance	-1.0	Net change in reserves	0.5
as % of GDP	-3.6	Level of reserves, end-Dec.	2.4
Foreign debt	16.4	Debt service	2.5
as % of GDP	31.5	as % of export earnings	13.3

Principal exports	$m fob	Principal imports	$m fob
Garments & knitwear	3,000.7	Textiles & yarn	1,556.8
Fisheries products	321.6	Machinery & transport equip.	969.9
Jute goods	318.3	Food	551.9
Leather	185.0	Chemicals	372.7
Raw jute	116.0	Fuel	320.6
Tea	38.3	Iron & steel	183.6

Main export destinations	% of total	Main origins of imports	% of total
United States	32.1	India	16.2
UK	11.4	China	10.3
Germany	10.2	Japan	8.6
France	6.9	Singapore	5.9
Netherlands	4.9	South Korea	5.8

Government
System Republic since 1971. The elected president is head of state and chief executive; the parliament includes 300 members directly elected every 5 years and 30 seats reserved for women elected by the other members.
Main political parties Awami League, Bangladesh National Party, Jatiya Party

Climate and topography
Tropical monsoon; monthly temperatures 21–28°C (70–82°F). Rainy season Jun–Sep. Cyclonic storms occur in the Bay of Bengal. Mostly flat with low-lying fertile flood plains and deltas of the Ganges and Brahmaputra.

People and society

Population m	120.4	% under 15	39.7
Pop. per sq km	920.0	% over 60	6.0
% urban	18.0	No. women per 100 men	97.0
% av. ann. growth 1980–95	2.2	Human Development Index	36.8
No. households m	...		

Life expectancy	yrs	Education	
Men	57	Spending as % of GDP	1.7
Women	58	Years of compulsory education	5
Crude birth rate	28	Adult literacy %	36.4
Crude death rate	10	Primary school enrolment %	111
Infant mortality		Secondary school enrolment %	19
per 1,000 live births	79	Tertiary education enrolment %	...

Workforce	% of total	Consumer goods ownership	
Services	18		per 1,000 people
Industry	16	Cars	0.3
Agriculture	65	Televisions	7.0
% of pop. over 15 in workforce	49	Mobile telephones	–
		Personal computers	...

Ethnic groups	% of total	Religious groups	% of total
Bengali	99	Muslim	85
		Hindu	7
		Buddhist	0.6
		Christian	0.3

Tourism		Health	
Tourist arrivals m	0.2	Spending as % of GDP	2.4
Tourism receipts $bn	0.04	People per doctor	12,884

a 1980.

BHUTAN

Druk-yul, or the Kingdom of Bhutan, is one of the world's poorest nations, landlocked in the high mountains of the Himalayas. In many ways its pastoral beauty is an illusion: the kingdom is vulnerable both to its own ethnic tensions and to outside pressures.

History: land of the Dragon People

Bhutan emerged as a distinct political area over three centuries ago, with the arrival of a Tibetan lama, Sheptoon La-Pha, as its ruler. Contact with the outside world came with the signing of a treaty in 1774 with the British East India Company, followed by a treaty in 1865 which granted Bhutan an annual subsidy. A new treaty in 1910 gave control of Bhutan's foreign policy to British India. This was transferred to independent India with the conclusion of a treaty with Delhi in 1949.

Politics: neighbourly influences

The first hereditary king was installed in December 1907. Today's ruler, the western-educated King Jigme Singye Wangchuck (the Druk Gyalpo, or Precious Ruler of the Dragon People), was crowned in 1972. Since the invasion of Tibet by China in 1959, Bhutan has absorbed several thousand Tibetan refugees. Meanwhile immigration from Nepal, which began a century ago, has continued despite a ban imposed in 1958. At least a quarter of the population is now of Nepalese origin.

Social and economic tensions led the king in mid-1988 to revive Bhutanese identity and culture, imposing Bhutanese dress, banning Nepali teaching and limiting foreign tourists. Despite an incipient pro-democracy movement, especially among students, Bhutan is in essence an absolute, indeed feudal, monarchy. There are no political parties, but since 1953 there has been an advisory National Assembly. Its 151 members meet twice a year and include 106 members popularly elected for three-year terms.

The economy: ever dependent

Bhutan has few resources other than natural beauty and some hydroelectric power. Tourism is the biggest earner of foreign exchange, but the economy relies on aid from India and international donor agencies. Most Bhutanese live as subsistence farmers, as will their children.

Total area	46,500 sq km	% agricultural area	7
Capital	Thimphu	Highest point metres	Kula Kangri
Other cities	Chirang, Paro, Sakden		7,554
		Main rivers	Amo Chu, Tongsa Chu

The economy

GDP $bn	0.3	GDP per head $	200
% av. ann. growth in		GDP per head in purchasing	
real GDP 1991–96	6.2	power parity $	1,260

Origins of GDP	% of total	Components of GDP	% of total
Agriculture	42	Private consumption	70
Industry	37	Public consumption	24
of which:		Investment	38
manufacturing	10	Exports	…
Services	31	Imports	…

Principal exports[a]	$m fob	Principal imports[a]	$m cif
Cement	40	Aircraft	34
Talcum powder	16	Fuel	22
Fruit	12	Rice	11
Resin	10	Motor vehicles	9

Government

System Modified constitutional monarchy. King is head of government and shares power with the council of ministers, the national assembly and the Buddhist head abbot.

Main political parties None

Climate and topography

Temperate, varying with altitude. Dry in the extreme north, hot and humid on the Duars plain. Average monthly temperatures in the valleys range from 5°C (41°F) in Jan to 17°C (63°F) in Jul. Flat, fertile valleys run north-south through the centre of the country. Mountainous in the north, with peaks of over 7,000 metres.

People and society

Population m	1.6	% under 15	40.7
Pop. per sq km	15.0	% over 60	3.0
% urban	…	No. women per 100 men	128
% av. ann. growth 1985–95	2.6	No. households m	…
Human Development Index	33.8		

Ethnic groups	% of total	Religious groups	% of total
Bhutia	61	Buddhist	70
Gurung	15	Hindu	25
Assamese	13	Muslim	5

a 1983.

BRUNEI

Negara Brunei Darussalam is one of the world's richest countries. But Brunei's population is small and its territory is split into two parts by the sliver of Sarawak. The task of the monarchy is to maintain economic strength as its petroleum reserves decline.

History: from empire to statelet

In the early 16th century Brunei's empire included all of Borneo and the Sulu archipelago and Palawan in the Philippines. But by the mid-19th century the European powers had reduced the sultanate to its present size. After a treaty with Britain in 1847 against piracy, Brunei became a British protectorate in 1888. In 1963 Brunei resisted British pressure to be part of the new Federation of Malaysia. Full independence came on January 1st 1984.

Politics: absolute power

His Majesty Paduka Seri Baginda Sultan Haji Hassanal Bolkiah Mu'izzidin Waddaulah (also called the world's richest man) wields absolute power: there is no legislature and parts of the constitution have been in abeyance since a revolt in 1962. The then sultan, Sir Omar Ali Saifuddin, abdicated in favour of his son in 1967.

Brunei is a member of ASEAN and is pro-western. The concept of the Melayu Islam Beraja (Malay Muslim Monarchy) has been stressed since 1990. The Brunei United National Party was formed in 1986 with the approval of the sultan (who in 1988 banned the only other party). However, public employees, two-thirds of the workforce, are forbidden to engage in politics. About 70% of the people are Malays and aboriginals; they are officially preferred over the business-minded Chinese, few of whom are citizens.

The economy: petroleum power

The government is trying to diversify the economy, but oil and gas account for about 70% of GDP and 99% of exports (just over half consist of liquefied natural gas to Japan). Officials hope that Brunei could become a banking centre.

Total area	5,765 sq km	% agricultural area	3
Capital	Bandar Seri Begawan	Highest point metres	Bukit Timah 177
Other cities	Seria	Main rivers	Limbang

The economy[a]

GDP $bn	3.9	GDP per head $	17,000
% av. ann. growth in real GDP 1991–96	...	GDP per head in purchasing power parity $	...

Origins of GDP[b]	% of total	Components of GDP	% of total
Agriculture	2.2	Private consumption	...
Industry	54.1	Public consumption	...
of which:		Investment	...
manufacturing	46.2	Exports	...
Services	43.7	Imports	...

Principal exports	Br$m	Principal imports	Br$m
Crude oil	1,786	Electrical & industrial machinery	339
LNG	1,591	Road vehicles	159
Refined products	122	Iron & steel	124

Government

System Absolute monarchy. The sultan governs by decree through appointed councils.

Climate and topography

Tropical: hot, humid and rainy. Flat coastal plain rises to mountains in east; hilly lowlands in west. Settlements are confined to river valleys and the narrow coastal plain, where mangrove swamps separate fertile areas of peat and alluvium.

People and society

Population m	0.29	% under 15	32.0
Pop. per sq km	54.0	% over 60	4.0
% urban	59.0	No. women per 100 men	92.0
% av. ann. growth 1980–95	...	No. households m	2.9
Human Development Index	88.2		

Ethnic groups	% of total	Religious groups	% of total
Malay	65	Muslim	63
Chinese	20	Buddhist	14
		Christian	10

a 1991.
b 1988.

CAMBODIA

Total area	181,035 sq km	Population	9.8m
GDP	$2.7bn	GDP per head	$270
Capital	Phnom Penh	Other cities	Kompong Som

Still scarred, socially and economically, by the horrors of the Khmer Rouge era and 13 years of civil war, Cambodia will benefit more than most from peace in Indochina. But this promise is by no means secure: unless rampant corruption is checked and the gap between the towns and the poor countryside narrowed, political stability and economic progress will remain uncertain.

History: from paradise to Sihanouk

Cambodia's recorded history began 2,000 years ago with the kingdoms first of Funan, and then Chenla, but its cultural greatness coincided with the Khmer kingdoms which began at the start of the 9th century and built the wondrous complex of shrines and temples at Angkor.

In the mid-15th century the Khmer dynasties began to lose their power. Their strength was sapped by constant wars with the neighbouring Thais and Vietnamese; often, the Khmers became the vassals of one neighbour or another. Salvation, of a sort, came in 1864, when Cambodia became a French protectorate.

French rule continued until independence in 1953 (the occupying Japanese in the second world war left the Vichy French administration in place), four years after Cambodia had become an Associate State of the French Union.

From Sihanouk to Pol Pot

The dominating figure of independent Cambodia has always been Norodom Sihanouk, an ebullient, charismatic and maddeningly mercurial individual whom the French installed on the throne in 1941. Sihanouk officially entered politics in 1955, abdicating in favour of his father, Norodom Suramarit, in order to found the Sangkum Reastr Niyum (Popular Socialist Community). This won all the seats in the National Assembly elections in 1955, 1958, 1962 and 1966. When King Suramarit died in 1960, Prince Sihanouk was elected head of state.

The prince refers to the 1960s as a golden age. In retrospect, its tarnish is plain. From 1964 the government was faced by the communist Khmer Rouge insurgents, who fed on the grievances of corruption and rural poverty. Meanwhile, it became increasingly difficult for Sihanouk, who strove for good relations with communist China and communist North Vietnam, to isolate his country from the war in neighbouring Vietnam.

Eventually, in March 1970, Sihanouk was deposed by the American-backed General Lon Nol, who in October 1970 proclaimed the Khmer Republic. But Lon Nol was never secure. On April 17th 1975 the Khmers Rouges seized Phnom Penh, bringing back Sihanouk in September from exile to become head of state once more. The following January Cambodia was renamed Democratic Kampuchea; in March a 250-member People's Representative Assembly was formed; and in April Sihanouk resigned as head of state. In 1977 the Kampuchea Communist Party was officially designated as the country's governing body.

The era of the Khmers Rouges was a nightmare. Their leader, Pol Pot, was determined to set the country back to "Year Zero", banning money and forcibly emptying the cities in the cause of an agrarian revolution. In the process probably 1m (some claims go as high as 3m) of the 7m or so Cambodians were killed, or died from starvation, disease and ill-treatment.

From Vietnam to the UN

The end of the nightmare came when Vietnam, now estranged from the Chinese-backed Khmers Rouges, invaded on December 25th 1978. On January 7th 1979 Vietnam's troops occupied Phnom Penh. Three days later the People's Republic of Kampuchea was established with Heng Samrin, a former Khmer Rouge, as president; the Kampuchean People's Revolutionary Party replaced the Communist Party.

But despite military backing from Vietnam and economic aid from the Soviet Union, the regime was unable to quell the resistance movement. This was dominated by the Khmers Rouges, in an uneasy alliance with the Khmer People's National Liberation Front of Son Sann and the army of Prince Sihanouk. The three resistance factions in 1982 formed the Coalition Government of Democratic Kampuchea and occupied Cambodia's seat at the UN.

The diplomatic and military logjam between the Phnom Penh government and the three resistance factions began to break in 1988, when all four factions met "unofficially" in Jakarta. The spur was the desire of Vietnam, pressed by the Soviet Union, to disengage itself from Cambodia. This was matched by the decision of China, now willing for a rapprochement with Vietnam, to urge the Khmers Rouges to the negotiating table. Another pressure for peace was the desire of Thailand, breaking ranks with the rest of the Association of South-East Asian Nations (ASEAN), to deal directly with the Phnom Penh prime minister, Hun Sen, in its quest for commercial advantage in Indochina. By September 1989 Vietnam had supposedly withdrawn all its forces, once as many as 200,000, from Cambodia.

The first result, after much difficulty, was a UN Security Council peace plan, adopted in November 1990, for a ceasefire and UN-supervised elections. After a difficult year the four Cambodian factions and 18 countries with an interest in the area met in Paris on October 21st–23rd 1991 to sign the Cambodian peace accord.

Politics: a nervous limbo

Sovereignty for Cambodia (as the country had been renamed) after the Paris accord lay in the Supreme National Council (SNC), led by Sihanouk as head of state. Of its 13 other members, 7 represented the Phnom Penh government; the remaining 6 were equally divided between the other three factions.

The SNC was a temporary arrangement, pending elections due, according to the Paris agreement, in the first half of 1993 and supervised by the United Nations Transitional Authority in Cambodia (UNTAC). The other duties of UNTAC were to monitor the ceasefire; oversee the demobilisation of the opposing armies (all factions agreed to cut their forces by 70% in the run-up to the elections); help resettle the 340,000 Cambodians who had sought refuge in Thailand; and man the main government ministries.

The May 1993 election, with a turnout of 90%, gave the royalist Funcinpec party a narrow victory over the Cambodian People's Party of Hun Sen. In September a new constitution was adopted, with Sihanouk becoming king. His son, Ranarridh, became "first" prime minister. However, in a June 1997 coup, the "second" prime minister, Kun Sen, assumed control, replacing Ranarridh with his Funcinpec colleague, Ung Huot.

A promising development in 1997 was the near-demise of the Khmers Rouges. Thousands defected to the government side; and Pol Pot himself was arrested by his own followers. Less promising has been Hun Sen's stifling of democratic dissent (blatant enough in 1997 to delay Cambodia's agreed entry into ASEAN).

Society: a traumatised nation

Cambodians are overwhelmingly from the Mon-Khmer ethnic group; most are Theravada Buddhists. There is a divide between the peasantry and the sophisticated urbanites, but a universal deference to the monarchy. All are in some way scarred by the Khmer Rouge era, when ethnic minorities were expelled, atheism became mandatory and Buddhist monks were forced to work in the fields. The killings during the Khmer Rouge period in part explain why so many of the present population are under the age of 15.

The economy: just beginning

Cambodia is one of the world's poorest countries. In "normal" times, agriculture – mainly subsistence farming – employs three-quarters of the workforce, but years of war and millions of mines in unmapped minefields have persuaded hundreds of thousands of peasants to seek shelter in the cities. There is very little manufacturing apart from some rubber and other agricultural processing; mineral resources appear scarce, although there is some gem mining in the west and some recent petroleum exploration by western companies. The biggest potential is probably in tourism.

Stability and charity

But economic progress depends on sustained political stability, especially since the collapse of the Soviet bloc has left Cambodia bereft of its traditional market and source of aid, so its future will depend on the charity of others. As soon as the Paris accords were signed, America lifted its trade embargo and Singapore its investment embargo. Japan also appears ready to help with aid, trade and investment. The challenge is to stop the influx of money from worsening Cambodia's corruption and increasing the disaffection the countryside feels for the towns. Until that challenge is met, the threat of the Khmers Rouges – or similar extremist groups – will persist.

Total area	181,035 sq km	% agricultural area	20
Capital	Phnom Penh	Highest point metres	Phnom Ausol
Other cities	Kompong Som		1,813
		Main rivers	Mekong, Tonle Sap

The economy[a]

GDP $bn	2.7	GDP per head $	270.0
% av. ann. growth in		GDP per head in purchasing	
real GDP 1991–96	...	power parity $	...

Origins of GDP	% of total	Components of GDP	% of total
Agriculture	51	Private consumption	82
Industry	14	Public consumption	11
of which:		Investment	19
manufacturing	6	Exports	11
Services	34	Imports	24

Structure of manufacturing

			% of total
Agric. & food processing	...	Other	...
Textiles & clothing	...	Av. ann. increase in industrial	
Machinery & transport	...	output 1991–96	...

Inflation and exchange rates

Consumer price 1996 av. ann. incr.	10.6%	CR per $ 1997 average	3,035.0
Av. ann. rate 1991–96	...	CR per $ end-1997	3,379.7

Balance of payments, reserves and debt

			$bn
Exports, goods & services	1.0	Net capital account	0.1
Imports, goods & services	1.4	Net portfolio & direct investment	0.0
Net income	-0.1	Other net investment	0.0
Net current transfers	0.3	Net errors & omissions	0.2
Current-account balance	-0.2	Net change in reserves	0.0
as % of GDP	-6.8	Level of reserves, end-Dec.	0.2
Foreign debt	2.0	Debt service	0.2
as % of GDP	52.0	as % of export earnings	0.6

Principal exports	$m	Principal imports	$m
Sawn timber	96	Gold	305
Logs	53	Cigarettes	192
Rubber	32	Petrol & diesel	109
Maize	4	Motorcycles	36
		Vehicles	22

Main export destinations[b]	% of total	Main origins of imports[b]	% of total
Thailand	36.2	Thailand	22.6
Japan	30.0	Japan	6.3
Germany	10.2	Indonesia	5.0
Malaysia	4.6	Hong Kong	3.9
Italy	1.5	China	2.6

Government
System Constitutional monarchy with king head of state. Legislative national assembly has 120 members elected for 5-year terms. Executive power is in the hands of the cabinet headed by the prime minister.
Main political parties FUNCINPEC, Cambodian People's Party, Buddhist Democratic Liberal Party

Climate and topography
Tropical and humid. There is a rainy season from Jun to Nov, with the heaviest rainfall in Sep. Temperature is generally between 20°C and 36°C (68–97°F). Around 90% of Cambodians live on the low alluvial plain around the Mekong and Tonle Sap Lake. East of the Mekong the land climbs gradually to forested mountains and plateaus.

People and society

Population m	9.8	% under 15	41.9
Pop. per sq km	57.0	% over 60	4.0
% urban	45.0	No. women per 100 men	108
% av. ann. growth 1980–95	2.9	Human Development Index	34.1
No. households m	...		

Life expectancy	yrs	Education	
Men	52	Spending as % of GDP	...
Women	54	Years of compulsory education	6.0
Crude birth rate	40	Adult literacy %	35.0
Crude death rate	13	Primary school enrolment %	...
Infant mortality		Secondary school enrolment %	...
per 1,000 live births	108	Tertiary education enrolment %	...

Workforce	% of total	Consumer goods ownership	
Services	19		per 1,000 people
Industry	8	Cars	7.6
Agriculture	74	Televisions	8.0
% of pop. over 15 in workforce	50	Mobile phones	1.5
		Personal computers	...

Ethnic groups	% of total	Religious groups	% of total
Khmer	93	Buddhist	88
Vietnamese	4	Muslim	2
Chinese	3	Christian	1

Tourism		Health	
Tourist arrivals[b] m	0.1	Spending as % of GDP	7.2
Tourism receipts $bn	0.12	People per doctor	11,996

a 1995.
b 1993.

CHINA

Total area	9,561,000 sq km	Population	1,218m
GDP	$824bn	GDP per head	$680
Capital	Beijing	Other cities	Shanghai, Tianjin, Shenyang, Wuhan

The People's Republic of China is home for one-fifth of mankind in an area slightly bigger than the United States of America. It boasts the world's oldest continuous civilisation, nuclear weapons and the world's largest armed forces. For most of the past four decades it has been the world's fastest growing economy. Yet it remains a poor country whose stress on unity masks divisions: between the peasantry and the cities; between the rich coast and the poor interior; between Marxist ideologues and reformist liberals. The challenge for the leadership is to press on with economic reforms without encouraging political instability. Only then will China wield influence worthy of its size.

History: a question of dynasties

China's first dynasty, the Xia, began around 2205 BC. This was followed from 1766 BC to 1122 BC by the Shang, or Yin, dynasty – when the Chinese developed writing – and then by the "Classical Age" of the Chou dynasty, nine centuries which included the flowering of Confucianism and Taoism but also wars between China's feudal states.

Unity came to China during the reign (221–206 BC) of Emperor Ch'in Shih Huang (from whose name "China" is derived). He began the Great Wall to keep out barbarian foreigners and also burned books and executed scholars in an early exercise of "thought control". The Ch'in dynasty was followed by the four centuries of the Han dynasty, which introduced examinations for the civil service, opened trade to the west and spread Chinese culture across Asia.

But China was too vast to remain stable. Successive dynasties made startling scientific, economic and cultural advances, from making steel and cannons to building huge irrigation systems, but only rarely was China united.

In 1280 Kublai Khan, the grandson of Genghis Khan, led the Mongol hordes from Central Asia into what is now Beijing and established the Yuan dynasty, the biggest empire the world had ever seen.

The Mongols, however, could not digest what they had swallowed; in 1368 they were displaced by the Ming (or "bright") dynasty. Despite Admiral Cheng Ho's seven seafaring expeditions, through South-East Asia and as far as Africa, between 1405 and 1431, the Ming emperors resented the arrival of traders from Europe and began to close China off from the world. They were unable, however, to resist the movement south of the Juchen tribes from Manchuria. Arriving under the pretext of helping the Ming emperor exterminate bandits, they soon displaced him and in 1644 established their own Manchu or Qing dynasty.

The impact of the West

The Manchus treated the European traders as barbarians bearing tribute. But the Europeans had greater power: when China objected to Britain paying for tea with opium instead of silver, Britain fought the Opium War of 1839–42, forcing China both to give Hong Kong Island to Britain in 1841 and to provide easier access for all western traders.

Indeed, the 19th century was a disaster for China. Britain and France pressed a second Opium war against China in 1857–60, and meanwhile the Russians, Germans and Japanese were all forcing "concession areas" for themselves in China's ports. As if that were not enough, religious fanatics waged the Taiping rebellion and formed a separate kingdom from 1851 to 1864; there was a war with Japan in 1894–95; and in 1900 there was the uprising of the "Righteous and Harmonious Fists", known as the Boxers.

By now Manchu rule, characterised by the scheming dowager empress, Zi Xi, was in terminal decay. In late 1911 Sun Yat Sen's Kuomintang (Nationalist Party, or KMT) overthrew the dynasty and on January 1st 1912 established the Republic of China. Nationalism was boosted in 1919 when the Treaty of Versailles proposed giving the Chinese territories of the defeated Germany to Japan.

Nationalism and communism

But regional warlords mocked the KMT's attempt to govern, and a KMT alliance in 1924 with the communists (the Chinese Communist Party was founded in Shanghai in 1921) foundered when in 1927 the KMT suddenly purged Shanghai's revolutionaries. The communists took to the countryside, and set up the Chinese Soviet Republic in southern China (with a population of 10m) in 1931. The KMT hit back, forcing the emerging communist leader, Mao Zedong, to escape north to Yenan with his forces on the "Long March" of 1934–35. However, the KMT was meanwhile suffering other reverses: Japan seized Manchuria in 1931 and invaded coastal China in 1937.

Although the communist guerrillas of Mao Zedong cooperated with the KMT army of Generalissimo Chiang Kaishek against the Japanese, as soon as the second world war ended civil war broke out between the communists and the nationalists. The outcome was defeat for the KMT government, which fled to the island of Taiwan. On October 1st 1949 Mao proclaimed the People's Republic of China.

Politics: the edifice of communism

Although there are a few token non-communist parties, power rests with the 50m-strong Chinese Communist Party. Its base consists of local and provincial party congresses and committees who send delegates to the National Party Congress, which meets every five years to approve long-term policy; choose a general secretary; and elect a Central Committee (of around 300 members). The Central Committee has two subcommittees: the Central Military Commission, which liaises with the People's Liberation Army, and the Central Audit Commission, composed mainly of retired politicians. The Central Committee also elects a Politburo, of around 20 members, which in turn has a standing committee of six or so members. This Politburo Standing Committee is at the apex of the party's pyramid.

The structure of government rests on a 3,000-member National People's Congress, which meets every five years as a rubber-stamp parliament for its executive organ, the State Council. Headed by the prime minister and a handful of vice-premiers, the State Council directs more than 40 ministries and important commissions, including a Central Military Commission running parallel to the party's one.

So much for the theory of power. In reality power belongs, as of old, to the individual who has claimed "the Mandate of Heaven" and who, in the case of Deng Xiaoping, held on to the mandate even after, at the end of the 1980s, giving up all his official posts.

The emperors of communism

Mao Zedong was one of the 20th century's great figures. He was born in Shaoshan village, Hunan Province, on December 26th 1893, to a rich grain dealer former peasant. He united, clothed and (most of the time) fed the world's most populous country; swept away the corrupt landowning class; established (with Soviet help) an industrial base; made China a nuclear-weapons state (despite Soviet opposition); and spread a Marxist theory of peasant revolution and "people's war" throughout the developing world.

But the costs were enormous. In 1956 Mao said "Let a hundred flowers blossom, a hundred schools of thought contend", and the next year launched a "rectification" campaign to crush all the dissidents who had emerged. In 1958–59, as Soviet aid declined, Mao launched the "Great Leap Forward", to catch up with America and Britain in industrial production within 15 years and to abolish individual agricultural effort in favour of "People's Communes". It was a disaster, worsened by natural catastrophes. Between 1959 and 1961 perhaps 26m Chinese died from famine.

Mao was unrepentant, telling the party in 1962: "Never forget class, class contradictions and class struggle." The result was the "Cultural Revolution", a decade of madness, beginning in 1966: moderates such as Deng Xiaoping were purged; fanatical Red Guards humiliated, imprisoned or killed hundreds of thousands; intellectuals were sent to work in the fields for their "re-education". Liu Shaochi, China's president, was dismissed for being a "capitalist roader"; Lin Piao, Mao's leftist second-in-command, died in an aircraft crash in Outer Mongolia in 1971, apparently fleeing after an abortive plot against Mao. In January 1976 the popular prime minister, Zhou Enlai, died, sparking massive demonstrations of sympathy in Beijing's Tiananmen Square which were implicit attacks on the regime. Only the army was keeping the Red Guards in check until finally the excesses ended with Mao's death in September 1976.

The revenge of the moderates was swift: in October 1976 they arrested Mao's widow, Jiang Qing, and the rest of the extremist "Gang of Four" for trying to "usurp party and state power"; Hua Guofeng became party chairman and China's leader; the Cultural Revolution was officially over.

The Deng era

Hua was just a stop-gap. Deng Xiaoping, who had been purged a second time in 1976 for allegedly orchestrating the Tiananmen Square demonstrations on Zhou's death, was "rehabilitated" in July 1977 and became vice-premier. In 1980 Hua resigned as prime minister in favour of an ally of Deng, and in 1981 was replaced as party chairman (later to become general secretary) by another Dengist, Hu Yaobang.

Although Deng contented himself with the chairmanship of the Central Military Commission, it was clear that he had won possession of "the mandate of Heaven" back in 1978, when he reversed the collectivisation of agriculture. Although all land still belonged to the state, under a "family responsibility" system the peasants could till for their own profit once they had fulfilled a quota of produce for the state. In 1984 the reforms were launched in the cities, with state-owned factories allowed to produce for their own profit once the state's quota had been filled. As Deng declared: "To get rich is glorious."

Tiananmen Square

But as some got rich much faster than others, the economy was overheating and the Communist Party was becoming increasingly corrupt. In April 1989 huge demonstrations took place in Tiananmen Square, the spiritual heart of post-revolution Beijing, after the death of the liberal Hu Yaobang, whom Deng in 1987 had ousted as general secretary in favour of Zhao Ziyang. The protesters demanded democracy, an end to corruption and the downfall of the hardline prime minister (and former education commission head), Li Peng. A meeting in Beijing of the Asian Development Bank, followed by the visit in May of the Soviet president, Mikhail Gorbachev, meant that retaliation against the students was, for the moment, out of the question.

The turning point came after Gorbachev's departure. On May 20th Beijing was put under martial law by Li Peng; during the night of June 3rd–4th the People's Liberation Army, using tanks, armoured cars and assault rifles, swept the demonstrators from the Square. The death toll, mostly civilian, was put at anything from 200 to over 1,000.

The Tiananmen tragedy proved that Deng would not let political liberalism threaten stability. The role of the party in the workplace and in government was once again stressed, reversing the measures of the 1987 Party Congress; students were "re-educated" with a year of military service.

But it was not a total victory for old-style Marxists. Deng remained committed to economic reform: Zhao Ziyang, who had disappeared from view on May 19th, was replaced as party boss by another economic liberal, Jiang Zemin. After Deng's death in February 1997 the challenge for Jiang was to consolidate his supremacy within a supposedly collective leadership that included potential rivals such as Li Ruihuan and Zhu Rongji. One measure of Jiang's triumph was his successful visit to America in October 1997.

Foreign policy: Moscow and Washington

China has always sought to protect its interests through a triangular relationship with Russia and America. Initially, as America supported Taiwan, this meant a close alliance with the Soviet Union, which gave immense economic and technical support to China. But by 1960, when Soviet aid was withdrawn, the friendship with Russia had collapsed, not least because Mao was determined that China should have nuclear weapons (which it achieved in 1964). A rapprochement came only after the visit to Beijing of Mikhail Gorbachev in 1989, which led to a Soviet troop withdrawal from the Mongolian border with China.

Relations with America were extremely hostile during the Korean war of the 1950s and through the 1960s, when Mao was trying to export revolution to the rest of the third world. Matters improved at the start of the 1970s: in 1971 China displaced Taiwan at the United Nations, and took a permanent seat in the Security Council; and in 1972 Mao welcomed President Nixon in Beijing. Since the "open door" policy of the 1980s China and America have increasingly regarded each other as friends, despite America's revulsion over Tiananmen Square.

In the 1990s, however, the collapse of the Soviet Union and European communism has revived fears of American "hegemonism", with China no longer able to use the "Russian card" to influence America. In compensation, China is wooing Japan, South Korea and countries that had been close to the Soviet Union – for example, India, with which it fought a border war in 1962, and Vietnam, which it briefly fought in 1979.

Potential points of conflict are the Spratly Islands, also claimed by Taiwan, the Philippines, Malaysia, Vietnam and Brunei; the border region with India; and Taiwan. Chinese belligerence would be worrying, since the 3m strong People's Liberation Army (reduced by Deng from 4m) constitutes the world's largest armed forces.

Society: the "Middle Kingdom"

The Chinese call their country "Zhongguo", the Middle Kingdom, at the centre of the world. This sense of superiority is at odds with the evidence of everyday life; and educated Chinese often feel uneasy over their admiration for foreign technology. Some 92% of the population is from the Han ethnic group; the rest belong to 56 "minorities", such as the often restive Tibetans and Muslim Uigurs. The minorities have been exempted from most of the strictures of the state's desire since the 1970s (earlier, Mao had believed the more children the better) to limit population growth. This involves late marriage and more or less compulsory abortion for all but the first child.

Although China has some of the world's biggest cities, more than 70% of the people live in the countryside. Northerners tend to think of southerners as crude and brash;

southerners see northerners as dull and arrogant. All, however, are imbued with a Confucian respect for hierarchy;
individualism is frowned on.

The economy: planned or free

Deng Xiaoping's goal was that by the end of this century
China should enter the lower ranks of middle-income
economies, which would mean doubling China's present
GDP per head in less than a decade.

And why not? After 1978 the commune system was
ended and peasants were allowed to farm land on long
leases (equivalent, indeed, to private ownership); once state
quotas had been met, extra produce could be sold on a free
market. The result was dramatic. Farm output, which had
grown by 2% a year from 1958 to 1978, now grew by 8% a
year in 1979–84; peasant incomes doubled in six years.

A similar leap in output came in 1984, when Deng
spread the reforms to the cities, allowing factories to negotiate a quota due to the state and then to sell the surplus on
the free market. The result was that in the 1980s economic
output per head rose by an average of 9.5% a year.

The invisible hand

The secret of this increase was the growth of a quasi-private
sector. In the late 1970s state factories, developed on the
Soviet model to make China as self-sufficient as possible,
accounted for around four-fifths of China's industrial output; by the early 1990s they accounted for only half, and
most were operating at a loss. The remaining industrial output was produced by township and rural enterprises, which
operate rather like private sector companies, and by joint
ventures with foreign companies. Capitalism has now gone
so far that companies can raise money on a handful of
stock exchanges; and the Shenzhen exchange is open to
foreign investors.

The foreign hand

Another reason for growth was Deng's "open door" policy.
In 1979 four Special Economic Zones – Xiamen, in Fujian
province, and Shantou, Shenzhen and Zhuhai in Guangdong province – were set up in China's coastal regions as
export zones, with tax incentives to attract foreign
investors. Hainan Island was designated as a fifth SEZ in
1991. In addition, in 1981 economic and technological
development zones, with their own financial lures to foreigners, were established in 14 coastal cities. The theory is

that wealth will spread inland from these regions. The practice is a sometimes tense divide between "have" provinces, particularly Guangdong, and the "have nots" in the interior.

Meanwhile, most western investors in China have been disappointed: profits are hard to make and difficult to repatriate. By contrast, investors from Taiwan and Hong Kong have done well, benefiting from family relationships and common languages. By the start of the 1990s it was reckoned that Hong Kong provided two-thirds of China's foreign investment and that Hong Kong companies, usually making clothes or toys, were employing up to 3m workers in factories in Guangdong, a province of 63m people whose economy during the 1980s grew by over 12% a year.

Problems of growth

The open-door policy has undoubtedly been good for China, putting consumer goods into most homes and more or less eliminating hunger. But there have been costs. "Dual pricing", for example, where the state guarantees the price of a fixed quota of a product and allows the rest to be freely priced, tempts many officials and party members into corrupt business deals. Another cost is that an economy growing so fast is bound to overheat, provoking unpopular austerity programmes every five years or so to cool inflation. Meanwhile the state industries are mismanaged and unprofitable – but their demise threatens huge unemployment.

Lastly, the open-door policy, which has made foreign trade equal to a third of China's GDP, has brought a dependence on America. China in 1996 enjoyed a trade surplus of some \$40 billion with America. Such a surplus provokes constant threats of retaliation, although no longer – following a decision by President Clinton – the withdrawal of China's "Most Favoured Nation" status, by which America gives China's exports favourable tariffs.

The challenge ahead

China's inherent contradiction is between its Marxist creed and the liberalising pressures of its economic growth and open-door policy. The gerontocracy of Deng Xiaoping associated political liberalism with chaos, which is why the country's human rights' record is among the world's worst. Historically, China's emperors have always feared provincial independence, linking it with "warlordism"; yet a federal China, with power devolved from the centre, seems the most rational future for such a vast and populous country. The challenge is to achieve it without the bloody convulsions that have scarred China through the ages.

Total area	9,561,000 sq km	% agricultural area	41
Capital	Beijing	Highest point metres	Mt Everest
Other cities	Shanghai, Tianjin,		8,848
	Shenyang, Wuhan	Main rivers	Yangtze Kiang,
		Huang He, Chang Jiang, Xi Jiang	

The economy

GDP $bn	824.0	GDP per head $	680
% av. ann. growth in		GDP per head in purchasing	
real GDP 1991–96	12.1	power parity $	3,120

Origins of GDP	% of total	Components of GDP	% of total
Agriculture	21	Private consumption	46
Industry	48	Public consumption	12
of which:		Investment	40
manufacturing	38	Exports	21
Services	31	Imports	19

Structure of manufacturing

			% of total
Agric. & food processing	13	Other	50
Textiles & clothing	13	Av. ann. increase in industrial	
Machinery & transport	24	output 1991–96	-0.4

Inflation and exchange rates

Consumer price 1996 av. ann. incr.	8.3%	Yuan per $ 1997 average	8.30
Av. ann. rate 1991–96	13.9%	Yuan per $ end-1997	8.40

Balance of payments, reserves and debt
$bn

Exports, goods & services	147.2	Net capital account	...
Imports, goods & services	135.3	Net direct & portfolio investment	34.6
Net income	-11.8	Other net investment	4.0
Net current transfers	1.4	Net errors & omissions	-17.8
Current-account balance	1.6	Net change in reserves	-22.5
as % of GDP	0.2	Level of reserves, end-Dec.	80.3
Foreign debt	118.1	Debt service	2.2
as % of GDP	16.4	as % of export earnings	9.9

Principal exports	$bn fob	Principal imports	$bn fob
Machinery & electrical equip.	53.7	Machinery & electrical equip.	36.0
Textiles & clothing	15.7	Chemicals	10.9
Base metals & metal manuf.	10.3	Base metals & products	10.4
Plastic & rubber articles	7.7	Precision instruments,	
Vehicles, aircraft & ships	5.2	clocks & watches	5.3
Chemicals	3.3	Crude petroleum	4.9
		Vehicles, aircraft & ships	4.6

Main export destinations	% of total	Main origins of imports	% of total
United States	23.2	Japan	26.9
Hong Kong	23.1	United States	19.5
Japan	11.8	Germany	4.9
Singapore	3.9	South Korea	4.1

Government

System Communist republic since 1949. 22 provinces, 5 autonomous regions and 3 municipalities. Political power is held by the Chinese Communist Party, whose congress elects a central committee and politburo every 5 years. Legislature is unicameral National People's Congress (NPC), with 3,000 indirectly elected deputies. The NPC elects a standing committee, an executive state council and a president who is head of state.

Main political parties Communist Party

Climate and topography

Subtropical in SE, continental in the interior. Up to 4,000mm (1,579in) of rain in SE, less than 250mm (10in) in NW. Winter temperatures range from -28°C (-18.5°F) in the extreme north, to 20°C (68°F) in the south; range smaller in summer, typhoon season. Plateau in SW is highest in world (over 4,000m). To its north and east are basins and plateaus. To the east rolling hills and plains are drained by rivers.

People and society

Population m	1,217.6	% under 15	25.1
Pop. per sq km	129.0	% over 60	10.0
% urban	30.0	No. women per 100 men	94.0
% av. ann. growth 1980–95	1.3	Human Development Index	62.6
No. households m	...		

Life expectancy	*yrs*	**Education**	
Men	68	Spending as % of GDP	2.6
Women	71	Years of compulsory education	9
Crude birth rate	17	Adult literacy %	80.9
Crude death rate	7	Primary school enrolment %	109
Infant mortality		Secondary school enrolment %	52
per 1,000 live births	34	Tertiary education enrolment %	6

Workforce	*% of total*	**Consumer goods ownership**	
Services	13		*per 1,000 people*
Industry	15	Cars	1.0
Agriculture	72	Televisions	250.0
% of pop. over 15 in workforce	59	Mobile telephones	3.0
		Personal computers	2.2

Ethnic groups	*% of total*	**Religious groups**	*% of total*
Han (Chinese)	92	Confucian	20
Zhuang	1	Buddhist	6
Manchu	1	Taoist	2
Hui	1	Muslim	2
Miao	1		

Tourism		**Health**	
Tourist arrivals m	46.4	Spending as % of GDP	3.8
Tourism receipts $bn	10.2	People per doctor	1,063.0

FIJI

Western interest in Fiji began in the early 19th century, with America's involvement in the sandalwood trade. The first Christian missionaries arrived in 1835; Britain appointed a consul in 1857 and in 1874, in an accord with the Christian chief, Cakobau, made Fiji a colony.

In the 1880s the British began large-scale sugarcane cultivation, importing Indian workers. Although the Indians eventually numbered half the population, colonial rule ensured that the Fijian chiefs maintained their social authority. Independence was granted in 1970 and Fiji became a dominion within the British Commonwealth.

Politics: indigenous rights

The political structure of independent Fiji was originally based on a 52-member House of Representatives, elected to five-year terms by universal suffrage, and a 22-man Senate appointed for six years by the governor-general on the advice of the Great Council of Chiefs, the prime minister, the leader of the opposition and the Council of Rotuma (an island annexed to Fiji in 1881). The aim was to safeguard the rights of the indigenous Fijians; in the House of Representatives 22 seats were reserved for Fijians, 22 for Indians and 8 for "general electors" (Europeans, Chinese and others, normally sympathetic to the Melanesian Fijians). The first election, in 1972, gave victory to the Fijian-dominated Alliance Party under Ratu Sir Kamisese Mara.

But in April 1987 the Alliance Party was defeated by a coalition led by Dr Timoci Bavadra, a Fijian whose colleagues were mostly Indian. On May 14th 1987 Colonel Sitiveni Rabuka deposed the government. Unhappy with a proposed constitution, he staged a second coup on September 25th 1987, and on October 7th declared Fiji a republic.

A constitution agreed on June 25th 1990 guaranteed Fijians 37 of the 70 seats in the House of Representatives, Indians 27 and 6 to the other races. Of the 34-member appointed Senate, 24 seats were for Fijians. The guarantee of a Fijian majority in parliament was to expire in 1998.

The economy: under ethnic stress

Racial tensions have hurt tourism, which provides one-fifth of GDP, and many of the Indian commercial class have emigrated. Sugar exports have been protected by quotas in America and the European Union, but the importance of sugar means that the industry can be a political weapon to be wielded by the farmers, most of whom are Indian.

Total area	18,274 sq km	% agricultural area	16
Capital	Suva	Highest point metres	Mt Victoria 1,324
Other cities	Labasa, Nadi	Main rivers	Rewa, Siga Toka

The economy[a]

GDP $bn	1.9	GDP per head $	2,440
% av. ann. growth in		GDP per head in purchasing	
real GDP 1991–96	…	power parity $	5,780

Origins of GDP	% of total	Components of GDP	% of total
Agriculture	20	Private consumption	67
Industry	44	Public consumption	20
of which:		Investment	14
manufacturing	11	Exports	56
Services	37	Imports	59

Principal exports	$m fob	Principal imports	$m cif
Sugar	215.0	Manufactured goods	255.0
Garments	135.3	Machinery	235.6
Gold	58.1	Food	139.0
Fish	32.5	Mineral fuels	132.0
Timber	20.8		

Government

System Republic since 1987. The head of state is the president. The constitution of July 1990 made way for a bicameral legislature, with an elected 70-seat House of Representatives and an appointed 34-member Senate. Under the constitution 37 seats in the House are elected by indigenous Fijians and 27 are elected by those of Indian descent.

Main political parties Soqosoqo ni Vakavulewa ni Taukei (SVT), National Federation Party, Fiji Labour Party

Climate and topography

Tropical, with temperatures from 16–32°C (60–90°F). Rainfall is heavy on the windward side. More than 300 islands, of which 100 are inhabited.

People and society

Population m	0.8	% under 15	34.7
Pop. per sq km	40.9	% over 60	3.5
% urban	40.0	No. men per 100 women	98.0
% av. ann. growth 1990–95	1.3	No. households m	…
Human Development Index	86.3		

Ethnic groups	% of total	Religious groups	% of total
Indian	50	Christian	50
Fijian	45	Hindu	41
European	2	Muslim	8

a 1995.

HONG KONG

Total area	1,074 sq km	Population	6m
GDP	$154.3bn	GDP per head	$24,440
Capital	Victoria	Other cities	Kowloon

Hong Kong is an economic miracle: a small territory of refugees and their children that has gone from poverty to prosperity in just 50 years. But from July 1st 1997 the British colony's sovereignty has belonged to neighbouring China. Can Hong Kong retain its dynamism and its way of life despite the change of landlord?

History: a barren rock

Originally a fishing village of fewer than 4,000 people, the island of Hong Kong, off the coast of southern China, had only one natural asset: a sheltered anchorage. On January 20th 1841 China ceded the island to Britain's Captain Charles Elliott, who was waging the first Opium war (1840–42) to compel China to allow greater access to foreign traders.

Britain's foreign secretary, Lord Palmerston, was famously unimpressed, calling Hong Kong "a barren island with hardly a house upon it", but Britain's occupation of the island was still confirmed "in perpetuity" by the Nanking Treaty of August 29th 1842. Stonecutter's Island and the tip of the Kowloon peninsula were then ceded to Britain, again for ever, by the Convention of Peking in 1860. Finally, in the tension that followed China's 1895 defeat by Japan, Britain demanded control of the land approaches to Hong Kong; this led to the Convention of 1898, under which China signed away the New Territories to Britain on a lease which would last for 99 years and give the colony 92% of its land area. Not surprisingly, the Chinese have ever since denounced these "unequal treaties".

From rags to riches

Hong Kong has always attracted refugees fleeing insecurity or poverty in China. In 1851 the population was 32,983 (31,463 of them Chinese); by 1931 it had risen to 878,947 (859,425 of them Chinese). When Japanese troops occupied Guangzhou (Canton) in 1938, at least 500,000 Chinese fled into Hong Kong, followed the next year by another 150,000.

At the start of the second world war, Hong Kong's population had swollen to 1.6m; when Japan had been forced out at the war's end the population had fallen to 600,000, only to rise because of civil war in China to 1.8m by the end of 1947. Then came the impact on cities such as Shanghai of Mao Zedong's Communist victory; by mid-1950 Hong Kong was home to 2.2m. In the 1960s and 1970s China's Cultural Revolution prompted another exodus to Hong Kong. No wonder Hong Kong has a "get rich quick" mentality: the present population of 6m consists almost entirely of refugees from China and their children.

Their genius is their adaptability. In 1951, when the United Nations imposed a trade embargo on China because of the Korean war, Hong Kong was cut off from its natural market, so its workers spun cloth or made cheap goods to sell to Europe, America and the British Commonwealth. Whereas in 1951 almost all of Hong Kong's exports had consisted of entrepot trade with China, by 1963 domestic exports (ie, goods made in Hong Kong, rather than re-exports) accounted for three-quarters of total exports, and by the early 1970s over 80%. Overseas critics, with justice, called Hong Kong the world's sweatshop; but today, Hong Kong is reckoned to have as many US dollar billionaires as Britain or France and incomes per person are as high as in parts of Europe.

The prosperity means the territory can no longer compete on the basis of cheap labour. Fortunately, China's economic reforms, begun in late 1978, have given Hong Kong a new lease of economic life. Once again, Hong Kong is the conduit for China's foreign trade; its companies employ up to 3m workers in Guangdong province, and then add value and expertise in Hong Kong. Well before the 1997 transfer to China's sovereignty, Hong Kong had made itself the economic and financial capital of South China.

Politics: freedom without democracy

Appointed by the British monarch, the Governor of Hong Kong had the powers of a dictator, choosing his own advisory cabinet, the Executive Council (Exco), from a dozen or so of the colony's leading figures. The Legislative Council (Legco) debates and passes bills passed to it by Exco (its only real power is to hold up financial bills). Less important bodies of government are the Urban Council; the Regional Council (for the "new towns", huge public housing developments in the New Territories); and the 19 District Boards, which until 1991 were the only institution chosen by direct election.

Historically (and almost without precedent in the British Empire), there was little or no demand by Hong Kong's citizens for representative government or for an end to colonial rule. But on September 26th 1984 Britain and China initialled a Joint Declaration on Hong Kong's future. Hongkongers suddenly realised that the colony's freedoms of speech, assembly, religion and travel had no legal protection. Could they be protected once the British left?

Joint Declaration and Basic Law

Britain's decision to depart became inevitable as the expiration of the lease on the New Territories approached. Investors were not prepared to advance money on an uncertain future; Hong Kong Island, although ceded in perpetuity, could not survive without the New Territories; China could always cut off Hong Kong's water supply.

The elegant solution, devised by China's senior leader, Deng Xiaoping, was that Hong Kong would become part of China, but with its own way of life: "One Country, Two Systems". At midnight on June 30th 1997 Hong Kong would become a Special Administrative Region of the People's Republic of China, but with "a high degree of autonomy, except in foreign and defence affairs" and with its way of life unchanged for the next 50 years. The governor would become a Hongkong Chinese "chief executive"; senior government and judicial posts would also be reserved for local Chinese. Hong Kong people would rule Hong Kong, officials from both sides proclaimed.

But how? The 57-man Legco consisted of the governor; his chief secretary, financial secretary and attorney general; 7 "official" members, representing various government departments; 20 members appointed by the governor; and 26 members elected by various functional constituencies, such as lawyers, teachers and doctors. Britain's solution was gradually to introduce direct elections. Beginning with the Legco election of 1991, Britain proposed to introduce 10 directly elected seats.

Then came the Tiananmen Square bloodshed in Beijing on June 4th 1989. Perhaps a million Hongkongers – a sixth of the population – demonstrated in sympathy with China's democracy movement. China suddenly viewed Hong Kong as a nest of liberals plotting to overthrow the Beijing government, while Hongkongers suddenly clamoured for the safeguard of more democracy.

The compromise was that in 1991 a 60-member Legco was chosen, with 18 members directly elected by universal adult suffrage (official members were limited to 3, functional representatives to 21 and appointed members to 18). A new 60-seat Legco was elected in 1995 with 20 directly elected members and 30 representing functional constituencies (the remaining ten would be chosen by an "election committee"). A "Basic Law", passed by China to be Hong Kong's post-1997 constitution, agreed that this Legco would sit through to elections in 1999. The Basic Law stipulates that directly elected seats will then rise to 24, and to 30 in the elections of 2003.

But Hong Kong's commitment to democracy is ambivalent. On the one hand, in the 1995 Legco election, the United Democrats of Hong Kong, led by an outspoken critic of China, emerged as the largest party. On the other hand, the electoral turnout was just under 40%.

The challenge for the last governor, Chris Patten, a former Conservative cabinet minister appointed in 1992, was to use his skills as a politician (predecessors were traditionally diplomats) to bolster Hong Kong's confidence in the period of transition. In practice his extension of democracy – he had insisted, for example, on making the franchises for the nine new functional constituencies extremely broad – infuriated China, which disbanded the 1995 Legco.

In its place was a 60-member Provisional Legislative Council, selected by a Chinese-appointed committee of 400 and preparing the way for new Legco elections in 1998. Democrats noted that the electorate for 30 functional constituencies (half of the total) was now 180,000, compared with 2.7m in the Patten-organised 1995 election.

Foreign policy: at others' command

Theoretically, Hong Kong has no foreign policy of its own. In practice, it has deferred not just to Britain but also to China. In past years, for example, it made it difficult for Taiwanese to visit Hong Kong, and almost impossible – because of the Sino-Soviet rift – for Russians and East Europeans. The antipathy to Taiwan seemed incongruous given the booming trade and indirect contact between China and Taiwan. The Joint Declaration allows Hong Kong to remain a separate member of the World Trade Organisation, but specifies that after 1997 China is responsible for the territory's foreign and defence policy.

Society: capitalist to the Cantonese core

About 97% of Hong Kong's residents are Cantonese Chinese, just over a third of whom were born in China. About half the population lives in subsidised public housing; about 300,000 live in squatter areas awaiting rehousing.

The largest foreign community (apart from Vietnamese boat people, most of whom were repatriated by 1997 as "economic" rather than "political" refugees but who in 1992 had numbered over 55,000) consists of over 50,000 domestic servants from the Philippines. The senior ranks of the civil service and the financial sector have traditionally been heavily populated with expatriate Britons; in the private sector there is a growing presence of Americans and Japanese, but probably the most influential non-Cantonese group are the Chinese businessmen who fled from Shanghai.

All sectors of society admit to an aggressive materialism (Hong Kong has the world's highest concentration of Rolls-Royces per head and per mile). Despite Hong Kong's reputation as an international city, relatively few Cantonese are fluent in English or, for that matter, in Mandarin (the official dialect of the mainland). However, with the approach of 1997, a knowledge of English became a valuable qualification for would-be emigrants. Around 60,000 Hongkongers, fearful of the Chinese takeover, left each year in the early and mid-1990s for Canada, Australia and America. To calm their fears, Britain in 1990 promised full citizenship to 50,000 commercially or politically important heads-of-family, the idea being that the "insurance policy" of the right of abode in Britain would persuade them to stay in Hong Kong.

The economy: the world's trader

With no natural resources other than its harbour (the container port is often the world's busiest), Hong Kong prospers thanks to the industry and ingenuity of its people and to a laissez-faire economic policy described by one financial secretary as "positive non-interventionism". Taxes are very low and customs duties are limited to oil, tobacco, alcohol and cosmetics. There are large disparities of wealth but very little real poverty and almost no unemployment.

The hongs

The economy has always been dominated by the "hongs", the big trading houses (from the Cantonese word for "shop"), such as Jardine Matheson (controlled by Britain's Keswick family), Swire Pacific (controlled by Britain's Swire family), the Wharf group and Hutchison Whampoa (whose chairman, Li Ka-shing, is reputed to be Hong Kong's richest man). Their activities range from airlines (Swire controls the colony's flag-carrier, Cathay Pacific) to telecommunications, shipping, container ports and supermarkets.

The hongs face two challenges: the need to expand beyond Hong Kong, which is too small to absorb all their energies, and the desire to protect their assets should Chinese rule prove disastrous. Jardine Matheson, even before the Joint Declaration, moved its corporate headquarters to

Bermuda (a move which dozens of other Hong Kong companies have since copied); Swire sold a shareholding in Cathay Pacific to China's state-owned CITIC group; the Hongkong and Shanghai Banking Corporation (which, with Standard Chartered, issued Hong Kong's currency) incorporated itself in London and bought Britain's Midland Bank; Hutchison bought Canada's Husky oil company.

The Chinese connection

For all the fears of 1997, Hong Kong's companies have long been tied to China. Several thousand Hong Kong companies now employ, directly or indirectly, about 3m workers in China's Guangdong province to make toys, garments and other low-tech items; they also provide two-thirds of China's foreign investment and act as the conduit for one-fifth of China's imports and two-fifths of its exports. Moreover, China is now the largest foreign investor in Hong Kong's stock market, Asia's biggest after Tokyo. The hope is that China, whatever its misgivings over Hong Kong's liberal politics, will not wish to kill "the goose that lays the golden eggs".

The airport

The hope, however, grows strong or faint depending on events in China. To restore confidence after the 1989 tragedy of Tiananmen Square, the governor announced a new "Port and Airport Development Scheme", costed originally at HK$127 billion ($16.3 billion) and including everything from new roads and an extended container port to a new airport. But bankers would not lend to the project unless it first had China's approval; China would not approve it because it suspected Britain of trying to empty Hong Kong's coffers before 1997. In 1991 China gave its backing in return for a guarantee of Hong Kong's financial reserves and health in 1997 and for a visit to Beijing by Britain's prime minister, John Major, to sign the agreement. Hongkongers saw it as a British kowtow, but a sensible one.

A future of hope and fear

The dream is that 1997 – despite a region-wide currency crisis soon after Tung Chee-hua became Hong Kong's first chief executive – will turn out to have been an innocuous date like any other and that Hongkongers will simply carry on making money; the nightmare is that Hong Kong after 1997 will be dispossessed just as Shanghai was after 1949. The most likely outcome, however, is that Hong Kong will continue as the richest and most comfortable city on the Chinese coast, but rather less efficient and much more corrupt.

Total area	1,074 sq km	% agricultural area	9
Capital area	Victoria	Highest point metres	Tai Mo Shan
Other urban areas	Kowloon		957
		Main rivers	–

The economy

GDP $bn	154.3	GDP per head $	24,440
% av. ann. growth in		GDP per head in purchasing	
real GDP 1991–96	5.3	power parity $	23,290

Origins of GDP	% of total	Components of GDP	% of total
Agriculture	1	Private consumption	59
Industry	17	Public consumption	9
of which:		Investment	35
manufacturing	9	Exports	147
Services	83	Imports	149

Structure of manufacturing

			% of total
Agric. & food processing	10	Other	33
Textiles & clothing	35	Av. ann. increase in industrial	
Machinery & transport	22	output 1991–96	-3.7

Inflation and exchange rates

Consumer price 1996 av. ann. incr.	6.0%	HK$ per $ 1997 average	7.8
Av. ann. rate 1991–96	8.1%	HK$ per $ end-1997	7.8

Balance of payments, reserves and debt

			$bn
Exports, goods & services	218.3	Net capital account	...
Imports, goods & services	220.5	Net current account	...
Net income	...	Other net investment	...
Net current transfers	...	Net errors & omissions	...
Current-account balance	...	Net change in reserves	-8.4
as % of GDP	...	Level of reserves, end-Dec.	63.8
Foreign debt	27.7	Debt service	1.5
as % of GDP	19.8	as % of export earnings	0.8

Principal exports	$bn fob	Principal imports	$bn fob
Clothing	9.0	Consumer goods	74.0
Electrical mach. & apparatus	3.9	Raw materials & semi-manuf.	69.9
Textiles	1.8	Capital goods	41.9
Watches, clocks &		Foodstuffs	8.4
photographic equipment	1.5	Fuels	4.2
Office machinery	1.3		

Main export destinations[a]	% of total	Main origins of imports	% of total
China	34.3	China	37.1
United States	21.2	Japan	13.6
Japan	6.5	Taiwan	8.0
Germany	4.2	United States	7.9
UK	3.3	Singapore	5.3
Singapore	2.7	South Korea	4.8

Government
System Special Administrative Region of China headed by chief executive appointed by China and assisted by an Executive Council. The 60-member Legislative Council (Legco) is formed by direct and indirect elections.
Main political parties Democratic Alliance for the Betterment of Hong Kong (DAB), Liberal Party (LP), Democratic Party (DP)

Climate and topography
Subtropical, with an annual average temperature of 21°C (70°F) and a rainfall of 2,160mm (85in), more than half of which falls in Jun–Aug. Winters are dry and sunny, summers humid. The mainland and islands of Hong Kong are a partly drowned old mountain range. Between Hong Kong island and the Kowloon peninsula is one of the great deep-water harbours of the world. The terrain is steep and hilly; land is at such a premium that much has been reclaimed from the sea. Inland, north of the Kowloon ridge, are the New Territories, the focus of agriculture and rapidly expanding dormitory towns.

People and society

Population m	6.0	% under 15	19.0
Pop. per sq km	6,252.0	% over 60	14.0
% urban	95.0	No. women per 100 men	92.0
% av. ann. growth 1980–95	1.4	Human Development Index	91.4
No. households m	1.7		

Life expectancy	yrs	Education	
Men	76	Spending as % of GDP	2.5
Women	81	Years of compulsory education	9
Crude birth rate	11	Adult literacy %	92.0
Crude death rate	5	Primary school enrolment %	102
Infant mortality		Secondary school enrolment %	64
per 1,000 live births	5	Tertiary education enrolment %	21

Workforce	% of total	Consumer goods ownership	
Services	62		per 1,000 people
Industry	37	Cars	34.0
Agriculture	1	Televisions	359.0
% of pop. over 15 in workforce	51	Mobile phones	129.0
		Personal computers	116.0

Ethnic groups	% of total	Religious groups	% of total
Chinese	97	Buddhist	18
British	0.5	Christian	18
		Taoist	14

Tourism		Health	
Tourist arrivals m	10.2	Spending as % of GDP	4.3
Tourism receipts $bn	10.8	People per doctor	1,211.0

a Including re-exports.

INDIA

Total area	3,287,590 sq km	Population	935.7m
GDP	$319.7bn	GDP per head	$340
Capital	New Delhi	Other cities	Bombay, Calcutta,
			Madras, Bangalore, Hyderabad

The Republic of India is the world's largest democracy, but it is also a country beset by political violence, poverty and sectarianism. Its challenge is to sustain a belated policy of economic liberalism, in the hope that Indian entrepreneurs can emulate the miracles of other Asian economies.

History: making the mosaic

India's first civilisation had taken root along the Indus valley, in the far north of the subcontinent (in what is now Pakistan), by 2500 BC. By 1750 BC it had collapsed, allowing the eventual invasion from the north by Aryan tribes between 1500 and 1200 BC. They developed cities along the Ganges valley; their Vedic religion was the foundation of Brahminism; and their Sanskrit tongue became a national language for the next 2,000 years. By the sixth century BC the Buddhist and Jain religions emerged; by the fourth century BC the Maurya dynasty formed the first Hindu empire in northern India, and within 100 years this had spread over two-thirds of the subcontinent. The Maurya empire eventually fragmented, but in the fourth century AD the north was again united under the Gupta dynasty.

The Muslim invasions began around AD 1000, and for a time Muslim, Hindu and Buddhist states co-existed in conflict. Then, in 1526, Babur established the Mughal empire, which, under Akbar the Great (1556–1605), spread Muslim power over most of India until, in the late 17th century, the Hindu Marathas challenged Mughal supremacy.

Meanwhile, Europe was seeking influence. Vasco da Gama's voyage to India in 1497 led to a century-long monopoly on trade with Europe by Portugal, until in the 17th century Holland, Britain and France began to compete.

The British raj

The British East India Company emerged triumphant. It established settlements from 1600 onwards, including a formal government for Bengal in 1700. By 1757 it had defeated the Mughals, and in 1784 Britain decided to bring the company under its formal control. Two years later, Britain appointed the first governor-general, but the company continued to rule India, subduing the Marathas in 1818.

This period was marked by increasing westernisation,

much of it, such as the Christian missions and the attempts to emancipate women, resented. In April 1857 Indian troops (sepoys) employed by the East India Company rose in revolt in Bengal, by refusing to use cartridges for the new Enfield rifle because they had first to bite off the ends and these had apparently been lubricated with a mix of pigs' and cows' lard, which was offensive to Muslims and Hindus equally. By May 10th the sepoys had seized Delhi, nominally restoring to power the retired Mughal emperor, Bahadur Shah II. There followed desperate fighting in Delhi, Cawnpore and Lucknow, with brutality on both sides, until on July 8th 1858 the uprising was officially declared over.

One result of the mutiny was an administrative reorganisation: the East India Company's powers were abolished and its functions and forces transferred to the British Crown. Another result was a policy of consultation: a new Legislative Council was formed in 1861 with Indian members nominated to it. But the most lasting consequence was an acceptance that the West could not be excluded: from this came the emergence of a westernised class system, whose middle and upper class ironically became the first Indian nationalists.

Seeking independence

Nationalism found its expression in 1885 in the Indian National Congress, which was dominated by Hindus, and then in 1906 in the All-India Muslim League. Most Muslims had co-operated with the British after the Mutiny, but after the first world war and the break-up of the Ottoman empire (which was Muslim), they began to oppose British rule.

In 1917 Congress (most Indians abbreviate the party's title) was taken over by its "extremist" Home Rule wing. Then in the 1920s and 1930s Mohandas K. Gandhi (later known as Mahatma) began a policy of peaceful non-co-operation in protest at the limited powers given to India under the Government of India Acts of 1919 and 1935. When Britain made India fight in the second world war, Congress declared it would not support the war effort unless granted full independence, and in 1942 it organised mass civil disobedience to force Britain to "quit India".

Partition

However, the independence issue became complicated by the demand by the Muslim League in 1940 for a separate Muslim nation. When Britain finally conceded independence, on August 15th 1947, its Indian Empire was partitioned between the new Muslim country of Pakistan and the rest of India. This process led to the movement of some 12m refugees, extreme sectarian violence and the integration of the former princely states into a federal Indian structure (the maharajahs had been given the choice of accession to the federation or independence). It also led to a perpetually festering dispute with Pakistan over Kashmir, where a Hindu prince ruled a Muslim majority.

Politics: free but fractious

Since January 26th 1950 India has been a republic within the British Commonwealth, accepting the British monarch as the head of the Commonwealth. India's head of state is now a president (with largely ceremonial powers) of a federal union of 25 states and 7 union territories. The upper house of Parliament is the Rajya Sabha (Council of States), which has not more than 250 members, most of them indirectly elected (a few are appointed by the president) by the state assemblies for a term of six years, with one-third retiring every second year. The lower house is the Lok Sabha (House of the People), almost all of whose 545 members are elected by universal suffrage on a "first past the post" system (a few can be nominated by the president to represent the Anglo-Indian community). The Lok Sabha's term is five years, unless the prime minister decides to call an early general election. The legislative, executive and judicial functions of the union are duplicated at the state level: the states of Bihar, Jammu and Kashmir, Karnataka, Maharashtra and Uttar Pradesh have bicameral legislatures; the other states have single-chamber bodies.

The first family

Although India has many parties, from the Hindu right-wing Bharatiya Janata Party to two separate communist parties, government has generally been by the Congress Party. The first exception was the 1977–80 government of the Janata (People's) Party under Morarji Desai, followed by the Janata Dal coalition government of Viswanath Pratap Singh in December 1989 and the minority government of Chandra Shekhar from November 1990. Congress regained power after the elections of May–June 1991, but lost it in the 1996 elections (when the Hindu-chauvinist Bharatiya Janata Party failed to assert a majority, a coalition "United Front" government was formed under the Janata Dal's H.D. Deve Gowda).

Congress traditionally espoused Fabian socialism, secularism and nationalism. However, its ideology was often subservient to personalities, not least because it became over the years almost the private fief of a single family. Jawaharlal Nehru was India's prime minister, and so Congress's dominating force, until his death in 1964. After the brief prime ministership, ended by his death, of Lal Bahadur Shastri, Nehru's daughter, Indira Gandhi (a purely fortuitous link to the Mahatma), in 1966 became Congress leader and prime minister. In 1969 Congress split and a group of party leaders, led by Morarji Desai, expelled her. In 1971, however, Mrs Gandhi's "New Congress Party" returned to power.

Unhappily, the Gandhi government became excessively authoritarian. In 1975 after a court found she had violated election laws, she declared a state of emergency. When elections were held in March 1977 Congress was defeated and she herself lost her seat. In January 1978 she formed the "real" Congress, under the name Congress-I (for Indira), and in November regained a seat in parliament. In January 1980 she once again was prime minister. When she was assassinated in October 1984 by a Sikh extremist, her successor was her son Rajiv (her favourite son and political adviser, Sanjay, had died in an air crash in June 1980).

When Rajiv was himself assassinated, in May 1991, allegedly by Tamil extremists, it seemed as if the Nehru clan's dominance of Congress was over, not least because Rajiv's Italian-born widow, Sonia, at the time refused the party leadership. However, in March 1998 she finally accepted the post and it seemed that her daughter, Priyanka, would also follow a political path.

The Rao government

After Congress's win in the 1991 federal election, P.V. Narasimha Rao was the compromise choice of squabbling Congress factions to succeed the assassinated Rajiv Gandhi as party leader. As prime minister of a minority government he went on to confound the sceptics. Not only did he introduce the most sweeping programme of economic reform in India's history, but he also kept Congress united. One example of his political skill was to accept in September 1991 the recommendations of the Mandal Commission that 27% of public service jobs be reserved for lower castes, in addition to the 22.5% already reserved for untouchable castes and tribal people. This neatly hijacked the chief policy proposal of V.P. Singh's Janata Dal. Moreover, to placate the upper castes (who had rioted against the proposal during Mr Singh's government) Mr Rao said a further 10% should be reserved for the upper-caste poor.

Hindu chauvinism

Although Congress regained power in the 1991 election the biggest gains were made by the Bharatiya Janata Party (BJP), using its appeal to Hindu fundamentalism. Moreover, in state elections the BJP gained control of Madhya Pradesh, Rajasthan, Uttar Pradesh and Himachal Pradesh. True, it failed to form a government after the 1996 election, but it was the largest single party and the "United Front" coalitions in 1996 and 1997, under first Deve Gowda and then Inder Kumar Gujral (also of the Janata Dal), both proved unstable, notably because of Congress's attitude.

The BJP, however, has a problem. Its appeal to Hindu chauvinism, as exemplified by a campaign to demolish the Babri mosque at Ayodhya and build a Hindu temple there (it is the birthplace of the god Ram), risks being too strident for moderate Hindus. But if it tones down this appeal, it loses ground to extremists such as the Vishnu Hindu Parishad (World Hindu Council).

Communal violence

The rise of the BJP – again the largest party in the 1998 election – could well threaten the secular ideal of Nehru's India. This is already strained by several separatist movements, for example in Nagaland, Assam and Tamil Nadu. The most dangerous, however, is the call by the Akali Dal for a Sikh state – Khalistan – in Punjab. It was the storming of a Sikh separatist stronghold within the Golden Temple at Amritsar in 1983 which led to Mrs Gandhi's assassination by a Sikh bodyguard in October 1984.

Foreign policy: a change of climate

Within its own region India is the dominant power, assuming the lead in the South Asian Association for Regional Co-operation (which also includes Pakistan, Nepal, Bhutan, Sri Lanka, Bangladesh and the Maldives) through the weight of its armed forces and population. Indeed, in 1987 India sent troops to Sri Lanka, in an abortive effort to suppress the Tamil Tigers. This ended with the troops' withdrawal by March 1990. In 1988 troops were also sent to foil a coup in the Maldives. Similar strength of Indian purpose was shown in 1989–90, when India virtually blockaded Nepal in protest at Nepal's improving relationship with China.

But the benchmark of India's foreign policy is its relationship with Pakistan, with whom it has fought wars immediately after partition (over the fate of Kashmir); again in 1965; and lastly in 1971, when India helped East Pakistan secede and become Bangladesh. The running sore of Kashmir – where the Pakistani and Indian armies face each other across a ceasefire line (the "line of control") between Azad, or Free, Kashmir, controlled by Pakistan, and the Indian-controlled two-thirds of the area – is especially difficult to heal. Pakistan argues that a plebiscite must be held on Kashmir's future; India maintains that Kashmir has been a part of the Union of India since 1963. The Indo-Pakistan relationship is made still more tense by the threshold nuclear capability on both sides: India exploded a "peaceful" nuclear device in 1974 and Pakistan is determined not to let India enjoy a permanent advantage.

Nuclear tangles

One attempt to defuse the problem was a proposal in 1991 by Pakistan for talks between Pakistan, India, America, Russia and China, with the aim of ending nuclear proliferation. This idea was taken up by America, which was anxious that India sign the Nuclear Non-Proliferation Treaty. India was not impressed, arguing that the treaty was biased in favour of those countries that already admitted to possessing nuclear weapons, notably, from India's point of view, China. This view is hard to dismiss, since India fought a war with China in 1962 over the Aksai Chin plateau near Tibet and since Sino-Indian border disputes remain unresolved near both Tibet and Nepal.

The Soviet demise

India's regional relationships, however, have always taken place within a larger context. Traditionally, India was supported by the Soviet Union, with which it signed a Treaty of Peace and Friendship in 1971. The USSR was seen as both an economic ally and a counter to China and to the American-backed Pakistan. All this changed at the end of the 1990s with the collapse of the Soviet Union. Initially, India felt alarmed. However, it was soon comforted by the realisation that with the end of the Afghanistan war, America no longer felt an obligation to support Pakistan.

Society: mixed

India is perhaps the world's most complex nation. Ethnically, it has Caucasoid, Mongoloid, Australoid and Negroid strains, with the yellow-skinned people near Tibet totally different, for example, from the very dark Tamils in the south. The country is the birthplace of many religions and the host of others: Hindus are about 83% of the population;

Muslims 11%; Christians 3%; Sikhs 2%; and Buddhists 1%. The main division among people is not just religion but language. Hindi, spoken by about 30% of the people, is the official language, with English an associate language for many official purposes. The Indian constitution also recognises 16 regional languages: of these Bengali, Marathi and Telegu are spoken by about 8% each; and Tamil and Urdu (which is similar to Hindi) by 5% or more each.

Caste marks

Indian society is also distinguished by the caste demarcations of Hinduism. There are basically four categories: at the top are Brahmans, or priests; then Kshatriyas, or warriors; then Vaisyas, or merchants; and lastly Sudras, or artisans and labourers. However, over the course of 3,000 odd years these have divided into about 3,000 castes and 25,000 sub-castes. At the very bottom of the social heap are the "outcastes", or "scheduled castes", whose occupations (for example, as latrine attendants) are thought to pollute them. Mahatma Gandhi tried to redeem their status by calling them *Harijan*, or Children of God. One untouchable leader, B.R. Ambedkar, preferred the more pugnacious term *dalit*, or downtrodden. Beyond the caste system are also some 600 tribal minorities. In theory, discrimination on the basis of caste is illegal; in practice, it is rife, which is why the constitution also guarantees parliamentary seats for the scheduled castes and the tribals.

The economy: aroused at last

By some measures, India is an economic giant: it is one of the world's dozen biggest industrialised economies; and its technological capability runs from offshore oil-drilling to satellite-launching. By other measures, the country is hardly developed: three-quarters of its people rely on agriculture for their living; literacy rates are low; population growth is high (despite vigorous – and, in the mid-1970s, almost forced – programmes of contraception and sterilisation); and perhaps a third of the people described by the World Bank as the world's "absolute poor" live in India.

The industrial size is the result of a series of five-year plans by economists who, in the first years of independence, were imbued with the liberal socialism of the London School of Economics and who also saw the Soviet Union as a model for the development of a vast, heavily populated landmass. Added to this was the Gandhian philosophy of self-sufficiency. In retrospect, however, it can be seen that India suffered badly from this autarkic approach. While the countries of South-East Asia enjoyed decades of fast growth, India's economic growth rate dawdled at 3.4% a year from 1950 to 1973, equal to only 1.2% per head.

The dawdling was an inevitable consequence of some of the world's most protectionist policies. For example, imports of all but the most essential items were forbidden, or subject to high tariffs; licences were required for virtually any form of production, including the right to change it or increase it; and it was made almost impossible to close a loss-making factory or sack a redundant workforce. On top of this came the collapse of the Soviet Union, with which India had enjoyed subsidised trading links.

Dr Singh's cure

Arguably, the Rao government in 1991 had no choice but to adopt radical reforms, since these were the prerequisite of emergency help from the International Monetary Fund. Even so, the measures taken by Mr Rao's finance minister, Manmohan Singh, were dramatic.

Part of Mr Singh's policy was simple austerity, designed to bring the budget deficit from 8% of GDP to an IMF-agreed target of 6.5% of GDP in 1991–92 and to less than 6% in 1992–93. The rest of his policy amounted to abandoning the economic philosophy that had prevailed since independence. In its place is an increasingly free-market approach. In February 1991, in his second budget in eight months, Mr Singh made the rupee partly convertible; abolished non-tariff curbs on most imports; legalised gold imports; encouraged foreign participation in oil and gas; and allowed foreign pension funds to invest in Indian stockmarkets. The question is how well successor governments will continue his liberal measures (the I.K. Gujral government made a valiant – if short-lived – attempt in 1997).

Lingering maladies

While such measures will undoubtedly improve India's economic performance, complete success may yet prove to be elusive. The curse of India's open democracy is the need for political compromise. For India to achieve its full potential, it must privatise or close many state-owned factories and adopt an "exit policy" to allow both the public and private sectors to make workers redundant. In a poor country with strong unions, that will be difficult.

Total area	3,287,590 sq km	% agricultural area	60
Capital	New Delhi	Highest point metres	Nanda Devi
Other cities	Bombay, Calcutta,		7,871
	Madras, Bangalore, Hyderabad	Main rivers	Ganges, Indus, Brahmaputra

The economy[a]

GDP $bn	319.7	GDP per head $	340.0
% av. ann. growth in		GDP per head in purchasing	
real GDP 1991–96	...	power parity $	1,400

Origins of GDP	% of total	Components of GDP	% of total
Agriculture	29	Private consumption	68
Industry	29	Public consumption	10
of which:		Investment	25
manufacturing	19	Exports	12
Services	41	Imports	15

Structure of manufacturing

			% of total
Agric. & food processing	11	Other	51
Textiles & clothing	13	Av. ann. increase in industrial	
Machinery & transport	25	output 1991–96	7.2

Inflation and exchange rates

Consumer price 1996 av. ann. incr.	8.9%	Rupees per $ 1997 average	36.80
Av. ann. rate 1991–96	9.5%	Rupees per $ end-1997	39.23

Balance of payments, reserves and debt

			$bn
Exports, goods & services	39.7	Net capital account	...
Imports, goods & services	48.5	Net current account	...
Net income	-4.5	Other net investment	...
Net current transfers	7.5	Net errors & omissions	...
Current-account balance	-5.8	Net change in reserves	...
as % of GDP	-1.8	Level of reserves, end-Dec.	12.1
Foreign debt	93.8	Debt service	4.1
as % of GDP	22.6	as % of export earnings	27.9

Principal exports	$bn fob	Principal imports	$bn fob
Gems & jewellery	5.3	Petroleum & petroleum products	7.2
Textiles	3.8	Capital goods	6.6
Garments	3.7	Gems	2.1
Engineering goods	3.6	Iron & steel	1.4
Chemicals	3.0	Fertilisers	1.3

Main export destinations	% of total	Main origins of imports	% of total
EU	26.5	EU	26.6
UK	6.3	Germany	8.6
Germany	6.2	UK	5.2
Belgium	3.5	Belgium	4.6
United States	17.4	United States	10.5
Japan	7.0	Japan	6.7

Government

System Federal republic. Each of the 25 states has its own elected legislature and governor appointed by the federal president. The legislative parliament has a Council of States (Rajya Sabha), with no more than 250 members elected for 6 years by the state assemblies, and a 545-member House of the People (Lok Sabha) elected for 5 years from single-member constituencies. The chief executive is the prime minister. Head of state is the president, elected by a college of parliament and the state assemblies.

Main political parties Bharatiya Janata Party, Congress

Climate and topography

Tropical, monsoon season Jun–Oct. Annual rainfall 750–1,500mm (30–60in) in most areas. Average annual temperatures from around 13°C (55°F) in northern highlands to 25–30°C (77–86°F) on coast. South of the Himalayas a wide and densely populated alluvial plain contains the main rivers. Peninsular India consists of the Deccan plateau fringed by a coastal plain.

People and society

Population m	935.7	% under 15	35.0
Pop. per sq km	313.0	% over 60	8.0
% urban	27.0	No. women per 100 men	94.0
% av. ann. growth 1980–95	2.0	Human Development Index	44.6
No. households m	178.5		

Life expectancy	yrs	Education	
Men	62	Spending as % of GDP	2.9
Women	63	Years of compulsory education	8
Crude birth rate	26	Adult literacy %	51.2
Crude death rate	9	Primary school enrolment %	105
Infant mortality		Secondary school enrolment %	...
per 1,000 live births	68	Tertiary education enrolment %	...

Workforce	% of total	Consumer goods ownership	
Services	20		per 1,000 people
Industry	16	Cars	2.0
Agriculture	64	Televisions	61.0
% of pop. over 15 in workforce	43	Mobile phones	0.1
		Personal computers	1.3

Ethnic groups	% of total	Religious groups	% of total
Indo-Aryan	72	Hindu	83
Dravidian	25	Muslim	11
Mongoloid	3	Christian	3
		Sikh	2
		Buddhist	1

Tourism		Health	
Tourist arrivals m	1.8	Spending as % of GDP	3.5
Tourism receipts $bn	3.0	People per doctor	2,459

a 1995.

INDONESIA

Total area	1,904,569 sq km	Population	193.8m
GDP	$227.4bn	GDP per head	$1,175
Capital	Jakarta	Other cities	Surabaya, Bandung

Indonesia's large population and petroleum wealth give it the foundation to be a regional power. The challenge is to secure the country's future with steady economic growth that will overcome the problems of a multi-ethnic nation that spreads across some 13,700 islands.

History: unity from diversity

Indonesia's cultural origins lie first in the Malay kingdom of Srivijaya, which from the 7th to the 12th centuries spanned the Malay peninsula, Sumatra and the western part of Java. The Srivijaya kingdom and the Majapahit kingdom which took power in Java at the end of the 13th century were influenced by Hinduism and Buddhism.

Islam arrived from India in the 13th century. Over the next two centuries the faith spread throughout the archipelago, except for Bali, which remained Hindu.

But the Muslim kingdoms were unable to resist the pressures of Europe's naval powers. The Portuguese arrived in the Moluccas (Spice Islands) in 1510, and were followed by the Spanish, Dutch and British. By the end of the 17th century the British had gone and the Portuguese remained only in Timor. Meanwhile the Dutch East India Company had gained colonial sway over Java, Sumatra and the Moluccas. Dutch control, apart from a brief interruption from 1806 to 1815, lasted until the Japanese invasion of 1942.

The fight for independence

The Japanese were welcomed by most Indonesians almost as liberators from Dutch colonialism. The anti-colonial movement had begun with the founding in 1927 of the Indonesia Nationalist Party (PNI) under Sukarno. When Japan surrendered in 1945, Sukarno promptly declared, on August 17th, Indonesia's independence. The Dutch tried through a mix of war and negotiation to regain control but in December 1949 were forced to grant independence in a nominal union of Indonesia with the Netherlands. Indonesia dissolved the union with the Netherlands in 1954 in protest at the Netherlands' continuing control over Irian Barat, or West New Guinea. In October 1962, the Netherlands transferred Irian Barat to the United Nations; but in May 1963 Indonesia annexed the area as Irian Jaya. The final step in creating today's Indonesia was the occupation of East Timor in 1975 on the departure of the Portuguese, and then its annexation in 1976 (which, pending the determination of the inhabitants' own wishes, is not recognised by the United Nations).

Sukarno and Suharto

Indonesia's modern founder, Sukarno, was a charismatic populist intent on making Indonesia a leader of the Non-Aligned Movement (whose genesis can be traced back to a conference in Bandung in 1955, six years before the NAM's formation). In the process Sukarno was friendly with local communists and the China of Mao Zedong, and suspicious of the West. This showed in Indonesia's military "confrontation" in the early 1960s with the British-backed federation of Malaysia (Sukarno proposed in its place "Maphilindo", Indonesia, Malaya and the Philippines).

But much of the foreign policy activism was to divert attention from Sukarno's corruption and mismanagement of the economy. In September 1965 an abortive coup, apparently involving the Indonesian communist party, PKI, took place. Sukarno's own role remains obscure, but the military, led by its chief of staff, General Suharto, crushed the coup with extreme ruthlessness, killing at least 500,000. In March 1966 Sukarno was forced to transfer emergency powers, and then in February 1967 full powers, to Suharto. Finally, in March 1968, Suharto was inaugurated as Indonesia's president.

Politics: pulling the strings

Governing such a huge and diverse country as Indonesia is a matter of checking extremism and carefully balancing different interest groups. The liberal democracy established in 1950 was marred by regional revolts and unstable cabinets, persuading Sukarno in 1959 to bring back the country's 1945 constitution. This is based on the five principles of Pancasila: belief in one god; humanitarianism; Indonesia's unity; popular democracy; and social justice. Sukarno then replaced the elected House of Representatives with a provisional People's Consultative Assembly composed of his own appointees from the various nationalist, religious and communist groups. Sukarno called this system "guided democracy".

But it led only to the coup of 1965, which marked the end of what was subsequently called the Old Order. In its place Suharto established the New Order, still formally based on the 1945 constitution. Supreme power is theoretically held by the People's Consultative Assembly, which has

1,000 members and sits at least once every five years to elect the president. Half of the assembly consists of members appointed by the government from the 27 provinces, from the political parties and various "functional" groups (in proportion to the general election results), and from the armed services. The other half of the assembly is the House of Representatives, a legislative body which sits at least once a year. This consists of 400 members chosen by general election every five years, and 100 representatives of the armed forces. In other words, the president and the armed forces have an unbreakable grip on power.

Suharto made that grip stronger in 1973 by forcing the various political parties (other, of course, than the banned PKI) to merge. The Indonesian Democratic Party (PDI) combined three former nationalist and Christian parties; the United Development Party (PPP) represented four Muslim groups; and Golkar was a coalition of functional groups such as teachers, civil servants and retired soldiers. Since 1985 – a year after the Muslim social organisation, Nahdlatul Ulama, withdrew from the PPP – all political parties and mass organisations have had to adopt Pancasila as their only ideological basis; constitutional amendments need a two-thirds majority in the People's Consultative Assembly and 90% approval in a popular referendum. In every election so far, Golkar has won at least three-fifths of the vote.

The army's functions

The guarantor of this structure is the 276,000-strong Indonesian armed forces (ABRI). From the struggle against the Dutch to the suppression of the 1965 coup and on to the present, ABRI has had an institutionalised *dwifungsi* (dual function), a role not just in external defence but also in internal politics. Senior officers of the armed forces, either on secondment or after their retirement, fill posts in the bureaucracy as well as the People's Consultative Assembly; they also operate many large business enterprises.

Stresses and strains

Pancasila and the emphasis on consensus have kept Indonesia remarkably stable since the 1965 coup attempt. But there are stresses that threaten the system. Islamic fundamentalism is particularly strong in Aceh, at the northern end of Sumatra, where there is a separatist movement; and Islamic extremism is said to have been behind violent riots in Jakarta's port area of Tanjung Priok in 1984. In Irian Jaya there is a stubborn Melanesian separatist movement, the Organisasi Papua Merdeka (Free Papua Organisation). In

East Timor the Fretilin guerrilla movement survives to harass the Indonesian army. In November 1991 the armed forces killed scores of peaceful demonstrators at the funeral of a separatist sympathiser in Dili, the capital of East Timor.

Foreign policy: more friends than foes

East Timor, which draws attention to Indonesia's sometimes casual attitude towards human rights, is the only subject over which the rest of the world takes issue – albeit quietly – with Indonesia. Suharto has been at pains to develop good relations with his neighbours and with the West. In 1967, for example, Indonesia became a founding member of the Association of South-East Asian Nations (ASEAN).

This does not, however, mean that foreign relations are always smooth. Diplomatic links with China, which was blamed for the 1965 coup attempt, were not restored until 1990; relations with Australia were soured for a time in the mid-1980s because of Australian press reports of corruption and the Suharto family; and western criticism of the Dili massacre led Indonesia to dissolve the combination of foreign aid donors known as the Inter-Governmental Group on Indonesia (credit was, after all, still readily available).

As the association's largest country Indonesia also plays its own role in ASEAN. Its good relations with Russia meant that it had a diplomatic access to Vietnam in the 1980s that other ASEAN members lacked. It has also had a somewhat ambivalent attitude towards America's security presence in the region, advocating instead a Zone of Peace, Freedom and Neutrality (ZOPFAN).

Society: unity from diversity

Indonesia is now the fourth most populous country in the world and one-third of its people are aged under 15. Three-fifths of the people are concentrated on the islands of Java, Madura and Bali, which together account for only 7% of Indonesia's land area. Indonesia has not only a family-planning policy but also a policy of transmigration, granting land and financial incentives to those willing to move to thinly populated areas such as Kalimantan and Irian Jaya.

Indonesia is a mosaic of ethnic groups and cultures, with dozens of different languages. There are, for example, Malays, Bataks and Minangkabaus in Sumatra and hundreds of different tribes – some still in the Stone Age – in Irian Jaya and Kalimantan. Political power, however, rests with the Javanese. The largest non-indigenous group is the Chinese, comprising the *peranakan* who have been in Indonesia for generations and the late arrivals known as *totok*. The Chinese form only 2–3% of the population, but they control business (often acting as *cekong*, or agents, for Indonesian officials and politicians). This makes them a scapegoat during times of unrest or hardship. Some 88% of Indonesians are Muslims; there are Christian minorities on several islands (Roman Catholics are found in many important posts); and Hinduism is the majority religion on Bali. The government is ever alert to prevent the growth of Islamic fundamentalism. The government's methods include a mix of suppression and the co-option of Islamic thinkers into the carefully controlled political process.

Pancasila is a deliberate attempt to ensure that the ethnic and religious mosaic does not fragment. So too is the adoption of Bahasa Indonesia (in essence the same as Malay) as a unifying official language, and the insistence that Chinese Indonesians should adopt Indonesian names.

The economy: resources aplenty

The basis of development is petroleum. Reserves of oil are between 8.5 billion barrels (proven) and 50 billion (unproven); natural gas reserves are at least 80 trillion cubic feet. Indonesia is the world's second largest producer (after Malaysia) of palm oil, and is a leading producer of rubber, pepper, cloves, nutmeg, tobacco, tea, coffee, timber and tin.

The challenge is to avoid an overdependence on primary products and to bring a growing population out of poverty. After the Sukarno era, when budget deficits equalled 50% of government spending and inflation reached 640% a year, Suharto sought to meet the challenge with a series of five-year plans, or Repelitas.

Repelita I, from 1969 to 1974, concentrated on agriculture in an effort to lessen the dependence on rice imports (self-sufficiency was reached in 1984). Repelita II embraced the 1974 and 1979 price hikes of the Organisation of Petroleum Exporting Countries (of which Indonesia is a member). Although oil revenue rose dramatically, it was offset by a financial scandal in Pertamina, the state oil and gas company, and by the higher import and development bills that followed the OPEC price shocks. Subsequent plans sought to move from import-substituting industries to export-oriented industries. Underlying all recent plans is the need to stimulate job creation for a labour market that grows by more than 2m a year.

Diversification

The development effort has been reasonably successful over the past quarter century. The proportion of the population living beneath the poverty line, for example, had fallen from 40% in 1967 to about 15% at the start of the 1990s.

The secret has been to diversify. Oil and gas (the main buyers are Japan, South Korea and Taiwan) account for a fifth or more of export earnings, but there has been a rapid growth in the export of manufactured goods, such as shoes, textiles, garments and in the tourism industry (especially of Bali). In addition, the export of unprocessed timber was progressively banned during the 1980s in order to build the exports of a domestic plywood and furniture industry. Because wages are among the lowest in ASEAN, and because the rupiah has been progressively devalued, manufactured exports are likely to expand their market share.

Problems

Development, however, has not been painless. With agriculture accounting for about a fifth of economic output, most Indonesians are farmers only just above the subsistence level; industrial areas are polluted; some 45% of the workforce is said to be underemployed; and foreign debt is worryingly high. Moreover, corruption permeates society in all aspects, including business. One result of crony capitalism was a serious financial crisis in 1997 and 1998, triggering the intervention of the IMF and a promise by Indonesia to improve banking supervision and further deregulate the economy. Another long-term problem is illegal or badly controlled logging, especially in Kalimantan (Borneo).

Opportunities – and challenges

Whatever the problems, Indonesia's potential is almost boundless. The opportunity was spotted by Singapore, which in the late 1980s talked of "growth triangles", joining parts of Indonesia with Singapore and Malaysia (for example, Indonesia's Batam Island, Singapore and Malaysia's Johore).

The challenge is to maintain a stable political environment. President Suharto was re-elected for a seventh term, at the age of 76, in the presidential election of 1998. This prolonged rule may increase disquiet, including among the military, at the failure of Suharto to prepare a successor (B.J. Habibie was a controversial choice as vice-president). As the local saying goes: "Nothing grows in the shade of the banyan tree", and the banyan tree is the symbol of Golkar.

Total area	1,904,569 sq km	% agricultural area	18
Capital	Jakarta	Highest point metres	Puncak Jaya
Other cities	Surabaya, Bandung,		5,030
	Medan	Main rivers	Hari

The economy

GDP $bn	227.4	GDP per head $	1,175
% av. ann. growth in		GDP per head in purchasing	
real GDP 1991–96	7.3	power parity $	3,800

Origins of GDP	% of total	Components of GDP	% of total
Agriculture	17	Private consumption	56
Industry	42	Public consumption	8
of which:		Investment	38
manufacturing	24	Exports	25
Services	41	Imports	27

Structure of manufacturing

			% of total
Agric. & food processing	26	Other	46
Textiles & clothing	15	Av. ann. increase in industrial	
Machinery & transport	12	output 1991–96	...

Inflation and exchange rates

Consumer price 1996 av. ann. incr.	8.0%	Rupiah per $ 1997 average	2,497.0
Av. ann. rate 1991–96	8.6%	Rupiah per $ end-1997	3,275.0

Balance of payments, reserves and debt

			$bn
Exports, goods & services	51.2	Net capital account	0.0
Imports, goods & services	53.2	Net direct & portfolio investment	3.7
Net income	-5.8	Other net investment	2.5
Net current transfers	0.8	Net errors & omissions	2.3
Current-account balance	-7.0	Net change in reserves	-1.6
as % of GDP	-3.1	Level of reserves, end-Dec.	14.9
Foreign debt	107.8	Debt service	8.7
as % of GDP	54.5	as % of export earnings	30.9

Principal exports	$bn fob	Principal imports	$bn fob
Crude oil & products	7.3	Machinery & transport equip.	17.5
Natural gas	4.5	Other manufactures	6.6
Plywood	3.6	Chemicals	6.0
Ready-made garments	3.6	Food, drinks & tobacco	4.2
Textiles	3.0	Fuels & lubricants	3.7
Rubber	2.2	Raw materials	3.5

Main export destinations	% of total	Main origins of imports	% of total
Japan	25.9	Japan	19.8
United States	13.6	United States	11.7
Singapore	7.8	Germany	7.0
South Korea	6.6	Singapore	6.7
China	4.1	Australia	5.9
Netherlands	3.3	South Korea	5.6

Government
System Military-dominated republic. The president, who is both chief executive and head of state, is elected for 5-year terms. The 1,000-member People's Consultative Assembly includes a legislative House of Representatives, with 500 government appointees, 100 members of the armed forces and 400 elected members.
Main political parties Golkar, United Development Party, Indonesian Democratic Party

Climate and topography
Tropical: hot and humid, but more moderate in the highlands. There are nearly 14,000 islands, 930 of them inhabited. Most are rugged, sometimes volcanic, and covered with rain forest. Sumatra, Java, Southern Borneo, Sulawesi and Irian Jaya contain the majority of the population. Most live in river valleys, alluvial coastal plains or on terraced mountain sides.

People and society

Population m	193.8	% under 15	33.0
Pop. per sq km	107.0	% over 60	7.0
% urban	34.0	No. women per 100 men	100.0
% av. ann. growth 1980–95	1.8	Human Development Index	66.8
No. households m	40.7		

Life expectancy	yrs	Education	
Men	62	Spending as % of GDP	1.3
Women	66	Years of compulsory education	6
Crude birth rate	23	Adult literacy %	83.2
Crude death rate	8	Primary school enrolment %	114
Infant mortality		Secondary school enrolment %	43
per 1,000 live births	51	Tertiary education enrolment %	10

Workforce	% of total	Consumer goods ownership	
Services	31		per 1,000 people
Industry	14	Cars	5.0
Agriculture	55	Televisions	147.0
% of pop. over 15 in workforce	44	Mobile phones	1.1
		Personal computers	3.7

Ethnic groups	% of total	Religious groups	% of total
Javanese	40	Muslim	88
Sudanese	15	Christian	7
Indonesian	12	Hindu	2
Madurese	5		

Tourism		Health	
Tourist arrivals m	3.9	Spending as % of GDP	1.5
Tourism receipts $bn	6.1	People per doctor	7,028

JAPAN

Total area	377,708 sq km	Population	125.8m
GDP	$4,600bn	GDP per head	$36,575
Capital	Tokyo	Other cities	Yokohama, Osaka, Sapporo, Nagoya

Japan is the world's most successful industrial economy. But its economic weight and financial clout have yet to be translated internationally into political and military muscle. This discrepancy seems likely to erode over time, in which case the challenge for Japan's politicians is to find an appropriate role for Japan on the world stage, a quest which, ironically, disquiets the Japanese people as much as their neighbours in Asia.

History: pride before the fall

Japanese tradition holds that the nation began with the accession of the emperor Jimmu in 660 BC, but historical records ascribe the unification of the country to the Yamato clan in the early 5th century AD. The emperor was given a genealogy to link him to the Sun goddess. During this period, Japan was influenced by the culture of China and by the Buddhism imported from Korea.

By the 9th century, however, Japan had acquired its own literature, script and cultural identity. At the same time powerful families emerged to form a "samurai" military class which increasingly manipulated the emperors. In 1192 the samurai Minamoto Yoritomo established the first military government, or shogunate, at Kamakura, a form of government which lasted until 1867.

The Kamakura shogunate was marked by Mongol invasions launched from Korea in 1274 and 1281. Both were defeated by the sudden appearance of typhoons, the Kamikaze (Divine Wind), confirming the belief that Japan was somehow divinely protected. Even so, the cost of maintaining a military alert against the Mongols virtually bankrupted the Kamakura shogunate. It was succeeded in 1333 by a three-century long period of rival shogunates, led by the Ashikaga shoguns of Muromachi, in Kyoto.

Not until the end of the 16th century did a warrior, Oda Nobunaga, emerge strong enough to begin to impose unity on Japan. His successor, Toyotomi Hideyoshi, launched a disastrous invasion of Korea in 1592 (so imprinting a bitterness which still marks relations between the two countries).

Edo isolation

A united Japan was finally achieved by Tokugawa Ieyasu,

who defeated his rivals in the battle of Sekigahara in 1600, and then, in 1603, was appointed shogun, with his headquarters in the village of Edo (the modern Tokyo). The Tokugawa shogunate was a police state: Christianity, which had arrived in the middle of the 16th century, was virtually eradicated in favour of Confucianism, which stressed a man's loyalty to his master; all foreigners, except for a few Dutch and Chinese traders in Nagasaki, were expelled; and Japanese were forbidden to travel abroad.

The isolationism of this Edo era had several results. One was a flowering of Japanese culture; another was the rise of the merchant houses, many of which still dominate Japan. This was ironic, since the merchants were at the bottom of the social order, but they grew powerful by lending money to the samurai, who were at the top of society but had nothing to do in a period of extended peace.

The rise of the merchants, and the impoverishment of the government, strained the feudal system. So, too, did the pressure of the West. In 1854 Commodore Matthew Perry sailed into Edo harbour and by the implicit threat of military action forced Japan to begin diplomatic relations with America and grant trading rights. This, in turn, led to a civil war, the end of the Tokugawa shogunate and, in 1868, the restoration of the emperor's power by the accession of the Emperor Meiji (who renamed Edo Tokyo).

Meiji mischief

The Meiji period was one of modernisation. Perceptive leaders from the south-west of the country (they were later known as the *genro*, or elder statesmen) sent fact-finding missions to the West in search of technologies and ideas.

One result in 1889 was the Prussian-inspired Meiji Constitution, which instituted a constitutional monarchy with a two-chamber Diet (parliament). Another result was an imperialist drive in which Japan first defeated China in 1895 and then Russia in 1905. Annexation of Formosa (Taiwan), parts of Russia and then Korea all followed. As the world slipped into depression in the 1930s, so Japan saw militarism as its salvation. In 1931 Japan seized Manchuria, renaming it Manchukuo; in 1937 Japanese troops went on to occupy Beijing, Tianjin, Shanghai and Nanking (where they killed and raped thousands upon thousands); by 1940 Japan had occupied northern Indochina, and the following year, all of Indochina. Finally, on December 7th 1941, Japan, by now formally allied to Nazi Germany, sent aircraft to attack the American fleet in Pearl Harbor, Hawaii. It seemed that Japan was well on the way to creating its

"Greater East Asia Co-prosperity Sphere", an industrial bloc centred on Japan, Korea and northern China which would draw its raw materials from South-East Asia.

Atomic catastrophe

In retrospect, however, the Pearl Harbor attack – devastatingly successful at the time – was a colossal blunder because it brought America into the second world war. Although Japan's land forces went on in 1942 to conquer the Philippines, Singapore and the rest of South-East Asia, the navy and then Japan's own cities were increasingly exposed to counterattack. In April 1945 American forces landed in the southern Japanese island of Okinawa. Then, on August 6th and 7th 1945, American aircraft dropped atom bombs on Hiroshima and Nagasaki. On August 8th the Soviet Union declared war on Japan and occupied Manchuria; the following week the Pacific war was over, and on September 2nd 1945 a Japanese surrender document was signed aboard the USS *Missouri* in Tokyo Bay.

In little more than 50 years Japan had gone from backward feudalism to industrial and military greatness, and then to humiliating defeat and occupation by foreign forces. Those forces did not leave until 1952, having restructured Japan to their liking.

Politics: the "peace constitution"

Technically the "peace constitution", devised for Japan in 1947 by the Allied Occupation under General MacArthur, is simply an amendment to the Meiji constitution. But instead of specifying the emperor as the source of sovereign power, it stipulates that sovereign power rests with the people. The other two guiding principles are pacifism and human rights.

As part of a design to decentralise power, the executive consists of a prime minister elected from the Diet with a cabinet selected mainly from the Diet. The Diet itself consists of a House of Representatives, originally composed of 512 members elected for four-year terms, and a less powerful upper body, the House of Councillors. Under reforms agreed in 1994 and first applied in the 1996 elections, the lower house now has 300 single-seat constituencies and 200 with members chosen by proportional representation, so largely replacing the multi-seat constituencies that had fostered "money politics". The upper house has 252 members, elected for six-year terms, with half the seats contested every three years; 100 of the seats are chosen by proportional representation, the rest coming from prefectural elections. The upper house's power is essentially limited to delaying legislation, although normally a compromise will be worked out if there is initial disagreement with the lower house.

LDP rules

Decentralisation did not happen. By 1955 various left-wing parties had merged into the Japan Socialist Party (now confusingly renamed the Social Democratic Party of Japan), and the conservative Japan Democratic Party had merged with the Liberal Party to form the Liberal Democratic Party (LDP), which has dominated Japan ever since.

Although the opposition was not irrelevant, the LDP for almost four decades made Japan a one-party state. However, because Japan is a consensus-minded society, the LDP rarely used its majority to force through legislation. Instead, it made deals with various parties of the weak and divided opposition. This was especially true after 1989, when the LDP lost its majority in the upper house thanks to the imposition of an unpopular consumption tax; and thanks also to public disgust at a scandal in which the Recruit company gave shares in return for political favours.

After 1993, when the LDP suffered a spate of defections, Japan's political parties entered a period of confusion, changing names – and indeed policies – with a rapidity that showed personalities counted for more than ideas. Unusually in capitalist Asia, there is a legal communist party. There is also a tradition of student radicalism in Japan; this helped spawn the Japanese Red Army, which waged international terrorism in the 1970s and early 1980s.

Money and factions

The LDP's success was always based on the support of rural Japan (which is grossly overweighted in terms of constituencies), the retail sector and Japan's industrialists. However, this success could not have been sustained without money. In multi-seat constituencies patronage won votes, which meant that campaigning was expensive, especially since several candidates from the same party might be campaigning against each other. Once elected, a candidate needed to replenish the campaign coffers, which encouraged corrupt links with business.

This "money politics" bred factions within the LDP. These are based not on ideology but on family ties or money, and the prime minister, his term usually limited by the party to two years (occasionally renewed), has rarely been the most important man in the LDP. Real power belonged to party barons, who might hold no official positions, and to senior civil servants, who on retirement "descend from heaven" to take top jobs in business.

Reform

But in 1993 the LDP's stranglehold was broken. One pressure was the decline in the rural population; as constituency boundaries were changed to reflect demographic reality (at the start of the 1990s a rural vote was worth three times an urban one in terms of representation in the Diet), so the LDP had to appeal to the more fickle urban voter. A second pressure was public resentment at the financial (and sex) scandals that had dogged the party's leaders.

Toshiki Kaifu, prime minister from 1989 to 1991, pledged to reduce "money politics" by changing many of the multi-seat constituencies into single-seat ones with their members chosen on a "first past the post" basis; other seats would be allotted by proportional representation. But the faction leaders in October 1991 sacked Mr Kaifu. His successor, Kiichi Miyazawa, failed to keep the LDP united. Financial scandals mounted; dissidents defected to form new parties such as the Japan Renewal Party. Finally, in the general election of July 18th, 1993, the LDP was forced into opposition. The new coalition of Morihiro Hosokawa managed in January 1994 to limit campaign financing and to pass reforms – implemented after the 1996 election – so that for the lower house there would be 300 single-member constituencies and 200 members from 11 multi-member constituencies. However, in April 1994 Mr Hosokawa resigned after a financial scandal. He was succeeded by Tsutomu Hata. In June the LDP became part of a coalition government led by the left-wing Social Democrat Tomiichi Murayama. But after the 1996 election the LDP took charge of the coalition, with Ryutaro Hashimoto as prime minister.

Foreign policy: shy but serious

Defeat in 1945 placed Japan firmly in the western camp, with a mutual security treaty being signed with America in 1951. This has provided ever since for the presence of American bases in Japan, including in Okinawa (which was not handed back to Japanese sovereignty until 1972). From America's point of view, Japan was a crucial part of the western posture against the Soviet Union in the cold war; for Japan, which depends on imported energy, America was the ultimate security guarantor, not least because article 9 of the "peace constitution" forbids the possession of war potential and renounces the right to belligerency.

However, this coincidence of interests no longer holds so true. With the cold war ended, some Americans – angry over the perennial Japanese trade surplus with America – accuse Japan of not shouldering its share of international responsibility. This was especially so after Iraq's invasion of Kuwait in 1990. Constrained by its constitution and domestic opposition, the Japanese government was able, belatedly, to provide only financial assistance (to the tune of $14 billion) to the American-led coalition. The only material assistance was the dispatch of minesweepers to the Gulf long after the conflict had ended. Only in June 1992 did the Diet pass a law allowing Japanese troops to participate abroad in United Nations peacekeeping operations. Critics say the law is so hedged with restrictions that it will have little practical value.

Overseas initiatives

This is true, but also unfair. The law is a sign of Japan's increasing willingness to play an international role. By 1989 Japan had become the world's largest aid donor. Moreover, at the start of the 1990s Japan was taking a leading diplomatic role to achieve peace in Cambodia (indeed, after the Cambodian accord of October 1991 a Japanese, Yasushi Akashi, headed the UN mission to Cambodia). In June 1992 Japan's generosity at the environmental summit in Rio de Janeiro upstaged America. Meanwhile, Japan's bureaucrats make no secret of their desire for Japan to become a permanent member of the UN Security Council.

Overseas obstacles

But how acceptable is an internationally active Japan? The impetus comes from America and Europe. Japan's neighbours still harbour fears of a resurgent Japan. They note that despite limiting its military expenditure to around 1% of GDP, Japan's economy is so large that its military might is already considerable. In addition, although various prime ministers have formally apologised to countries such as South Korea and the Philippines for Japan's wartime brutality, Japanese society – unlike Germany's – has made no attempt to come to terms with its war record. Indeed, the ministry of education has rewritten history so that Japan's schoolchildren should not know that record.

Japan's own hope is that it can achieve its foreign-policy objectives by trade and aid. The carrot of economic help has been dangled in the 1990s to persuade North Korea to halt its nuclear programme. It is also being used to persuade Russia to hand back a group of four islands and islets at the south of the Kuriles chain which were occupied by Soviet troops at the end of the second world war. Japan claims these "Northern Territories" on the basis of a Russo-Japanese treaty in 1855; Russia's claim is that it was given the Kuriles by the Potsdam agreement of 1945, which Japan accepted in its 1951 peace treaty with America.

Society: conformist and Confucian

The Japanese like to think of themselves as a homogeneous people (even though much Chinese and Korean blood is, in fact, mixed in their veins). Society is structured on the hierarchical lines favoured by Confucius. At the bottom are the *burakumin*, some 2m "untouchables" stigmatised by their dirty work as tanners and butchers in the pre-Meiji period. Foreigners are considered innately inferior, including the 620,000 ethnic Koreans who were born in Japan (often from parents brought from Korea as slave labour) but have no rights of citizenship.

In line with Confucianist thinking, consensus is favoured and confrontation frowned on; the group has greater importance than the individual (hence the saying: "The nail that sticks up must be hammered down."). Add to this the pressure to excel at school in order to get on the correct career path, and it is easy to see Japan as a stressful society.

The judgment, however, is too trite. Japanese society copes with stress by being highly organised, and most big companies try to give their employees jobs for life. What is true, though, is that Japanese society is changing: young Japanese, especially those who have travelled abroad, are far more individualistic than their parents, and may even switch from one employer to another. In addition, the government is determined that Japanese should work fewer hours and take longer holidays, not for their own sakes, but to appease Japan's deficit-plagued trading partners.

One factor forcing the pace of change is urbanisation. In 1950 only half the population lived in cities; today, over three-quarters do. Another factor is the ageing of Japan's population, thanks to a lower birth-rate and high life expectancy. The proportion of the population aged over 65 was 7.1% in 1970; it had doubled by 1995. It remains to be seen how Japan will cope with the financial pressure of so many old people in the population, especially if personal savings rates fall.

The economy: a modern miracle

Japan boasts the world's biggest banks, as well as the

largest life-insurance company and biggest-selling automobile industry. These, in combination with an internationally dominant electronics industry, make Japan the world's most successful industrialised economy, with weaknesses in very few areas (one being aerospace). Such a prospect would have seemed impossible less than 50 years ago, when most of the country's industrial facilities had been destroyed in air raids and when the occupying authorities had deliberately broken up the powerful *zaibatsu* conglomerates such as Mitsui, Mitsubishi and Sumitomo.

The achievement has been helped by Japan's pre-war status as an industrial power, but most of all it has been the result of hard work and good planning. This planning included "guidance" to both the private and public sectors; tacit restrictions on imports and domestic competition; and subsidised credit for favoured industries. Much of this was organised by the Ministry of International Trade and Industry (MITI) and the Ministry of Finance, leading to foreign accusations of a mercantilist "Japan Incorporated".

Such charges are now outdated, and were always somewhat exaggerated (especially since domestic competition was often fierce). In the 1950s Japan concentrated on basic industries such as textiles; in the 1960s it moved on to steel and shipbuilding; in the 1970s to cars, cameras and consumer electronics; and in the 1980s to computers and robotics. The challenge for Japan in the 1990s and beyond is to succeed in sophisticated industries such as biotechnology and aerospace, taking account of rising labour costs which might erode Japan's competitive edge.

Flexibility

The post-war progress has been all the more remarkable for Japan's ability to absorb severe economic shocks. When OPEC quadrupled oil prices in 1973–74, Japan's industry streamlined itself so efficiently that unemployment stayed below 3% of the workforce. During the second oil shock, in 1979–80, Japan still managed real economic growth of 5.3% in 1979 and 4.3% in 1980. A third example came in the mid-1980s: under pressure from trading partners to reduce its exports, Japan agreed in New York's Plaza Hotel in September 1985 to let the yen appreciate against the American dollar. By the end of 1987 the yen had doubled in value (a strengthening known as *endaka*), and yet Japanese industry increased its productivity and marketing skills so that exports were barely dented. Indeed, Japan's trade surplus is perennial, and perversely becomes worse at times of economic slowdown when there is less demand for imports. In

1995, for example, the trade surplus reached around $135 billion, $45 billion of it accounted for by America.

Frictions

The Plaza Hotel meeting was but one example of how Japan's success has bred resentment. Much of the resentment is justified. To protect its farmers, Japan has consistently refused to allow significant imports of rice, forcing domestic consumers to pay up to eight times the world price. The same applies to lesser degrees to other foods, such as beef and wheat. Virtually the only countries with which Japan has trading deficits are energy suppliers such as Brunei.

The resulting frictions are most concentrated in the relationship with America, which is the largest single market for Japan's exports, and, after Canada, Japan is the largest market for America's exports. The mutual dependence goes further: when America during the Reagan years turned from a net creditor to the world's largest debtor, it was rich Japan that lent America the money to finance its federal deficit.

For many Americans this implies a shameful inferiority, made worse by the surge in Japan's direct investment in America, with the purchase of assets such as the Rockefeller Center in Manhattan. Although their reaction is economically illogical (not least because the British and Dutch both "own" more of America, and the Americans themselves are great foreign investors), it contributes to outbreaks of "Japan-bashing" by American politicians and businessmen (who note Japanese purchases doubled between 1992 and 1996).

Salves

The need to ease the frictions was first recognised by the prime minister, Yasuhiro Nakasone, in the mid-1980s, as America and various European countries extracted "voluntary restraint agreements" from Japan to limit the exports of its cars and electrical goods (which did nothing to force American and European producers to be more competitive). Anti-dumping measures by the European Union and the sanction of "Super 301", a section of America's 1988 trade legislation, have underlined the problem.

One solution is regular trade talks between Japan and America, which in 1989 became the "Structural Impediments Initiative", designed to "level the playing field" – as the jargon had it – with Japanese action on some 200 items, from allowing foreign retailers to compete with Japan's "mom and pop" stores to renewing Japan's inadequate infrastructure (which would increase domestic demand). The Japanese also committed themselves to reducing annual work hours from 2,100 in 1987 to 1,800 by 1996 (the Germans in 1992 managed only an estimated 1,600).

Patience

A better solution is probably time. Through the 1980s Japan invested overseas to combat the rising yen and increased labour costs, and also to circumvent trade barriers. In the four decades to 1990 Japan's direct investment abroad amounted to some $254 billion, of which half had been committed during the second half of the 1980s. The prime destination was America, but Japan was also the largest investor in almost every country in South-East Asia. Increasingly, therefore, Japanese factories abroad will export to Japan, so reducing Japan's trade surplus. That, in turn, will reduce the capital Japan has available to export. Indeed, in 1992 Japan turned into a net importer of capital.

Bursting the bubble

One reason for this was the half-controlled bursting at the start of the 1990s of the "bubble economy", a speculative rise in share and real estate prices which drove some companies' price/earnings ratios above 100 and ludicrously valued part of Tokyo at the same price as all of California. As banks increased their capital base to meet the March 1993 requirement of 8% of assets laid down by the Bank for International Settlements in Basle, so credit became tighter. By mid-1992 the Tokyo and Osaka exchanges had lost half of their value in less than three years. In short, Japan was reacting to economic forces, and will continue to do so as its economy opens to the world. There remain, however, underlying problems of bad loans by the financial sector (several banks and securities houses failed in 1997) and insufficient domestic demand.

Beyond 2000

One solution is to carry out the long-promised "big bang" full deregulation of the financial sector, but the challenge will be to match geopolitical reactions with economic ones. In 1965 Japan's economy was only a tenth the size of America's; by 1990 it was three-fifths. It may never match America's in size, and even if it does, the mantle of the world's political leadership will not instantly go from America to Japan. Yet in terms of finance, industry and business Japan is by a long way Asia's leading country. It will be hard pressed to avoid the challenge of political leadership and, in the long term, the rivalry of Asia's other emerging powers, China and India.

Total area	377,708 sq km	% agricultural area	15
Capital	Tokyo	Highest point metres	Mt Fuji 3,776
Other cities	Yokohama, Osaka, Nagoya, Sapporo	Main rivers	Ishikari, Kitakami

The economy

GDP $bn	4,599.7	GDP per head $	36,575
% av. ann. growth in real GDP 1991–96	1.4	GDP per head in purchasing power parity $	22,110

Origins of GDP	% of total	Components of GDP	% of total
Agriculture	2	Private consumption	60
Industry	38	Public consumption	10
of which:		Investment	29
manufacturing	24	Exports	9
Services	60	Imports	8

Structure of manufacturing

			% of total
Agric. & food processing	10	Other	48
Textiles & clothing	4	Av. ann. increase in industrial	
Machinery & transport	38	output 1991–96	-0.8

Inflation and exchange rates

Consumer price 1996 av. ann. incr.	0.2%	Yen per $ 1997 average	120.99
Av. ann. rate 1991–96	0.7%	Yen per $ end-1997	129.95

Balance of payments, reserves and aid

			$bn
Exports, goods & services	464.5	Net capital account	-2.3
Imports, goods & services	419.9	Net direct & portfolio invest.	-58.7
Net income	44.4	Other net investment	-6.0
Net current transfers	-7.7	Net errors & omissions	14.3
Current-account balance	111.2	Net change in reserves	-58.6
as % of GDP	2.2	Level of reserves, end-Dec.	192.3
Foreign debt	...	Debt service	...
as % of GDP	...	as % of export earnings	...

Principal exports	$bn fob	Principal imports	$bn fob
Motor vehicles	50.7	Mineral fuels	60.6
Office machinery	29.3	Foodstuffs	50.8
Chemicals	28.8	Textiles	25.6
Scientific & optical equipment	17.4	Chemicals	23.3
Iron & steel products	15.2	Wood	9.6

Main export destinations	% of total	Main origins of imports	% of total
United States	27.2	United States	22.7
South Korea	7.1	China	11.6
Taiwan	6.3	South Korea	4.6
Hong Kong	6.2	Indonesia	4.4
China	5.3	Taiwan	4.3
Singapore	5.1	Australia	4.1

Government
System Constitutional monarchy. The emperor is head of state. Executive power is vested in a cabinet and prime minister. The 500-member House of Representatives is elected for 4 years, and its decisions are largely rubber-stamped by the 252-member House of Councillors.

Main political parties Liberal Democratic Party, Social Democratic Party, Shinto Sakigake (New Party Harbirger), Shinshinto (New Frontier Party), Communist Party

Climate and topography
Pacific coast has hot, humid summers and cold, dry winters. Sea of Japan coast has heavy winter snowfalls. Hokkaido has cold winters, down to -10°C (14°F), and short, warm summers. Southern Kyushu is subtropical. The archipelago has 4 main islands (Honshu, Shikoku, Kyushu, Hokkaido) and about 4,000 small ones. It lies on a fault line; there are over 1,000 earth tremors annually and occasional major quakes. Of the land area 33% is mountainous and thickly forested; only 15%, mostly the coastal plains, is cultivable, and is intensively used for largely arable agriculture. Industrial and urban development is concentrated along Honshu's south coast.

People and society

Population m	125.8	% under 15	16.4
Pop. per sq km	333.0	% over 60	20.0
% urban	78.0	No. women per 100 men	103.0
% av. ann. growth 1980–95	0.5	Human Development Index	94.0
No. households m	40.6		

Life expectancy	yrs	Education	
Men	77	Spending as % of GDP	5.0
Women	83	Years of compulsory education	9
Crude birth rate	10	Adult literacy %	99.0
Crude death rate	7	Primary school enrolment %	102
Infant mortality		Secondary school enrolment %	96
per 1,000 live births	4	Tertiary education enrolment %	30

Workforce	% of total	Consumer goods ownership	
Services	59		per 1,000 people
Industry	34	Cars	355.0
Agriculture	7	Televisions	619.0
% of pop. over 15 in workforce	52	Mobile phones	81.5
		Personal computers	152.5

Ethnic groups	% of total	Religious groups	% of total
Japanese	99	Shinto[a]	87
		Buddhist[a]	73

Tourism		Health	
Tourist arrivals m	3.3	Spending as % of GDP	7.0
Tourism receipts $bn	4.1	People per doctor	608

a Most Japanese profess both.

KAZAKHSTAN

Vast and thinly populated, the Republic of Kazakhstan has found independence from the former Soviet Union a mixed blessing. But the development of its oil and gas reserves could yet bring prosperity.

History: under Russia's shadow

The Kazakhs, whose beginnings were as Turkic-speaking nomads roaming the great plains of central Asia, were part of the Mongol empire in the 13th century and then were dominated by the Tartars until, in 1730, they first came under Russia's influence, with one of the three Kazakh tribal confederations asked the Tsar for protection from the Kalmyks to the south. What followed was the slow, at times bloody, absorption of the Kazakh lands into the Russian empire. After the Tsars were overthrown in the communist revolution of 1917, the Kazakhs declared an autonomous republic, but by 1920 the Bolsheviks had regained control and in 1936 the region officially became the Kazakh Soviet Socialist Republic.

In 1991 Kazakhstan was the last of the former Soviet republics to declare independence following the dissolution of the Soviet Union in 1991; but it was not welcomed by the Kazakh communist party leader, Nursultan Nazarbaev (an ethnic Kazakh who had replaced Gennadi Kolbin, a Russian, in 1989). Mr Nazarbaev, the sole candidate to be the first president, had feared the possible resentment of Kazakhstan's Russians (a third of the population) and was aware of the country's economic dependence on Russia. Politics is dominated by President Nazarbaev, who in 1995 masterminded a 95.6% vote by popular referendum to cancel the 1996 presidential election and extend his term until 2000.

The economy: changing the balance

Although Mr Nazarbaev skilfully used the presence on Kazakh soil of Soviet nuclear weapons (they were not finally removed until 1995) to extract foreign aid, the first years of independence were economically disastrous. One reason was the loss of "captive" Soviet export markets; another was the inefficiency of the country's heavy industry; a third was sheer mismanagement. By 1994 the country was forced to begin an IMF stabilisation programme. Kazakhstan's long-term need is to exploit its oil and gas reserves by a system of foreign-built pipelines to the Black Sea, but its short-term challenge is to liberalise the economy while lessening rampant corruption.

Total area	2,717,300 sq km	% agricultural area	15
Capital	Akmola	Highest point metres	Zhengis Shingy
Other cities	Almaty		7,439
		Main rivers	Volga

The economy[a]

GDP $bn	22.1	GDP per head $	1,330
% av. ann. growth in		GDP per head in purchasing	
real GDP 1991–96	...	power parity $	3,010

Origins of GDP	% of total	Components of GDP	% of total
Agriculture	12	Private consumption	65
Industry	30	Public consumption	15
of which:		Investment	22
manufacturing	6	Exports	34
Services	57	Imports	37

Principal exports	% of total	Principal imports	% of total
Oil & oil products	33.0	Energy & fuels	19.0
Metals	30.6	Machinery	12.3
Food	7.9	Metals	9.1
Chemicals	6.8	Vehicles	7.1
Machinery	2.5		

Government

System Republic with bicameral national legislature. Universal suffrage over age 18 for presidential and lower house elections. Senators are elected partly by the regions and partly by the president.

Main political parties Party of National Unity, People's Congress of Kazakhstan, People's Co-operative Party, Democratic Progress Party

Climate and topography

Continental, with cold winters and hot summers; arid and semi-arid. The country extends from the Volga river to the Altai mountains, encompassing plains in western Siberia and oasis and desert in central Asia.

People and society

Population m	16.4	% under 15	...
Pop. per sq km	6.0	% over 60	11.0
% urban	60.0	No. women per 100 men	106.0
% av. ann. growth 1980–95	0.7	No. households m	...
Human Development Index	70.9		

Ethnic groups	% of total	Religious groups	% of total
Kazak	42	Muslim	47
Russian	37	Russian Orthodox	44
Ukrainian	5	Protestant	2
German	5		

a 1995.

KIRGIZSTAN

In Central Asia the Kirgiz Republic, sandwiched between Kazakhstan and China, has survived the downfall of the Soviet empire better than most – yet the road to prosperous democracy remains dauntingly long.

History: beyond Black Kirgiz

The Turkic-speaking Kirgiz, traditionally one of Central Asia's great nomadic groups, were gradually colonised in the 19th century by the Russian empire (a fifth of the population remains ethnically Russian) in an advance which has left a disputed border between Kirgizstan and China. The present republic dates back to the establishment in 1924 of the Kara-Kirgiz ("Black Kirgiz") Autonomous Oblast of the Russian Soviet Federative Socialist Republic (the Kirgiz, as opposed to Kara-Kirgiz, Oblast later became Kazakhstan). Twelve years later the status was raised to that of a full republic of the Soviet Union. In the succeeding decades of communist rule all dissent was eliminated and a new, entirely "Sovietised" Kirgiz elite took charge. This elite feared it might be dispossessed when the Soviet Union was dissolved in 1991 and Kirgizstan became independent. In practice most of the elite, and certainly many of their less-than-democratic attitudes have survived unscathed.

Askar Akaev, appointed president almost a year before the republic became independent, at first espoused liberal political and economic ideas – but within narrowing limits. The Communist Party was banned for plotting against him in the summer of 1991, and in the direct elections held in October 1991 for the independent republic's first president he refused to allow any opposition candidate to register. Mr Akaev was re-elected in 1995 for a further five years.

One excuse for Mr Akaev's increasing authoritarianism has been his need to balance the interests of the Russian minority with the demands of the Kirgiz nationalists.

The economy: trying to be good

Although agriculture is the dominant sector, the economy was badly affected by the loss of Soviet markets for its industrial output. Even so, Mr Akaev (a professed disciple of Adam Smith) launched an ambitious privatisation programme in 1992. It succeeded only in part – but enough to attract foreign approval and aid, and to achieve better economic growth rates than most the region.

Total area	198,500 sq km	% agricultural area	7
Capital	Bishkek	Highest point metres	Tien Shan 7,000
Other cities	Osh, Djalal-Abad	Main rivers	–

The economy[a]

GDP $bn	3.2	GDP per head $	700
% av. ann. growth in		GDP per head in purchasing	
real GDP 1991–96	...	power parity $	1,800

Origins of GDP	% of total	Components of GDP	% of total
Agriculture	44	Private consumption	67
Industry	24	Public consumption	23
of which:		Investment	16
manufacturing	...	Exports	26
Services	32	Imports	32

Principal exports	% of total	Principal imports	% of total
Food & agricultural produce	29.2	Mineral products	37.4
Textiles	19.3	Food & agricultural produce	18.8
Base metals	16.9	Machinery & equipment	12.1
Mineral products	11.8	Base metals	6.9

Government

System The Soviet-era 313-member Jogorku Kenesh was changed by referendum in 1994 into a 4-year term, 2-chamber parliament. There are 35 full-time deputies in the lower house, the Legislative Assembly, and 70 in the Assembly of People's Representatives, which meets twice a year to approve the lower house's laws.

Main political parties Social Democratic Party, Democratic Movement of Kirgizstan, National Unity, Communist Party

Climate and topography

Dry continental to polar in the high Tien Shan; subtropical in the south-west (Fergana valley); temperate in the northern foothills. The peaks of Tien Shan and associated valleys and basins encompass the entire country.

People and society

Population m	5.0	% under 15	...
Pop. per sq km	24.0	% over 60	9.0
% urban	39.0	No. women per 100 men	104.0
% av. ann. growth 1980–95	1.5	No. households m	...
Human Development Index	63.5		

Ethnic groups	% of total	Religious groups	% of total
Kirgiz	52	Muslim	70
Russian	22	Russian Orthodox	20
Uzbek	13		

a 1995.

LAOS

Total area	236,800 sq km	Population	4.7m
GDP	$1.9bn	GDP per head	$390
Capital	Vientiane	Other cities	Savannakhet, Paksé

The People's Democratic Republic of Laos is among the world's ten poorest nations. This unhappy status is unlikely to be permanent, first because the government in 1986 began to liberalise the economy, and second because a more open Laos is likely to benefit from the growing prosperity of its neighbours, especially Thailand and Vietnam, and from its entry into the Association of South-East Asian Nations (ASEAN) in July 1997.

History: "Kingdom of a Million Elephants"

Laos first emerged as a united country in 1353 when Fa Ngum, a Lao prince who had grown up in the Khmer capital of Angkor, returned with Cambodian troops to force Lao fiefdoms to join in the Kingdom of Lan Xang (a Million Elephants). Apart from a period of Burmese rule, from 1574 to 1637, this lasted until 1713, when it split into the kingdoms of Vientiane, Luang Prabang and Champassak.

But landlocked Laos was bound to be dependent on others. Surrounded by Thailand, Burma, China, Vietnam and Cambodia, it was little more than a Thai vassal state during the 18th century. Then in the 19th century France gained primacy over the area east of the Mekong river and, by the early 20th century, had formally made Laos a protectorate. Independence from France was declared by the Japanese (who had invaded in 1941) in March 1945, but was revoked with Japan's subsequent defeat in the second world war.

Independence came from the Geneva Conference in 1954. But the country was immediately racked by fighting between the American-backed Royal Lao government and the communist Pathet Lao (Lao Country) movement. Attempts to form coalition governments in 1957 and 1962 failed; a third was established in 1974 but in the following year, with the victory of communist forces in Vietnam and Cambodia, the Pathet Lao set up the People's Democratic Republic of Laos, governed by the Lao People's Revolutionary Party (LPRP) under Prince Souphanouvong (the "Red Prince") as president.

Politics: Pyrrhic victory

The rapid introduction of socialism, combined with the

withdrawal of American aid, led to economic chaos. Salvation, such as it was, came through aid from the Soviet Union and Vietnam. Under a Treaty of Friendship and Co-operation signed in 1977, Vietnam stationed some 50,000 combat troops and 6,000 advisers in Laos.

Recognising the need for change, the ruling LPRP – in tandem with its Vietnamese counterpart – in 1986 announced economic reforms. It has since also sought better relations with Thailand, with which it fought a bitter border war in 1988, and with other countries, such as China, France and America. Improved relations with China coincided with the withdrawal of Vietnam's troops.

Society: dispersed and divided

One problem for Laos is its small population, which in a large country makes development spending per person very expensive (hence the government's ban in 1976 on contraception). The lowland Lao, wet-rice farmers, make up just over half the population; the upland Lao are migrant slash-and-burn cultivators; other highland Lao include the Man and Hmong (who worked with America's CIA against the Pathet Lao during the Vietnam war). At the start of the 1990s there were about 45,000 Hmong among the 60,000 Laotians living in holding centres in Thailand. Business in the towns is dominated by immigrants from China, Vietnam and the Indian subcontinent.

The economy: in need of capitalism

With about 85% of the population living by subsistence agriculture, there are not enough skilled workers to exploit resources such as tin, gold and iron ore. Exports are mainly of hydroelectric power to Thailand, timber (much of it from illegal logging) and drugs. Laos, part of the "Golden Triangle", is a major producer of opium and America has accused the authorities of participating in drug trafficking.

Prompted by Vietnam, the government abandoned agricultural collectivisation in 1979 and in the early 1980s introduced wage, price and trade reforms. But this was not enough to improve the economy, hence the decision in 1986 to forsake central planning and the transfer in 1989 of collectively managed land to family management.

Laos depends on aid to cover its development spending; in 1988 it passed a foreign investment law to attract foreign capital. Most investment is likely to come from Thailand, in effect making Laos again a Thai vassal, this time within ASEAN.

Total area	236,800 sq km	% agricultural area	7
Capital	Vientiane	Highest point metres	Sao 2,590
Other cities	Savannakhet, Paksé	Main rivers	Mekong

The economy

GDP $bn	1.9	GDP per head $	390
% av. ann. growth in		GDP per head in purchasing	
real GDP 1991–96	2.6	power parity $	...

Origins of GDP	% of total	Components of GDP	% of total
Agriculture	52	Private consumption	...
Industry	18	Public consumption	...
of which:		Investment	...
manufacturing	14	Exports	...
Services	30	Imports	...

Structure of manufacturing

			% of total
Agric. & food processing	...	Other	...
Textiles & clothing	...	Av. ann. increase in industrial	
Machinery & transport	...	output 1991–96	...

Inflation and exchange rates

Consumer price 1996 av. ann. incr.	13.1%	Kip per $ 1997 average	1,256.7
Av. ann. rate 1991–96	11.0%	Kip per $ end-1997	2,009.0

Balance of payments, reserves and debt

			$m
Exports, goods & services	0.4	Net capital account	–
Imports, goods & services	0.7	Net direct & portfolio investment	–
Net income	–	Other net investment	–
Net current transfers	–	Net errors & omissions	–
Current-account balance	-0.2	Net change in reserves	0.2
as % of GDP	-12.1	Level of reserves, end-Dec.	0.1
Foreign debt	2.2	Debt service	1.5
as % of GDP	42.9	as % of export earnings	5.8

Principal exports	$m fob	Principal imports[a]	$m fob
Coffee	225.0	Machinery & raw materials	218.0
Timber & wood products	127.0	Rice & foodstuffs	60.0
Textiles & garments	65.0	Imports for re-export	43.0
Electricity	31.0	Petroleum products	41.0

Main export destinations[b]	% of total	Main origins of imports[b]	% of total
Thailand	25.7	Thailand	60.0
Japan	10.0	Turkey	8.2
France	9.8	Singapore	5.5
Turkey	8.9	Japan	5.0
Germany	7.5	Vietnam	4.3

Government

System Communist republic since 1975. The president is head of state, exercising executive power through a council of ministers. Members of the national assembly are elected for a 5-year term. The Lao People's Revolutionary Party is the only legal party.

Climate and topography

Tropical, with a monsoon season lasting from May to Oct. The population is concentrated on the east bank of the Mekong and the Bolovens plateau in the south.

People and society

Population m	4.7	% under 15	45.2
Pop. per sq km	21.0	% over 60	5.0
% urban	22.0	No. women per 100 men	103.0
% av. ann. growth 1980–95	2.8	Human Development Index	45.9
No. households m	...		

Life expectancy	yrs	Education	
Men	51	Spending as % of GDP	1.6
Women	54	Years of compulsory education	5
Crude birth rate	44	Adult literacy %	55.8
Crude death rate	14	Primary school enrolment %	107
Infant mortality		Secondary school enrolment %	25
per 1,000 live births	90	Tertiary education enrolment %	2

Workforce	% of total	Consumer goods ownership	
Services	16		per 1,000 people
Industry	6	Cars	...
Agriculture	78	Televisions	7.0
% of pop. over 15 in workforce	50	Mobile phones	0.1
		Personal computers	...

Ethnic groups	% of total	Religious groups	% of total
Lao	99	Buddhist	58

Tourism		Health	
Tourist arrivals m	...	Spending as % of GDP	2.6
Tourism receipts $bn	-0.05	People per doctor	4,446

a 1994.
b 1995.

MACAU

Macau, a tiny Portuguese enclave on China's coast, faces the same challenge as its bigger neighbour, Hong Kong: how to ensure its capitalist way of life continues after its sovereignty reverts to China.

History: in Hong Kong's shadow

The first Portuguese ship anchored in Macau in 1513, and by 1553 it had become an official trading post, dominating trade with China and Japan. In 1845 the Portuguese declared Macau a free port; in 1887 they signed a treaty under which China recognised Portugal's rule over Macau and its two islands, Coloane and Taipa; and in 1951 they proclaimed Macau an overseas province.

In 1949 China's communist government denounced the treaty as "unequal", but in the late 1960s (anxious not to alarm Hong Kong) it did not allow its Cultural Revolutionaries to overrun Macau. In 1974 post-revolutionary Portugal offered to give Macau back. The Chinese refused, wanting first to settle Hong Kong's future. In 1987 it was agreed that in 1999 (two years after Hong Kong) Macau would become a Special Administrative Region of China, retaining its existing way of life.

Politics

The Portuguese governor is assisted by a Legislative Assembly of 23 members: 8 directly elected, 8 indirectly and 7 appointed by the governor. The population is 95% Cantonese Chinese, but politics and the civil service have been dominated by the Macanese (Portuguese-speaking Eurasians) and Portuguese expatriates. The challenge is to train enough local Chinese before 1999.

The economy

Like Hong Kong, Macau is a conduit between China and the outside world, exporting textiles, garments and toys. Thanks to land reclamation, it is also growing; its land area has increased by a third since 1912. What makes Macau unique in Asia, however, is its casinos. Controlled by Stanley Ho, a Hong Kong-based Eurasian, these are patronised mainly by Hongkongers and Taiwanese, who – along with tourists visiting Hong Kong – make day or weekend trips to Macau. Gambling accounts for a third of the territory's revenue and it is unclear what China's attitude to gambling (often fraught with gang violence) after 1999 will be.

Total area	17.32 sq km	% agricultural area	–
Capital	–	Highest point metres	Coloane 174
Other cities	–	Main rivers	–

The economy[a]

GDP $bn	...	GDP per head $	...
% av. ann. growth in real GDP 1991–96	...	GDP per head in purchasing power parity $	...

Origins of GDP	% of total	Components of GDP	% of total
Agriculture	0	Private consumption	30
Industry	63	Public consumption	8
of which:		Investment	28
manufacturing	40	Exports	...
Services	37	Imports	...

Principal exports	$m fob	Principal imports[a]	$m cif
Clothing & textiles	1,545.0	Raw materials & semi-manufactured goods	1,079.0
Toys	72.0	Consumer goods incl foodstuffs, beverages & tobacco	565.0
Electronic goods	51.0	Capital goods	285.0
Footwear	41.0	Mineral fuels & oils	104.0

Government

System Portuguese governor assisted by a 23-member legislative assembly, 8 directly elected, 8 indirectly and 7 appointed by the governor.
Main political parties None, but a number of civic associations exist

Climate and topography

Subtropical, with an annual average temperature of 21°C (70°F) and a rainfall of 2,160mm (85in), more than half of which falls in Jun–Aug. Winters are dry and sunny, summers humid.

People and society

Population m	0.4	% under 15	52.1
Pop. per sq km	20,750.0	% over 60	6.5
% urban	100.0	No. women per 100 men	103.0
% av. ann. growth 1980–95	...	No. households m	...
Human Development Index	...		

Ethnic groups	% of total	Religious groups	% of total
Chinese	95	Buddhist	95

a 1995.

MALAYSIA

Total area	329,749 sq km	Population	20.7m
GDP	$99.3bn	GDP per head	$4,800
Capital	Kuala Lumpur	Other cities	Ipoh, George Town, Johore Bahru

The Federation of Malaysia, blessed with rich natural resources, has immense economic potential. But it will be fully exploited only in an atmosphere of political harmony. In multi-racial Malaysia, where politics is defined by ethnic groups, no government can take that harmony for granted.

History: Malay kings and British rajas

Modern Malaysia is in two parts, West and East, separated by 400 miles of the South China Sea. Together, they are the centre of a Malay sphere whose ethnic influence spreads along the Malay peninsula and then through the Malay archipelago from Indonesia in the south to the Philippines in the north.

Historically, West and East Malaysia were separate. The peninsular west was dominated in the 15th century by the Muslim city-state of Malacca, which in 1511 was captured by the Portuguese who in turn gave way in 1641 to the Dutch. Elsewhere, the city-states of Selangor and Johore were founded in the 18th century by invading Bugis from the Celebes island. Meanwhile, from the early 16th century Sabah and Sarawak, the two states of East Malaysia on the giant island of Borneo, were ruled by the sultans of Brunei.

By the 19th century, however, all these areas had come under the control of Britain, which set about establishing rubber, cocoa and palm oil plantations, and brought in Indian and Chinese workers to help man them. After founding a settlement on Singapore island in 1819, the British in 1826 joined it with Malacca and Penang, on the west coast of the Malay peninsula, to form the "Straits Settlements". In 1867 the Straits Settlements formally became a British crown colony. In 1896 the Malay states accepted British advisers, and the sultans of Perak, Selangor, Negri Sembilan and Pahang joined to form a loose union known as the Federated Malay States. Under looser control by Britain were the states of Kelantan, Trengganu, Perlis and Kedah, which were transferred from Thai control in 1909 and were known as the Unfederated Malay States.

Sabah came under British control in 1877 when a private syndicate (given a charter in 1881 as the British North Borneo Company) obtained a land grant from the sultans of Brunei and Sulu. Sarawak had been under Britain's control since 1841, when, as a reward for his help in suppressing a revolt by the Iban tribes, the sultan of Brunei installed a British adventurer, Sir James Brooke, as the "raja", or ruler. There followed a dynasty of "white rajas" from the Brooke family until Japan occupied both the Malay peninsula and Borneo in 1941–42. After Japan's defeat, the last raja, Sir Charles Brooke, defied family and local opposition and, on July 1st 1946, formally ceded Sarawak to Britain.

Independence: from emergency to *merdeka*
The British returned to a rather different Malay peninsula: the communist guerrillas who had fought against the Japanese now turned against the old colonial ruler. Britain reacted by dissolving the Straits Settlements and joining them with Malay states into a new Malayan Union; Singapore became a separate colony and so did Sarawak (thanks to Sir Charles) and British North Borneo (Sabah).

The Malay states felt their status had been reduced, and their opposition to the Union led in 1948 to the establishment in its place of the Federation of Malaya, consisting of the nine Malay states of the peninsula, Malacca and Penang, and to the promise by Britain of independence.

First, though, the British had to fight the Communist Party of Malay. The guerrilla struggle – euphemistically called an "emergency" since civil war would have meant a loss of insurance cover – was not finally defeated until 1960. In the meantime, the rising nationalism of the United Malays National Organisation (founded in 1946) prompted the British to introduce local elections in 1951. UMNO solved the problem of the country's ethnic divisions by forming the Alliance, first with the Malayan Chinese Association and then the Malayan Indian Congress. In the first federal elections, in 1955, the Alliance won 51 of the 52 seats contested and UMNO's leader, Tunku (Prince) Abdul Rahman was appointed the federation's first chief minister. In August 1957 Britain succumbed to the Alliance's pressure and gave peninsular Malaya its *merdeka*, or independence.

From Malaya to Malaysia
The idea of expanding the federation to include Singapore (which had in 1959 achieved internal self-government) and the British possessions in Borneo was first mooted in public by the Tunku in 1961. It immediately aroused the antagonism of the Philippines, which had a claim to Sabah, and Indonesia, which viewed it as a plot by Britain to retain influence. But a United Nations mission to Borneo reported public opinion was in favour of the federation and on

September 16th 1963 Singapore, Sabah and Sarawak – but not Brunei, which declined the invitation – joined the new Federation of Malaysia.

All was not yet plain sailing. Indonesia's President Sukarno, who had proposed a federation of "Maphilindo", to join Malaya, the Philippines and Indonesia, launched a policy of *"konfrontasi"*, or confrontation, with armed attacks on both West and East Malaysia. At the same time, the Tunku, who had welcomed Singapore's inclusion lest it otherwise become a base for communist infiltration, now feared that Lee Kuan Yew's People's Action Party would attract votes from the Alliance; moreover, UMNO worried that the presence of Singapore's Chinese might challenge Malay political supremacy and upset the federation's racial balance. The Tunku's solution was to arrange for Singapore to leave the federation in 1965. The following year Indonesia ended the confrontation, and the Philippines formally recognised Malaysia.

Politics: a Malay matter

Malaysia is a constitutional monarchy with a difference: the sultans of nine states of peninsular Malaysia (Perlis, Kedah, Perak, Selangor, Negri Sembilan, Johore, Pahang, Trengganu and Kelantan) elect one of their number as king, or Yang di Pertuan Agong, for a five-year period. The sultans are considered above the law, a concept which has occasionally caused tension with the government. The king appoints the governors of the "non-Malay" states of Melaka, Penang, Sabah and Sarawak for terms of four years. Each state has its own constitution and assembly. The federal parliament in Kuala Lumpur consists of a 192-member House of Representatives (Dewan Rakyat), chosen by general election for a term of up to five years, and a Senate (Dewan Negara) of 26 elected members (2 from each state) and 42 appointed by the king.

The Malay half of the population has a "special position" constitutionally but resents the economic dominance of the Chinese third of the population, which in turn resents the Malays' political supremacy. The Indians, a tenth of the population, cover the economic spectrum from plantation workers to barristers, but have no political clout. Serious race riots in 1969 showed that the social and political balance can never be taken for granted.

Managing this balance since independence has been the task of a governing coalition (known since 1969 as the Barisan Nasional, or National Front), led by the United Malays National Organisation (UMNO). The other main parties are the Malaysian Chinese Association (MCA), the Malaysian Indian Congress, the largely Chinese Gerakan Party and Sarawak's Parti Pesaka Bumiputera Bersatu. Sabah's dominant party, the Parti Bersatu Sabah, dropped out of the coalition before the 1990 election. The opposition is led by the Democratic Action Party, which espouses non-racial politics but is, in fact, mainly Chinese.

UMNO's power and problems

Although the fundamentalist Islamic party, Parti Islam se Malaysia (PAS), is strong in the north, UMNO has always been the first choice of the Malay voters. The result is that the UMNO president is the prime minister: Tunku Abdul Rahman, until 1970; Tun Abdul Razak until 1976; Dato' Hussein bin Onn until 1981; and then Dr Mahathir Mohamad.

The Mahathir era has been marked with controversy: corruption scandals in the MCA led many Chinese to vote for the DAP, so weakening the ruling coalition; divisions within the coalition have weakened its rule in Sarawak; and UMNO itself has been divided, partly by Dr Mahathir's confronta-tional style. This came to the surface in 1987, when Tengku (Prince) Razaleigh Hamza challenged Dr Mahathir for the UMNO presidency, and almost succeeded. In October and November, allegedly to prevent racial riots, 106 people, including the DAP's leader, Lim Kit Siang, were detained for up to 18 months under the Internal Security Act.

The following February the High Court ruled that the 1987 UMNO elections should be declared null and void and that UMNO was "an unlawful society". Dr Mahathir's reaction was to form UMNO (Baru) – or "New UMNO" – with all the assets of the defunct UMNO. Tengku Razaleigh's was to form Semangat '46 (Spirit of '46, when UMNO was founded).

In the event, Dr Mahathir prevailed. In the general elec-tion of October 1990 the Barisan Nasional won 127 out of 180 seats, thus keeping the two-thirds majority necessary to make constitutional amendments. Semangat '46 won only 8 of the 61 seats it contested. In simultaneous state elections in peninsular Malaysia, the Barisan Nasional won every-where except in Tengku Razaleigh's state of Kelantan, where the alliance of Semangat '46 and the Muslim parties won all seats, at both federal and state level. In October 1996 Semangat '46 gave up the unequal struggle, and its members rejoined UMNO.

Foreign policy: looking east

As a founder member of the Association of South-East Asian

Nations (ASEAN), and with its experience of the "emergency", Malaysia is fiercely anti-communist. But under Dr Mahathir it has not wanted to be seen as pro-western. Moreover, Muslim Malaysia disapproves of American policy towards Israel. The closest relations are with Singapore – a fellow member of the Five Power Defence Arrangements, with Australia, New Zealand and Britain – but the interconnection of the two economies occasionally leads to tension. In the early 1980s Dr Mahathir instituted a "Look East" policy for trade, partly from admiration of Japan, partly out of anger with Britain (with whom relations improved in the late 1980s before again souring in 1994). Malaysia has argued for making the ASEAN area a Zone of Peace, Freedom and Neutrality (ZOPFAN); it also believes that there should be an East Asian Economic Grouping to link ASEAN with Japan as a counterweight to any emerging American and European trade blocks.

Society: the goal of growth

Political pride of place goes to the Malays and other "*bumiputra*", native "sons of the soil", such as the indigenous tribes of Sabah and Sarawak. These make up about 60% of the total population. Economic clout, however, is wielded by the Chinese, who are about 30% of the population; the Indians make up some 8% of the people. Dr Mahathir has often accused the Malays of being lazy and even genetically inferior, hence the need for affirmative action. He has a grand vision of increasing the population from about 20m now to 70m by the year 2095. This, he believes, would give Malaysia a domestic market big enough to sustain its industrial development.

The economy: divided blessings

Malaysia can boast of being the world's largest producer of rubber, palm oil, pepper, tropical hardwoods and (at least until the collapse in the world market in 1985) tin. Such natural bounty gives a good platform for economic growth. Much of Malaysia's economic effort is to achieve balanced growth by diversifying into manufacturing.

In part, the effort has been rewarded. Manufacturing, which accounted for only 10% of GDP in 1965, now accounts for over a third of GDP and three-fifths of exports; and the country has emerged as a major world source of basic electronics. Moreover, as Thailand runs out of absorptive capacity, more and more foreign investment, especially from Japan and Taiwan, has flowed into Malaysia, which (in contrast to Thailand) has a superb physical infrastructure. But there have been mistakes: lax banking practices, over-ambitious building projects and over-heated stock speculation. The result in 1997 was a currency crisis, made all the worse by Dr Mahathir's intemperate criticism of foreign speculators such as George Soros.

Sons of the soil

The preoccupation of the planners is not just with achieving growth (which averaged over 8% a year from the mid-1980s to the mid-1990s) but with distributing its benefits. The race riots of 1969 led in 1970 to the New Economic Policy (NEP). Its purpose was to increase the share of the corporate sector owned by the Malays and other *bumiputras* to 30% by 1990; other Malaysians would own 40%; and foreigners would own the remaining 30%. This target compared with a situation in 1969 in which *bumiputras* owned just 2.4% of the corporate sector; other Malaysians (mainly Chinese) owned 34.3%; and foreigners owned 63.3%. *Bumiputras* were also to be given preference in the labour market.

The target was missed. By 1990 the *bumiputra* share of corporate equity was only about 20%, and much of this was achieved either by quasi-state corporations and pension funds or by having Malays "front" for Chinese businessmen. Meanwhile, practical considerations weakened some of the NEP's resolve, with 100% foreign equity allowed since 1986 in some export-oriented industries.

Yet it is politically impossible for UMNO to abandon its commitment to positive discrimination for the Malays. The compromise, reached in June 1991, was the National Development Policy. This preserves the concept of Malay development and is to last until 2000, but emphasises growth for all races and does not impose a deadline for 30% *bumiputra* ownership of the corporate sector.

Balancing the future

Since the tensions of Malaysia are probably inherent, the challenge is to produce enough prosperity to soothe all the racial groups. The National Development Policy is supposed to run alongside an "Outline Perspective Plan". This envisages real growth of 7% a year during the 1990s and a lessening of households below the poverty line from 17% in 1990 to 7% by 2000. That will be a minor miracle (in 1970 the proportion was 52%); it is a credit to Malaysia that such a miracle is entirely possible.

Total area	329,749 sq km	% agricultural area	13
Capital	Kuala Lumpur	Highest point metres	Mt Kinabalu
Other cities	Ipoh, George Town,		4,101
	Johore Bahru	Main rivers	Rajang, Sungai Pahang, Kinabatangan

The economy

GDP $bn	99.3	GDP per head $	4,800
% av. ann. growth in		GDP per head in purchasing	
real GDP 1991–96	8.7	power parity $	9,020

Origins of GDP	% of total	Components of GDP	% of total
Agriculture	13	Private consumption	51
Industry	43	Public consumption	12
of which:		Investment	41
manufacturing	33	Exports	96
Services	44	Imports	99

Structure of manufacturing

			% of total
Agric. & food processing	9	Other	4.9
Textiles & clothing	6	Av. ann. increase in industrial	
Machinery & transport	36	output 1991–96	10.8

Inflation and exchange rates

Consumer price 1996 av. ann. incr.	3.6%	Ringgit per $ 1997 average	2.81
Av. ann. rate 1991–96	4.2%	Ringgit per $ end-1997	3.89

Balance of payments, reserves and debt

			$bn
Exports, goods & services	81.7	Net capital account	–
Imports, goods & services	86.2	Net direct & portfolio investment	2.7
Net income	-3.7	Other net investment	-1.2
Net current transfers	0.2	Net errors & omissions	-0.5
Current-account balance	-4.1	Net change in reserves	3.2
as % of GDP	-9.4	Level of reserves, end-Dec.	24.7
Foreign debt	34.4	Debt service	8.1
as % of GDP	38.6	as % of export earnings	7.8

Principal exports	$bn fob	Principal imports	$bn fob
Electronics & elec. machinery	38.8	Manufacturing inputs	30.2
Palm oil	4.1	Machinery	8.4
Petroleum & LNG	3.9	Transport equipment	3.4
Textiles, clothing & footwear	2.6	Metal products	2.3
Chemicals & chemical products	2.5	Construction inputs	2.2
Logs & timber	2.4	Consumer durables	2.2

Main export destinations	% of total	Main origins of imports	% of total
Singapore	20.5	Japan	24.5
United States	18.2	United States	15.5
Japan	13.4	Singapore	13.3
Hong Kong	5.9	South Korea	5.2
Taiwan	4.1	Taiwan	5.0

Government

System Federation of 13 states and 1 federal territory (Kuala Lumpur). Nine states have hereditary sultans and these elect one of their number king and head of state for 5 years. The legislature has 2 houses: the 192 members of the Dewan Rakyat are elected for 5 years; the Dewan Negara has 68 members, 26 elected by the state assemblies and the remainder royal appointees. Executive power is held by the prime minister and cabinet, responsible to the legislature.

Main political parties United Malays National Organisation, Malaysian Chinese Association, Malaysian Indian Congress, Democratic Action Party

Climate and topography

Tropical with two annual monsoons. The country comprises a mountainous peninsula and the northern part of the island of Borneo. Almost 45% of the land area is tropical rain or swamp forest. Most of the peninsular population is concentrated on the western coastal plain.

People and society

Population m	20.7	% under 15	37.8
Pop. per sq km	61.0	% over 60	6.0
% urban	54.0	No. women per 100 men	98.0
% av. ann. growth 1980–95	2.5	Human Development Index	83.2
No. households m	3.9		

Life expectancy	yrs	Education	
Men	69	Spending as % of GDP	5.3
Women	74	Years of compulsory education	11
Crude birth rate	26	Adult literacy %	83
Crude death rate	5	Primary school enrolment %	93
Infant mortality		Secondary school enrolment %	59
per 1,000 live births	12	Tertiary education enrolment %	...

Workforce	% of total	Consumer goods ownership	
Services	50		per 1,000 people
Industry	23	Cars	71.0
Agriculture	27	Televisions	231.0
% of pop. over 15 in workforce	39	Mobile phones	43.4
		Personal computers	39.7

Ethnic groups	% of total	Religious groups	% of total
Malay and aborigines	60	Muslim	53
Chinese	31	Buddhist	17
Indian	8	Chinese folk	12
		Hindu	7
		Christian	6

Tourism		Health	
Tourist arrivals m	7.5	Spending as % of GDP[a]	1.4
Tourism receipts $bn	3.9	People per doctor	2,441

a Public only.

MALDIVES

The Republic of Maldives has no pretensions to power and influence. Its challenge is to maintain its culture while seeking prosperity as a tourist haven.

History: from India to Islam

The 1,800 coral atolls and sandbanks that form the Maldive Islands were first inhabited around the 5th century BC by settlers from southern India and Ceylon (now Sri Lanka). Legend has it that an itinerant Muslim holy man converted the islanders to Islam in 1153 AD.

From 1558 to 1573 the islands were ruled by the Portuguese. In the 17th century government was by a sultanate, protected by the Dutch rulers of Ceylon. After the British took Ceylon in 1796 the islands became a British protectorate (formally so in 1887). Although the Maldive Islands were declared a republic in 1953, in the same year the country reverted to a sultanate. Full independence from Britain came in 1965, with the sultanate being replaced by a new republic in 1968.

Politics: the dominance of Gayoom

For most of the independent era politics has been dominated by Maumoon Abdul Gayoom, who became president when the Majlis removed Ibrahim Nasir from office in 1968. Gayoom's tenure has been marked by at least three attempted coups, including a 1988 attack by Sri Lankan Tamil mercenaries.

The economy: staying afloat

The 250,000 Maldivians, mostly Sunni Muslims, depend for their livelihood on tourism and fishing, which managed to produce economic growth of more than 10% a year in the second half of the 1980s (by the late 1990s annual growth was a still-impressive 6%). Government policy has been to segregate tourism from the mainstream of Maldives' life. Only about 20 islands have Maldivian populations of more than 1,000; foreign tourists (338,000 in 1996) are channelled towards some 86 specially developed resorts. The long-term question, however, is the continued existence of the islands. Most are no more than six feet above sea-level, and President Gayoom has warned the developed world that global warming, by melting the ice-caps, will literally submerge the republic.

Total area	300 sq km	% agricultural area	10
Capital	Male	Highest point metres	–
Other cities	–	Main rivers	–

The economy[a]

GDP $bn	0.3	GDP per head $	990
% av. ann. growth in real GDP 1991–96	...	GDP per head in purchasing power parity $	3,080

Origins of GDP	% of total	Components of GDP	% of total
Agriculture	...	Private consumption	...
Industry	...	Public consumption	...
of which:		Investment	...
manufacturing	...	Exports	...
Services	...	Imports	...

Principal exports	$bn fob	Principal imports	$bn fob
	...		...

Government

System The president is nominated by a 48-member Majlis (Citizens' Council) – 40 are elected from Male and the 19 atoll groups, and 8 are presidential nominees – and is confirmed in office by popular referendum for a renewable 5-year term. The president appoints the judiciary, which acts according to Islamic law. From January 1998 a constitutional change has allowed a contest within the Majlis for the presidential nomination (hitherto it had been illegal for anyone to propose himself as a candidate).

Climate and topography

Tropical: hot and humid with dry north-east monsoon (Nov–Mar) and rainy south-west monsoon (Jun–Aug). The land area is flat; the highest elevations are only 2.5 metres.

People and society

Population m	0.3	% under 15	...
Pop. per sq km	850.0	% over 60	...
% urban	...	No. men per 100 women	95.0
% av. ann. growth 1980–95	...	No. households m	...
Human Development Index	61.1		

Ethnic groups	% of total	Religious groups	% of total
Sinhalese	...	Sunni Muslim	100
Dravidian	...		
Arab	...		
African	...		

a 1995.

MONGOLIA

Mongolia has leapt bravely from communism into an unknown world of democracy and free markets. Whatever the system, there will always be problems for a tiny population in a country three times the size of France, sandwiched between Russia and China.

History: the land of Genghis Khan

Mongolia's greatness came under Genghis Khan, who united the tribes in the 13th century and founded an empire that conquered Central Asia, the Gulf, the southern Caucasus and China. But the empire was short-lived. From 1691 to 1911 "Outer" Mongolia, as it was known, was a Chinese province; from 1912 to 1919 an autonomous state under Russian protection; and from 1919 to 1921 once again a province of China. Then in March 1921 a provisional government proclaimed independence and with Russia's Red Army drove out the Chinese. The Mongolian People's Republic was proclaimed in November 1924, and finally recognised by China in 1946.

Politics: from communism to democracy

For seven decades the Mongolian People's Revolutionary Party led a one-party, communist state, loyal to the Soviet Union in its dispute with China. But as Soviet communism collapsed the clamour for democracy grew. In May 1990 the constitution legalised opposition parties and introduced a presidential system with a standing legislature, the State Little Hural, elected both directly and from the People's Great Hural. The elections of July 1990 gave the MPRP a majority in both houses. But reforms continued and in February 1992 Mongolia abandoned communism for a single-chamber (Great Hural) parliamentary democracy.

The economy: going for broke

Under communism Mongolia, an essentially pastoral economy, supplied the Soviet Union's industry with raw materials and received aid in exchange. Meanwhile, meat was rationed in a land where livestock outnumbers people by at least ten to one. The end of Soviet aid in 1991 has forced dramatic economic reforms: free prices, privatisation and a stockmarket. But market reforms of themselves will not bring prosperity to such an isolated country. Fortunately, America, Japan and others are willing to be Mongolia's new friends. They are needed.

Total area	1,565,000 sq km	% agricultural area	80
Capital	Ulan Bator	Highest point metres	Turgen Uul
Other cities	Houd		4,116
		Main rivers	Ideriyn Gol

The economy

GDP $bn	1.0	GDP per head $	405
% av. ann. growth in		GDP per head in purchasing	
real GDP 1991–96	...	power parity $	1,950

Origins of GDP	% of total	Components of GDP	% of total
Agriculture	...	Private consumption	...
Industry	...	Public consumption	...
of which:		Investment	...
manufacturing	...	Exports	...
Services	...	Imports	...

Principal exports[a]	$m fob	Principal imports[b]	$m cif
Fuels, minerals & metals	49.7	Machinery & spares	172.4
Consumer goods	20.0	Petroleum products	134.0
Foodstuffs	6.6	Consumer goods	85.1
Agricultural goods	5.3		

Government

System Republic with president, who is directly elected for a 4-year term, as head of state. Single chamber legislature, the Great Hural, has 76 members, who elect the prime minister.

Main political parties National Democratic Party, Social Democratic Party, Mongolian People's Revolutionary Party

Climate and topography

Continental, with very cold, dry winters and warm summers; low rainfall. Largely high, rolling steppes with mountains to the north and the Gobi Desert in the south.

People and society

Population m	2.0	% under 15	40.0
Pop. per sq km	2.0	% over 60	6.0
% urban	60.0	No. men per 100 women	98.0
% av. ann. growth 1980–95	0.5	No. households m	...
Human Development Index	66.1		

Ethnic groups	% of total	Religious groups	% of total
Khalka	84	Shamanist	31
Kazakh	5	Buddhist	2
Durbet	3	Muslim	1

a 1990.
b 1991.

MYANMAR

The Union of Burma – or Myanmar, to use the name officially adopted in June 1989 – has wasted its abundant natural resources through autarkic socialism. But will the military junta ever accept the popular pressure for democracy?

History: from riches to rags

The first Burmese empire was founded at the start of the 11th century; real unity came with the dynasty established in 1757. But expansionist policies led in 1824, 1852 and 1885 to war with Britain and to Burma's incorporation as a province of British India. The second world war brought occupation by Japan. Independence from Britain came on January 4th 1948 with the Anti-Fascist People's Freedom League, led by U Nu, as the first government.

In 1962 General Ne Win, fearing concessions by the faction-riven government to the country's minorities, launched a military coup. In 1974 he declared a one-party state under the Burma Socialist Programme Party.

Politics: democracy disappointed

In July 1988 Ne Win resigned as chairman of the BSPP. Huge demonstrations, demanding multi-party elections, followed. The army reacted with brutal suppression. On September 18th 1988 it established the State Law and Order Restoration Council (SLORC) – with Ne Win behind the scenes.

The SLORC allowed elections on May 27th 1990. The National League for Democracy won 392 of the 485 People's Assembly seats contested, but the SLORC ignored the result and imprisoned most NLD politicians. The NLD's leader, Aung San Suu Kyi, daughter of an independence hero and under house arrest from July 1989 to July 1995, was awarded the Nobel Peace Prize in 1991.

The SLORC, renamed the State Peace and Development Council (SPDC) in November 1997, subsequently appealed to Buddhist Burmese chauvinism, attacking the Karen rebels and driving the Rohingya Muslims into Bangladesh.

The economy: desperate times

Although the country emerged slightly from its isolation in the 1980s, Myanmar in 1987 reduced its claim to high literacy in order to qualify for the UN's Least Developed Country status. The government talks of expanding exports, but this will mean depleting the forests which cover 40% of the country's land area and contain most of the world's teak.

Total area	676,552 sq km	% agricultural area	32
Capital	Yangon (Rangoon)	Highest point metres	Doi Inthanon
Other cities	Mandalay		2,595
		Main rivers	Irrawaddy, Chindwinn, Sittoung

The economy

GDP $bn	...	GDP per head $	...
% av. ann. growth in real GDP 1991–96	...	GDP per head in purchasing power parity $	...

Origins of GDP	% of total	Components of GDP	% of total
Agriculture	63	Private consumption	89
Industry	9	Public consumption	...
of which:		Investment	12
manufacturing	7	Exports	2
Services	28	Imports	2

Principal exports	$m fob	Principal imports	$m cif
Pulses & beans	213.9	Machinery & transport equip.	268.4
Prawns	82.2	Base metals & manufactures	178.9
Rice	60.1	Electrical machinery	168.1
Fish & fish products	33.3	Edible oils	81.0
Rubber	29.3	Cement	40.5

Government

System Republic ruled by military junta, the State Peace and Development Council (SPDC).

Main political parties National League for Democracy, National Unity Party

Climate and topography

Tropical, with an average temperature of 27°C (80°F) and monsoon rains from May to Oct. Most Burmese live in the valley and delta of the Irrawaddy, which is hemmed in by mountains and steep plateaus.

People and society

Population m	45.0	% under 15	37.5
Pop. per sq km	69.0	% over 60	7.0
% urban	27.0	No. men per 100 women	101.0
% av. ann. growth 1980–95	1.9	No. households m	...
Human Development Index	47.5		

Ethnic groups	% of total	Religious groups	% of total
Burman	68	Buddhist	87
Shan	7	Christian	6
Karen	7		

NEPAL

The Kingdom of Nepal has belatedly become a multi-party democracy. But stability is not guaranteed: Nepal, poor and landlocked, is perennially vulnerable to domestic dissent and foreign pressure.

History: royals and Ranas

The origins of modern Nepal go back to 1769, when Prithvi Narayan conquered the Nepal valley. From 1846 to 1951, however, royalty took second place to prime ministers from the Rana family, who took pains to please the British in India and to provide them with Gurkha soldiers.

Royal power was restored, with India's help, in 1951 and parliamentary elections were held in 1959. A year later King Mahendra dismissed the government and established a three-tier system of village, district and national *panchayats* (assemblies), answerable to him.

The *panchayat* system could not, however, still popular discontent. In April 1990, after violent demonstrations, King Birendra (who had succeeded his father in 1972) abolished the *panchayat* system, agreed to a constitutional monarchy and, after a ban of 39 years, legalised political parties.

Politics: important neighbours

The elections of May 15th 1991 gave 110 seats in the 205-member House of Representatives (the upper house is a semi-elected National Assembly) to the Nepali Congress Party. The United Communist Party of Nepal–United Marxist-Leninist coalition won 69 seats. In November 1994, however, the communists were elected, only to be replaced – after a no-confidence vote – by a Congress-led coalition 11 months later. A similar anti-communist coalition took power in 1997, but headed by the National Democratic Party. Since Nepal is sandwiched between India and China, any government has to be on good terms with both. This is not easy. In 1989 India, annoyed that Nepal had purchased arms from China for a time, closed all but two of its border posts with Nepal.

The economy: farming and foreign aid

Some 90% of the people depend on agriculture, which provides more than 40% of GDP. Population growth is depleting the country's forests. Nepal's best chance of lessening the dependence on foreign aid is tourism. The country, which divides into the world's highest mountains and the lush Terai plain, is a land of astonishing beauty.

Total area	140,797 sq km	% agricultural area	30
Capital	Kathmandu	Highest point metres	Mt Everest
Other cities	Pokhara		8,848
		Main rivers Buria Gandak, Sun Kosu	

The economy

GDP $bn	4.4	GDP per head $	200
% av. ann. growth in		GDP per head in purchasing	
real GDP 1991–96	4.9	power parity $	1,170

Origins of GDP	% of total	Components of GDP	% of total
Agriculture	42	Private consumption	79
Industry	22	Public consumption	8
of which:		Investment	23
manufacturing	10	Exports	24
Services	36	Imports	35

Principal exports	NRs bn fob	Principal imports	NRs bn cif
Woollen carpets	8.2	Machinery & transport equip.	15.3
Garments	5.4	Chemicals & drugs	8.8
Pulses	0.3	Mineral fuels & lubricants	5.6
Jute goods	0.5	Food & live animals	5.5
Hides & skins	0.4	Crude material	6.0

Government

System Parliamentary monarchy. Under the 1990 constitution parliament has a 205-member House of Representatives elected for 5-year terms, and a 60-member House of Estates of which 10 members are nominated by the king.
Main political parties Nepali Congress Party, United Communist Party of Nepal, National Democratic Party

Climate and topography

Subtropical on the plain, temperate in the mountain valleys, alpine or arctic on the peaks. Annual rainfall 1,500–2,000mm (60–80in) in the east, half that in the west. Most of Nepal is ruggedly mountainous with glacial basins. The only lowland is the fertile Tarai plain along the southern border.

People and society

Population m	21.9	% under 15	43.2
Pop. per sq km	157.0	% over 60	5.0
% urban	14.0	No. women per 100 men	96.0
% av. ann. growth 1980–95	2.5	Human Development Index	34.7

Ethnic groups	% of total	Religious groups	% of total
Nepali	54	Hindu	90
Bihari	19	Buddhist	5
Tamang	6	Muslim	3
Newari	4		
Tharu	4		

NEW ZEALAND

Total area	268,676 sq km	Population	3.6m
GDP	$65.9bn	GDP per head	$18,455
Capital	Wellington	Other cities Christchurch, Auckland	

The Dominion of New Zealand, 1,100 miles south-east of Australia, its nearest neighbour, is one of the more remote outposts of Europe's imperial reach. Divided into the North Island and South Island by the narrow Cook Strait, the country is twice the size of England but has less than half the population of London. Dependent on exporting to distant markets, the economic challenge is to be competitive enough to sustain the high quality of life that New Zealanders have traditionally taken for granted.

History: Cook's recipe

The first inhabitants of New Zealand were the Maori, Polynesian migrants who had sailed south from their Pacific islands. But so isolated is New Zealand that the Maori probably did not reach its shores until about the 10th century AD. The first European to arrive was the Dutch explorer, Abel Tasman, whose landing party on the South Island in December 1642 was bloodily rebuffed by the Maori.

The next visitor, in 1769, was Britain's Captain James Cook. His voyages led to European settlement, with New Zealand acting as a base for the whaling ships of New South Wales, Australia's convict settlement. Where the traders went, so did the Christian missionaries. From June 1839 to May 1841 New Zealand was legally part of New South Wales. This European impact, however, was of doubtful value: new diseases depleted Maori numbers from their peak of several hundred thousand; new religious values undermined social cohesion.

From Waitangi to Wellington

Before Britain formally annexed New Zealand in 1841, it first signed a treaty in February 1840 at Waitangi with the Maori chiefs. Under the treaty the Maori ceded sovereignty to the British crown, but in return for protection and the guaranteed possession of their lands, which they agreed to sell only to the crown.

The worthy intention of the treaty had, however, already been undermined by European land-grabbing before its signing; there were, too, many dubious cases of land transfer after the signature. These helped cause three decades of intermittent war and racial strife, with the Maori eventually losing most of their best land (in 1985 the Labour government gave the Waitangi Tribunal power to hear past breaches of the treaty and recommend compensation).

New Zealand became a dominion of the British crown in 1907, and demonstrated its loyalty in the Allied forces in both world wars. Independence came in 1947.

Politics: two-party consensus

The political foundation of modern New Zealand was laid between 1891 and 1912. Successive Liberal Party governments opened up more land for farming, protected domestic industry with import tariffs, encouraged trade unions, set up a labour code to protect workers and established a system of compulsory arbitration to end industrial unrest. There was even, in 1898, an Old Age Pensions Act. Such measures turned New Zealand into one of the world's earliest examples of a managed economy and welfare state.

The Liberal Party, however, began to lose rural support at the same time as urban followers broke away to create the Labour Party. In 1927 it was succeeded by the United Party, which in 1931 teamed up with the Reform Party in a coalition government ended by a Labour victory in 1935.

Governments since the second world war have been formed by either the Labour Party or the National Party, established in 1936 as the successor to the United-Reform alliance. The Labour Party draws its support from the trade unions and urban workers; the National Party relies on rural voters and urban conservatives.

In practice, differences between the two parties are of nuance rather than fundamental disagreement. This turned out to be true even in the 1980s, when the Labour government of David Lange made startling changes in both foreign and economic policy. In consequence, elections, which must take place every three years, to the one chamber House of Representatives tend to be unemotional affairs. Although popular support for the two parties has usually been more or less balanced, Labour has had fewer years in office. In the parliament elected in October 1990, the National Party won 67 seats; Labour 29; and the New Labour Party just one. In the November 1993 election the National Party retained its majority – but by just one seat. Voters also chose in future to use a system of proportional representation, rather than first-past-the-post. Its flaws were immediately revealed in the election of October 1996, when neither big party won enough seats to govern outright. Instead, the National Party formed a coalition government with the small New Zealand First party.

The challenge for the main parties in the future is to maintain social cohesion after a period in which the Labour governments of David Lange and Geoffrey Palmer and then the National government of Jim Bolger progressively deregulated the economy and dismantled the welfare state. These measures were taken to reverse the erosion of the country's competitiveness; it remains to be seen whether they will convince the electorate of their worth.

Foreign policy: loyal but independent

For most of its history New Zealand has displayed an instinctive loyalty to Britain, the "mother country". In the first world war its soldiers fought at Gallipoli and then in France; in the second world war, they fought again in Europe, as well as in North Africa. Subsequently, they fought against the Communist Party of Malaya, and joined Britain and Australia in the 1971 Five Power Defence Arrangements to support the integrity of Malaysia and Singapore, fellow members of the Commonwealth.

This loyalty to Britain and the crown is likely to remain fundamentally strong (certainly in comparison with Australia, whose more open immigration policy is swiftly weakening the links of kinship and culture with the United Kingdom). But the loyalty can no longer be blind: in 1973 Britain's entry into the European Economic Community was a devastating blow to the New Zealand economy and a warning that Britain saw its own interests to lie more in Europe than the Commonwealth.

For its part, New Zealand had long been aware of the changing balance of world power. America's Pacific presence during the second world war taught New Zealand to see itself as part of a bigger western alliance, hence its participation in the Korean war and its signing in 1951 of the ANZUS pact, a defence alliance with Australia and America. New Zealand also joined the South-East Asia Treaty Organisation in 1954, and then sent its soldiers to fight alongside Americans in Vietnam.

The Pacific identity: "no nukes"
But New Zealand, which administered Western Samoa from 1920 to 1962 and which still administers the island of Tokelau and retains links of "free association" with the Cook Islands and the island of Niue, increasingly sees itself as a Pacific nation and so at times, therefore, its interests are at odds with those of the West.

This became clear when the Labour government of

David Lange took office in July 1984 and pledged not to allow ships carrying nuclear weapons or powered by nuclear energy to dock in New Zealand. A furious America in August 1986 suspended its obligations to New Zealand under the ANZUS treaty.

Rainbow Warrior

Mr Lange's stance was popular both at home and with the smaller Pacific nations, and became more so when French secret service agents in July 1985 blew up the *Rainbow Warrior*, the flagship of the anti-nuclear environmentalist group, Greenpeace. The ship, which was moored in Auckland Harbour, was to have led a flotilla to Mururoa Atoll to protest against nuclear testing in French Polynesia. One crewman was killed in the explosion.

The diplomatic strains eventually eased. In February 1990 America announced it would resume ministerial contacts, which had been broken off in 1985. A month later the National Party, then still in opposition, said it would maintain Labour's anti-nuclear policy. Meanwhile, the French government apologised for the sinking of the *Rainbow Warrior* and paid compensation (in return its two agents were transferred for detention on a French Polynesian atoll, from which in May 1988 both were spirited off to France).

Society: more porridge than garlic

New Zealand often seems to be a throwback to a Britain that no longer exists. Its original immigrant stock, with a strong Scottish flavour, was overwhelmingly from the United Kingdom. Although immigration policy has recently been eased to attract skilled Asians, there is little of the cultural mix of southern Europe, the Middle East and Asia that now characterises Australia's big cities. As a result, New Zealanders are sometimes scorned as narrow-minded Philistines obsessed with rugby and cricket. Given the problems of a small population sprinkled over a large country, the criticism is a little unfair.

One problem for the future may be the position of Polynesians in New Zealand. Relations between the whites and the 296,000 Maori are generally harmonious, not least because of a rate of intermarriage which next century will ensure that a majority of New Zealanders will have some Maori blood. At the bottom of the social heap, however, there are around 100,000 Pacific Island Polynesians, mainly Samoans and Cook Islanders. In a country that is proud of its egalitarianism, they suffer disproportionately from unemployment, bad housing and poor education and risk becoming a disaffected underclass.

The economy: breaking free

Before the second world war more than 80% of New Zealand's exports were to Britain; at the end of the 1980s the proportion had fallen to 7%. The difference demonstrates the adjustment New Zealand had to make thanks to changes in the world economy and Britain's accession to the European Community (butter exports to Britain were given guaranteed access for five years).

But the adjustment is neither easy nor complete. Farm products account for 70% of New Zealand's exports and more than 6% of GDP, making the country vulnerable to foreign protectionism (especially the European Union's Common Agricultural Policy) or to changes in demand. In 1990–91, for example, the world wool price collapsed because China, a main buyer, decided to save foreign exchange and Japan decided to use up stocks. New Zealand, which has 60m sheep and accounts for 70% of world wool trade, could not avoid being hurt.

Wrong remedies

In the 1960s and 1970s the challenge of adjustment was met by diversification (land that once grazed cows might be used to grow kiwi fruit) and industrialisation, with a goal of self-sufficiency.

It was an expensive effort: the OPEC oil-price rises of the 1970s affected the economy badly at the same time as taxpayers were protecting manufacturing with high import tariffs. Meanwhile, the foreign debt rose. From 1974 to 1982 the economy grew by less than 1% a year; from 1982 it grew by only 1.6% a year. Although in 1989 New Zealand was still the 19th ranking country in the OECD in GDP per head, the population was clearly living beyond the country's means.

Labour's reckoning

The attempted cure was perhaps the fastest and most complete programme of deregulation ever experienced. It was initiated, despite its theoretical ideology, by the Labour government of Mr Lange. Subsidies to farmers, which in 1984 equalled 33% of the value of their output, were phased out; state-owned enterprises were privatised.

In the process, Mr Lange sacked Roger Douglas, his finance minister, for being too radical; Mr Lange was then replaced in August 1989 as party leader and prime minister by Geoffrey Palmer; he was followed in September 1990 by Michael Moore.

The National reckoning

Not surprisingly, an electorate dismayed by rising unemployment and soaring interest rates voted Labour resoundingly out of office in the October 1990 election. But the incoming National Party government under Jim Bolger agreed with Labour's economic diagnosis and simply continued the treatment: more privatisation; high interest rates; tight control of the money supply; the repeal of much employment legislation; and an end to compulsory union membership and centralised pay bargaining. Most controversially of all, Ruth Richardson, the finance minister, began to dismantle the structure of social welfare, reducing family and unemployment benefits and requiring payment, according to a means test, for medical and educational services. The split outcome of the 1996 election was a message to both Labour and the National Party that voters wanted an end to the economic and social revolution. One of the repercussions was the resignation from the National Party leadership in November 1997 of Mr Bolger. His successor, who took office in December 1997, was Jenny Shipley, the country's first woman prime minister – and with a right-wing reputation.

Salvation through pain?

Without doubt, the rigours since the mid-1980s have been a salutory lesson to New Zealanders that the outside world does not owe them a living. The question is whether the living they will have in the future can ever be both prosperous and secure.

If import tariffs are lowered further, New Zealand will be one of the world's least regulated or protected economies. The problem is that its economy is both small and remote, and so has no international clout. One attempt to redress this disadvantage is the Closer Economic Relationship signed with Australia in 1982, which by 1990 (five years ahead of schedule) had eliminated all bilateral trade barriers. Another attempt is membership of the Cairns Group of agricultural exporters. Unhappily, such efforts give New Zealand little of the weight it needs to fight for deregulation and free trade around the world.

Total area	268,676 sq km	% agricultural area	55
Capital	Wellington	Highest point metres	Mt Cook 3,764
Other cities	Christchurch, Auckland	Main rivers	Clutha, Waimakariri, Waikato

The economy

GDP $bn	65.9	GDP per head $	18,455
% av. ann. growth in		GDP per head in purchasing	
real GDP 1991–96	3.2	power parity $	16,360

Origins of GDP	% of total	Components of GDP	% of total
Agriculture	11	Private consumption	60
Industry	31	Public consumption	15
of which:		Investment	24
manufacturing	22	Exports	32
Services	58	Imports	30

Structure of manufacturing

			% of total
Agric. & food processing	27	Other	51
Textiles & clothing	8	Av. ann. increase in industrial	
Machinery & transport	14	output 1991–96	2.9

Inflation and exchange rates

Consumer price 1996 av. ann. incr.	2.3%	NZ$ per $ 1997 average	1.51
Av. ann. rate 1991–96	2.0%	NZ$ per $ end-1997	1.72

Balance of payments, reserves, aid and debt

			$bn
Exports, goods & services	17.8	Net capital account	1.2
Imports, goods & services	17.2	Net current account	1.9
Net income	-4.5	Other net investment	-1.4
Net current transfers	0.0	Net errors & omissions	2.3
Current-account balance	-3.8	Net change in reserves	-0.3
as % of GDP	-7.3	Level of reserves, end-Dec.	4.4
Foreign debt	...	Debt service	...
as % of GDP	...	as % of export earnings	...

Principal exports	$bn fob	Principal imports	$bn fob
Dairy produce	2.6	Machinery & mechanical	
Meat	1.8	appliances	2.2
Forest products	1.7	Vehicles & aircraft	2.0
Fruit & vegetables	0.7	Electrical machinery	1.5
Wool	0.7	Mineral fuels etc	0.9
Fish	0.6		

Main export destinations	% of total	Main origins of imports	% of total
Australia	20.3	Australia	23.5
Japan	15.3	United States	15.9
United States	9.1	Japan	13.5
UK	6.4	UK	5.1

Government

System Parliamentary monarchy. The head of state is the British monarch, represented by a governor-general. The legislative House of Representatives has 120 members elected on the basis of proportional representation. Head of government is the prime minister who appoints the cabinet.

Main political parties National Party, Labour Party, New Zealand First

Climate and topography

Temperate and sunny. Average annual temperature 9°C (48°F) in south, 15°C (59°F) in north. Annual rainfall 600–1,500mm (24–60in), more in mountains, evenly spread through the year. Two-thirds of New Zealand is covered with evergreen forest. There are two major and several smaller islands. South Island is mountainous, with glaciers, lakes and fast-flowing rivers; most settlement is on the alluvial east coast plains. North Island is less rugged but volcanically active, with many hot springs and geysers; the area to the north has poor soils and subtropical vegetation.

People and society

Population m	3.6	% under 15	22.9
Pop. per sq km	13.0	% over 60	15.0
% urban	84.0	No. women per 100 men	100.0
% av. ann. growth 1980–95	1.0	Human Development Index	93.7
No. households m	0.9		

Life expectancy	yrs	**Education**	
Men	73	Spending as % of GDP	4.4
Women	79	Years of compulsory education	9
Crude birth rate	16	Adult literacy %	99.0
Crude death rate	8	Primary school enrolment %	102
Infant mortality		Secondary school enrolment %	104
per 1,000 live births	7	Tertiary education enrolment %	58

Workforce	% of total	**Consumer goods ownership**	
Services	65		per 1,000 people
Industry	25	Cars	455.0
Agriculture	10	Televisions	508.0
% of pop. over 15 in workforce	48	Mobile phones	108.0
		Personal computers	222.7

Ethnic groups	% of total	**Religious groups**	% of total
European	87	Church of England	26
Polynesian (mostly Maori)	9	Presbyterian	16
		Roman Catholic	14
		Methodist	5
		Baptist	2

Tourism		**Health**	
Tourist arrivals m	1.4	Spending as % of GDP	7.5
Tourism receipts $bn	2.4	People per doctor	518.0

NORTH KOREA

Total area	120,538 sq km	Population	24m
GDP	...	GDP per head	...
Capital	Pyongyang	Other cities	Chongjin

With a record of extremism in foreign policy, North Korea has long been a dangerous (potentially nuclear-armed) threat to regional security. But economic crisis and the loss of its communist allies are forcing the North to emerge from isolation, and on terms that will be set mainly by the South and its friends, and which will lead – perhaps sooner rather than later – to the reunification of the Korean peninsula.

History: the "hermit kingdom"

The Korean identity goes back for at least 2,000 years (some Korean nationalists say 5,000), with its own culture, language and ethnic purity. But there have always been regional rivalries, with the North harking back to the Koguryo dynasty.

Sandwiched between China, Japan and Russia, Korea's instinct historically was to withdraw into itself, becoming the "hermit kingdom". This isolation was rudely ended by an expansionist Japan, which took control of the peninsula in 1905 and formally annexed Korea in 1910.

It was Japan's defeat in the second world war which led to the emergence of North Korea in 1945. Accepting equal responsibility for Japan's surrender, the Soviet Union and America divided the Korean peninsula along the 38th parallel; the North became a puppet of Soviet communism and the South an American client.

War was inevitable. On June 25th 1950 the North invaded the South and was turned back only when troops of the United Nations entered the fray, pushing their attack close to the Chinese border. At this point, China intervened, and the tide turned again. After about 4m deaths, 3m of them Koreans, an armistice was agreed in 1953, leaving the peninsula divided by a Demilitarised Zone drawn diagonally across the 38th parallel.

Politics: Great Kim and Dear Kim

North Korea's politics was dominated for almost five decades by its "Great Leader", Kim Il Sung, a nationalist who emerged under Soviet tutelage as the North's head of state in 1946 and then, in September 1948, as the first president of the Democratic People's Republic of Korea.

Until his death in July 1994, Kim was both the world's longest-serving political leader and, through his command of the armed services and the Korean Workers' Party, one of its most dictatorial. Radio and TV receivers were made to receive only the North's broadcasts; thousands were jailed for political errors; terrorists were dispatched to hit the South (a ministerial delegation from the South was blown up on a visit to Myanmar in 1983; a South Korean airliner was blown up in flight in 1987).

Kim's political heir was his son, the "Dear Leader" Kim Jong Il, who, lacking his father's charisma, has taken time to demonstrate an unchallenged authority, especially over the armed forces.

Foreign policy: the hermit finally emerges

The collapse at the start of the 1990s of its oldest ally, the Soviet Union (which in 1990 had, anyway, already recognised the South), has forced the North to reassess the outside world, not least because communist China, its other big ally, has since the late 1980s been keener on trade with the South. The result has been talks with Japan; the admission of the two Koreas as separate members of the UN in September 1991; an "agreement on reconciliation, non-aggression, co-operation and exchange" with the South in December 1991; and parliamentary approval in April 1992 for the North's nuclear facilities to be opened to international inspection. Before his death Kim Il Sung had publicly hoped for better relations with America, the guarantor of the South. Despite this, the nuclear programme remained shrouded in secrecy.

The economy: from riches to rust

North Korea's economic desperation (severe food shortages were reported at various times in the 1990s) stems from a Stalinist stress on heavy industry and from the Kim doctrine of *juche*, or self-reliance. But the mistakes were not immediately evident: industrial output expanded rapidly in the 1950s and 1960s, and as recently as 1973 the North could boast a higher GDP per head than the South.

However, the collapse in the late 1980s of Soviet bloc trade and aid revealed the underlying economic problems: out-of-date technology, inefficient state factories, severe power shortages and poor planning. One remedy proposed in 1991 was to set up investor-friendly Special Economic Zones, on the model of China. The only real remedy, however, will be reunification with the South and integration into the world trading system.

Total area	120,538 sq km	% agricultural area	19
Capital	Pyongyang	Highest point metres	Kwanmo-
Other cities	Chongjin		Bong 2,541
		Main rivers	Taedong, Yalu, Tumen

The economy

GDP $bn	...	GDP per head $	...
% av. ann. growth in		GDP per head in purchasing	
real GDP 1991–96	...	power parity $	...

Origins of GDP	% of total	Components of GDP	% of total
Agriculture	29.5	Private consumption	...
Industry	42.6	Public consumption	...
of which:		Investment	...
manufacturing	23.6	Exports	...
Services	27.9	Imports	...

Structure of manufacturing

			% of total
Agric. & food processing	...	Other	...
Textiles & clothing	...	Av. ann. increase in industrial	
Machinery & transport	...	output 1991–96	...

Inflation and exchange rates

Consumer price 1996 av. ann. incr.	...	Won per $ 1997 average	2.2
Av. ann. rate 1991–96	...	Won per $ end-1997	2.2

Balance of payments, reserves and debt

			$bn
Exports, goods & services	...	Net capital account	...
Imports, goods & services	...	Net current account	...
Net income	...	Other net investment	...
Net current transfers	...	Net errors & omissions	...
Current-account balance	...	Net change in reserves	...
as % of GDP	...	Level of reserves, end-Dec.	...
Foreign debt	...	Debt service	...
as % of GDP	...	as % of export earnings	...

Principal exports[a]	% of total	Principal imports	
Fuels, minerals & metals	31.0	...	
Manufactures	30.0		
Food & agricultural goods	29.0		
Machinery & equipment	5.0		
Textiles	5.0		

Main export destinations[b]	% of total	Main origins of imports[b]	% of total
Japan	27.9	China	32.6
South Korea	20.8	Japan	17.2
China	5.2	Russia	4.7
Germany	4.0	South Korea	4.3
Russia	1.2	Germany	2.9

Government
System Single-party communist state. Nominal constitutional authority is held by the unicameral legislature, the 687-member Supreme People's Assembly (SPA), elected for a 4-year term from a single list of candidates approved by the communist Korean Workers' Party.
Main political parties Korean Workers' Party

Climate and topography
Continental, with monthly average temperatures ranging from -3°C (27°F) to 24°C (75°F). Annual rainfall is 1,000mm (40in), most in Jun–Sep. Mountains run down the eastern side of the country. More than half the population is urbanised; major settlements are on the wide western and narrow eastern coastal plains.

People and society

Population m	24.0	% under 15	29.1
Pop. per sq km	198.0	% over 60	7.0
% urban	61.0	No. women per 100 men	103.0
% av. ann. growth 1980–95	1.8	Human Development Index	76.5
No. households m	...		

Life expectancy	yrs	Education	
Men	67	Spending as % of GDP	...
Women	74	Years of compulsory education	10
Crude birth rate	22	Adult literacy %	95
Crude death rate	6	Primary school enrolment %	...
Infant mortality		Secondary school enrolment %	...
per 1,000 live births	26	Tertiary education enrolment %	...

Workforce	% of total	Consumer goods ownership	
Services	31		per 1,000 people
Industry	31	Cars	13.0
Agriculture	38	Televisions	323.0
% of pop. over 15 in workforce	50	Mobile phones	–
		Personal computers	...

Ethnic groups	% of total	Religious groups	% of total
Korean	99	Shamanist	16
		Chundo Kyo	14
		Buddhist	2
		Christian	1

Tourism		Health	
Tourist arrivals m	...	Spending as % of GDP	...
Tourism receipts $bn	...	People per doctor	419.0

a 1978.
b 1995.

PACIFIC ISLANDS

American Samoa 195 sq km	Micronesia 700 sq km	Solomon Islands
Cook Islands 237 sq km	Nauru 21.3 sq km	27,556 sq km
French Polynesia 4,167 sq km	New Caledonia 19,103 sq km	Tonga 748 sq km
Guam 549 sq km	Niue 263 sq km	Tuvalu 26 sq km
Kiribati 689 sq km	Northern Mariana Islands	Vanuatu 12,173 sq km
Marshall Islands 180 sq km	457 sq km	Western Samoa 2,927 sq km

Sprinkled across the Pacific Ocean are the islands of Melanesia, Micronesia and Polynesia. Nine are independent nations, four are self-governing in association with their former colonial rulers and the remainder are dependencies of overseas powers. The biggest are the countries of Papua New Guinea and Fiji (see separate entries); the smallest is the country of Niue with 2,500 people on a coral atoll of 100 square miles. The Pacific nations are divided by different histories and different ethnic origins; they speak about 1,200 different languages. What unites them is a shared awareness of their vulnerability to the world beyond their horizon.

History: colonial serendipity

The first contact with the developed world came through the voyages of men such as Magellan, Tasman and Cook. The result was colonisation by Europe's maritime powers, and later by America and Japan. At the end of the second world war there were six colonial powers: Britain, America, France, the Netherlands, Australia and New Zealand (defeated Germany and Japan lost their colonies).

The colonial links in many cases remain: the Cook Islands, for example, are self-governing in association with New Zealand; the Federated States of Micronesia (Pohnpei, Truk, Yap and Kosrae), whose history includes rule from Spain, Germany, Japan and America, became a United Nations Trust Territory at the end of the second world war. In 1986 the Federated States became self-governing in association with America, which has a similar relationship with the Marshall Islands. Palau became fully independent in 1994, but America still administers American Samoa, Guam and the Commonwealth of the Northern Mariana Islands. France administers French Polynesia (including Tahiti). Britain and Australia have granted full independence to their Pacific islands.

Politics: colonial legacies

The independent or self-governing countries have usually based their political structures on the colonial powers. The exceptions are Tonga, where executive and legislative functions are vested in the king as well as parliament, and Western Samoa, where only the aristocracy (*matai*) may vote.

Most of the islands suffer from the tensions of development, ethnic rivalries and differences over property rights (colonial concepts of ownership were often imposed on communities whose traditions involved collective rights). In the French territory of New Caledonia there is a simmering – and in 1984-89 sometimes violent – struggle for political power between the indigenous Kanaks and French and South-East Asian immigrants. The Franco-British colonial condominium has bestowed differences of language and religion on independent Vanuatu.

Foreign policy: united we stand, divided we fall

The collapse of the Soviet Union, which in the mid-1970s attempted to forge links with some newly independent states, has arguably reduced the importance of the Pacific islands – and France in early 1996 stopped using the Mururoa Atoll to test nuclear weapons. America, however, has military facilities on Guam and others of its territories.

In recognition of their puny size as individual nations, the independent and self-governing islands in 1971 sought collective strength by setting up the South Pacific Forum with Australia and New Zealand. It has concentrated on the nuclear issue, the supervision of fishing rights and the quest for the independence of New Caledonia and other islands. A more recent cause for anger was the American decision in 1990 to move chemical weapons from Germany to be stored on Johnston Island. The Forum's influence, however, is limited: for almost 11 years France, Britain and America refused to sign the South Pacific Nuclear Free Zone Treaty ratified by eight of the Forum's members in December 1986.

The economy: externally dependent

The regional market consists of a mere 6m people (4m of them in Papua New Guinea; 800,000 in Fiji); distances to foreign markets are immense; arable land and fresh water are scarce; cyclones are frequent.

Traditional exports have been copra, sugar, coffee, cocoa and palm oil, none of which make for wealth. By contrast, Nauru has become rich from phosphate mining. Its reserves, however, will soon be depleted and it remains to be seen how well Nauru will live off its invested income. Most countries look to tourism, fishing and foreign aid for their long-term earnings.

American Samoa
Area 195 sq km   **Pop.** 46,800   **GDP** $190m[a]   **GDP per head** $5,410[a]
Major industries Fishing, fish-canning, handicrafts, dairy farming
Major imports Food, fuel, building materials, textiles, transport equipment
Major exports Canned tuna, pet food, fresh fish, aluminium

Cook Islands
Area 237 sq km   **Pop.** 19,000   **GDP** $62m   **GDP per head** $3,281
Major industries Fishing, farming
Major imports Food & live animals, fuel, transport equipment
Major exports Food & live animals, crude materials

French Polynesia
Area 4,167 sq km   **Pop.** 199,100   **GDP** $2,761m   **GDP per head** $14,350[c]
Major industries Coconut oil, oilcake, beer, printed cloth, Japanese sandals
Major imports …
Major exports Fresh fruit, vanilla, coconut oil, cultured pearls

Guam
Area 549 sq km   **Pop.** 132,726   **GDP** $1,364m[e]   **GDP per head** $10,276[e]
Major industries Fishing, tourism, petroleum refining
Major imports Foodstuffs, fuel, transport equipment
Major exports Petroleum products, iron and steel scrap, eggs

Kiribati
Area 689 sq km   **Pop.** 74,788   **GDP** $36.8m   **GDP per head** $492
Major industries Fishing, handicrafts
Major imports Foodstuffs, fuel, transport equipment
Major exports Copra, fish

Marshall Islands
Area 180 sq km   **Pop.** 43,355   **GDP** …   **GDP per head** …
Major industries Subsistence agriculture, fishing
Major imports Foodstuffs, building materials
Major exports Coconut products, fish, handicrafts

Micronesia
Area 700 sq km   **Pop** 100,000   **GDP** $150m[d]   **GDP** per head $1,500[e]
Major industries Public works, tourism, fishing
Major imports …
Major exports Copra, coconut oil, fish, pepper, handicrafts

Nauru
Area 21.3 sq km   **Pop.** 9,350   **GDP** $80.7m[a]   **GDP per head** $8,631
Major industries Phosphate mining
Major imports ….
Major exports Phosphate

a 1985.   b 1991.   c 1989.   d 1986.   e 1988.   f 1984.   g 1987.

New Caledonia
Area 19,103 sq km   **Pop.** 164,173   **GDP** $2,233m   **GDP per head** $13,400^c
Major industries Nickel ore production
Major imports Petroleum products, solid mineral fuels, cement
Major exports Ferro-nickel, nickel ore, nickel matte

Niue
Area 263 sq km   **Pop.** 2,267   **GDP** $3.3m^e **GDP per head** $1,456^f
Major industries Subsistence agriculture, honey
Major imports Food & live animals, fuel, transport equipment
Major exports Fruit & vegetables, miscellaneous manufactures

Northern Mariana Islands
Area 457 sq km   **Pop.** 43,345   **GDP** $512m^c **GDP per head** $11,812^c
Major industries Garment manufacture
Major imports Foodstuffs, construction materials, cars, beverages,
petroleum products
Major exports Garments

Solomon Islands
Area 27,556 sq km   **Pop.** 360,000   **GDP** $206m   **GDP per head** $572
Major industries Subsistence agriculture, fishing
Major imports Foodstuffs, fuel, transport equipment
Major exports Timber, palm oil & kernels, copra, fish

Tonga
Area 748 sq km   **Pop.** 100,000   **GDP** $97m   **GDP per head** $974
Major industries Fishing, fruit-farming
Major imports Food, machinery & transport equipment, fuel
Major exports Fish, coconut oil, vanilla beans, bananas

Tuvalu
Area 26 sq km   **Pop.** 8,229   **GDP** $3m^g **GDP per head** $326^g
Major industries Agriculture
Major imports Food & live animals, beverages and tobacco consumer
goods, machinery, transport equipment, fuel
Major exports Copra, cinematographic film

Vanuatu
Area 12,173 sq km   **Pop.** 174,574   **GDP** $180.6m   **GDP per head** $1,035
Major industries Fish-freezing, canneries, tourism
Major imports Food, consumer goods, machinery, transport equipment,
fuel
Major exports Copra, frozen fish, meat

Western Samoa
Area 2,927 sq km   **Pop.** 194,992   **GDP** $115m   **GDP per head** $590
Major industries Timber, tourism, light industry, fishing
Major imports Food, manufactured goods, machinery, fuel
Major exports Cocoa, timber, mineral fuel, bananas

PAKISTAN

Total area	746,045 sq km	Population	129.8m
	(excluding Jammu and Kashmir)		
GDP	$60bn	GDP per head	$465
Capital	Islamabad	Other cities	Lahore, Karachi

The Islamic Republic of Pakistan is a paradox: created as a Muslim state, its affinity supposedly lies with Afghanistan and the other Muslim countries to its west. In practice, the country feels at least as strongly the gravitational pull from the east of its giant (and often antagonistic) Hindu neighbour, India. The consequence is a troubled sense of national identity and an absence of the stability needed to promote economic growth.

History: seeking an identity

Pakistan's official existence began on August 15th 1947 with the partition of British India into the independent states of India and Pakistan. But the country's origins can be traced to the arrival of the British in the Indian subcontinent in the 18th century. This effectively ended six centuries of Muslim political dominance over the Hindus and other sects of India.

To protect their interests as a minority, the Muslims in 1906 founded the All-India Muslim League. In 1940, inspired by the poet Muhammad Iqbal and by the politician Mohammed Ali Jinnah, the League formally adopted the demand for an independent Muslim state of Pakistan as soon as the British raj should end.

It was, however, a bloody birth. Partition involved the panic-stricken transfer of up to 12m people, both Muslims and Hindus, across the new borders of West and East Pakistan, which were separated from each other by about 1,600km of Indian territory. War broke out between Indian and Pakistani forces over the fate of Jammu and Kashmir, whose mainly Muslim population was ruled by a Hindu princely family. A ceasefire-line was agreed in 1949, but Kashmir remains an area of high tension.

Of the states of British India, Pakistan inherited intact only the backward ones of Sindh, Baluchistan and the North-West Frontier; meanwhile, both the Punjab and Bengal were divided by partition. Moreover, while political and military power rested in West Pakistan, the majority of the population lived in East Pakistan, in Pakistan's share of Bengal. In 1971 this inherent contradiction led to civil war and the secession (with India's help) of the East, which named itself Bangladesh.

Politics: insecure foundations

Throughout the short history of Pakistan, political power has ultimately rested with the armed forces. In part, this is because the country has never felt truly secure. But it is also because civilian politicians have failed to solve underlying problems of feudalism and economic backwardness.

These failings became evident almost at once. Jinnah, whose strength and astuteness as the first governor-general were crucial, died in 1948; his prime minister (and ablest ally), Liaquat Ali Khan, was assassinated in October 1951. There followed a period of sustained tensions between religious factions; West and East Pakistan; governor-general and prime minister; and civilian politicians and the military. In 1956 a new constitution was agreed, making Pakistan, hitherto a dominion under the British monarchy, an Islamic Republic. Two years later, impatient with the failings of parliamentary democracy, the country's president, Major-General Iskander Mirza, abrogated the constitution, abolished political parties and declared martial law.

Military rule

The next decade was one of unquestioned military dominance. The "strongman" was General Mohammad Ayub Khan, who sent Mirza into exile in 1960. Ayub's strategy was to Islamicise the institutions of politics, by introducing "basic democracies", or local units chosen by direct election, while simultaneously promoting economic growth. But West Pakistan advanced in wealth while the East fell back, and Ayub's image was hardly helped by the 1965 war with India over Kashmir. In March 1969 Ayub handed power to General Agha Mohammad Yahya Khan, who imposed martial law ahead of a general election in December 1970 and ordered that the resulting National Assembly should produce a new constitution within 100 days.

Civil war

The election proved fatal for a united Pakistan. In the East, the Awami League of Sheikh Mujibur Rahman won a sweeping victory that would have given it 167 of the National Assembly's 300 seats; in the West, the Pakistan People's Party of Zulfikar Ali Bhutto was dominant. Sheikh Mujib envisaged a constitution which would have allowed the East total autonomy except in foreign policy. When Bhutto rejected this, Sheikh Mujib ordered a general strike throughout the East. The president, General Yahya, offered a compromise. When rebuffed, he sent troops from the

West to "re-occupy" the East in March 1971. The result was bloodshed and a huge exodus of Bengali refugees from the East to India. In December, Indian troops intervened and quickly defeated the Pakistani army. Sheikh Mujib was then free to proclaim independent Bangladesh.

The Bhutto era

General Yahya had little choice but to step down, leaving Zulfikar Ali Bhutto to be president of the now-truncated Pakistan, and then, after a new constitution in April 1973, its prime minister. Bhutto advocated a policy of "Islamic socialism" and nationalised many of the assets of the great feudal families. But as separatist tendencies increased in the North-West Frontier Province and Baluchistan, so he became increasingly repressive. The election of March 1977 gave Bhutto's PPP a sweeping victory, but amid accusations of widespread fraud and intimidation.

The consequences were a breakdown of law and order; the declaration by religious leaders that Bhutto was an unlawful ruler, liable for execution; and the imposition of martial law. On July 5th 1977 General Zia ul-Haq took over as martial law administrator. Two months later Bhutto was detained on a charge of attempted murder and Zia was proclaimed Pakistan's president.

The Zia era

General Zia's rule has left an indelible mark on Pakistan: his refusal, despite international protest, to reprieve Bhutto from execution in April 1979 ensured that revenge would be a lasting element in Pakistani politics; his introduction of Islamic laws pushed the country away from the secular political tradition it had inherited from the British raj. While Zia searched for a more "Islamic" way, political parties were banned and their leaders persecuted. In 1982 Zia established a 300-strong federal advisory council, the Majlis-i-Shura; in 1984 prayer wardens were appointed in every village to foster "Islamic democracy"; and in July 1985 interest-free Islamic banking was made compulsory.

Although Zia used a controversial referendum in December 1984 to claim support for himself and Islamisation, and amended the constitution in October 1985 to indemnify his regime's past actions, political and ethnic unrest mounted. In April 1986 Bhutto's daughter, Benazir, returned from almost three years' exile to strengthen the multi-party Movement for the Restoration of Democracy. Unable to contain ethnic strife and civil unrest, in May 1988 Zia dissolved the federal National Assembly and the four Provincial Assemblies and dismissed the cabinet. In July he announced that new elections would be held, but on a non-party basis, in November. His manoeuvring was in vain. On August 17th 1988 Zia died in a suspicious air crash.

Democracy returns

Zia's death automatically elevated to the presidency the president of the Senate, Ghulam Ishaq Khan, who proceeded, with the support of the army and the Inter-Services Intelligence department, to play his role with unexpected deftness and decisiveness. One of his first acts was to decree that elections would go ahead as scheduled, but with the political parties able to play a full role.

The result was a dramatic victory for Benazir Bhutto and the PPP over an opposition alliance called the Islami Jamhoori Ittehad (also called the Islamic Democratic Alliance, or IDA), whose main elements were the Pakistan Muslim League and the fundamentalist Jamaat-e-Islami.

Democracy spoilt

The PPP had only 93 of the 207 directly elected seats in the National Assembly (the IDA had 55), and so had to make alliances with other parties, notably the Mohajir Qaumi Mahaz (MQM), a movement representing the Urdu-speaking refugees from India who settled in Sindh Province in Karachi and Hyderabad. These alliances were inherently unstable: in September 1989 the MQM switched its support to the opposition. More damaging, however, was Miss Bhutto's inexperience, her failure to check corruption – which allegedly involved her husband, Asif Ali Zardari – and, crucially, the animosity and mistrust felt towards her by the army. As ethnic violence mounted and allegations of corruption spread, on August 6th 1990 the president dismissed the Bhutto government, dissolved the National Assembly and appointed Ghulam Mustafa Jatoi to lead a caretaker government until elections on October 24th 1990.

Those elections led to a victory for the IDA, falling only four seats short of an absolute majority. The new prime minister, Nawaz Sharif, was a Punjabi businessman eager to bring in economic reforms and skilled at balancing the demands for Islamisation with Pakistan's more liberal tradition (the 1991 Shariah Act, affirming the superiority of Islamic laws, was widely seen as a harmless sop to the extremists which would have little real impact).

Yet hopes in the Sharif government were disappointed. There were charges that the government's corruption spread to the prime minister's own family and was at least as bad as during Miss Bhutto's time. In elections held in October 1993 Miss Bhutto was returned to power for a second time – but her term was again marred by corruption and violence, and in 1996 she reacted with petulance to the entry into politics of the cricketer Imran Khan. In November 1996 President Farooq Leghari dismissed Miss Bhutto's government, citing corruption. Mr Sharif regained office in February 1997 and consolidated his power at the expense of the judiciary and of President Leghari, who resigned in December 1997.

Foreign policy: obsessed with India

Given the circumstances of Pakistan's creation, it is hardly surprising that India is the focus of the country's foreign policy. The two neighbours clash constantly in Kashmir (in 1963 India declared that the portion of Kashmir under its control was a full state of the Indian union). Where India was an ally of the Soviet Union, Pakistan was an ally of America. When Soviet troops occupied neighbouring Afghanistan in December 1979, Zia seized the opportunity to accelerate Pakistan's military build-up. America was Zia's supporter: Pakistan was a buffer against Soviet expansionism and a conduit for supplies to the anti-Russian Afghan *mujahideen* guerrillas.

In 1968 Pakistan, like India, refused to sign the Nuclear Non-Proliferation Treaty. Defeat by India in 1971 and India's explosion of a nuclear device in 1974 added urgency to Pakistan's secret nuclear programme, and American opposition to an "Islamic bomb" could be more or less ignored as long as America needed Pakistan to counter the Russians in Afghanistan.

Everything changed, however, with the Soviet withdrawal from Afghanistan in early 1989 and the ending of the cold war. In October 1990 President Bush cut off aid and military assistance to Pakistan. This was done under the terms of the 1985 Pressler Amendment, which requires the American president, before granting aid to Pakistan, to certify that it does not "possess a nuclear explosive device". As worrying, however, was the fear that America would now choose India, not Pakistan, to be its regional ally.

Society: divided by class and tribe

Although a common faith in Islam (mainly of the orthodox Sunni form) binds Pakistanis together, they are divided by cultural, ethnic and linguistic differences. The Pushtu-speaking Pathans of the North-West Frontier Province and the Federally Administered Tribal Areas are close to their

Afghan neighbours, as are the tribes of Baluchistan. In Sindh Province there is perennial conflict between indigenous Sindhi-speakers and the Urdu-speaking *mohajirs* (refugees) who came from India and now dominate Karachi and Hyderabad. Punjab, the most populated and relaxed province, has close cultural ties with India's Punjab.

These differences have often led to secessionist movements. Potentially as divisive, however, are Pakistan's social differences. Despite the growth of a lower-middle class in the cities, a feudal elite still dominates. Although some predict that social differences will lead to an Islamic revolution like that in Iran, religious fundamentalism is not a mass movement. The Jamaat-e-Islami, for example, draws its support not from the poor but from the lower-middle class.

The economy: trying to be free

Within days of coming to power in October 1990, the Sharif government announced sweeping economic reforms, involving the privatisation of 115 state-owned enterprises (only 15 of them making real profits), the abolition of foreign exchange controls, a reduction in import tariffs, an amnesty for tax-evaders and a less onerous but more efficient tax system, and a slashing of red tape.

Such reforms were needed. Government policy in the 1950s stressed industrialisation; in the 1960s the emphasis was on agriculture, too. But by the 1970s it was clear that the benefits had gone mostly to a feudal elite, hence Zulfikar Bhutto's decision to tap the populist yearning for social justice by nationalising much of the economy.

That remedy was as bad as the disease: economic growth slowed to 4% a year – with the population growing at more than 3% a year – and private investment disappeared. As Pakistan's energy bill soared because of OPEC price rises, all that saved the economy was foreign aid and remittances from Pakistanis working in the Gulf.

The odds against success

The question is whether Pakistan can translate good intentions into achievements. The economy has the potential for growth (it grew by 7% a year in the 1960s, despite the war with India), but this potential is dissipated by pervasive corruption and a constant state of insecurity. Perhaps the most serious problem, however, is the pressure of Pakistan's population. At the time of independence, in 1947, West Pakistan had 32.5m people. The same area now has around four times as many and almost half are below the age of 15.

Total area	746,045 sq km	% agricultural area	32
Capital	Islamabad	Highest point metres	Mt Godwin
Other cities	Lahore, Karachi		Austen (K2) 8,611
		Main rivers	Indus, Jhelum, Chenab

The economy

GDP $bn	60.2	GDP per head $	465
% av. ann. growth in		GDP per head in purchasing	
real GDP 1991–96	4.8	power parity $	2,230

Origins of GDP	% of total	Components of GDP	% of total
Agriculture	26	Private consumption	73
Industry	24	Public consumption	12
of which:		Investment	19
manufacturing	17	Exports	16
Services	50	Imports	19

Structure of manufacturing[a]

			% of total
Agric. & food processing	32	Other	37
Textiles & clothing	22	Av. ann. increase in industrial	
Machinery & transport	9	output 1991–96	3.3

Inflation and exchange rates

Consumer price 1996 av. ann. incr. 10.4%		Rupees per $ 1997 average	41.11
Av. ann. rate 1991–96	10.9%	Rupees per $ end-1997	44.50

Balance of payments, reserves and debt

			$bn
Exports, goods & services	8.3	Net capital account	...
Imports, goods & services	11.1	Net current account	...
Net income	-1.7	Other net investment	...
Net current transfers	2.4	Net errors & omissions	...
Current-account balance	-2.0	Net change in reserves	...
as % of GDP	-3.3	Level of reserves, end-Dec.	2.5
Foreign debt	30.2	Debt service	5.1
as % of GDP	38.4	as % of export earnings	35.3

Principal exports[b]	$bn fob	Principal imports[b]	$bn fob
Cotton yarn	1.5	Machinery excl. transport equip.	2.4
Cotton fabrics	1.1	Chemicals	1.6
Knitwear	0.7	Petroleum & products	1.6
Garments & hosiery	0.6	Edible oils	1.0
Synthetic textile fabrics	0.6	Motor vehicles	0.4

Main export destinations[b]	% of total	Main origins of imports[b]	% of total
United States	15.0	Japan	10.7
Hong Kong	7.5	United States	9.2
UK	6.8	Malaysia	8.4
Japan	6.7	Germany	6.2
Germany	6.4	Kuwait	5.6
United Arab Emirates	4.4	Saudi Arabia	4.9

Government

System Bicameral legislature: National Assembly has 207 directly elected members plus 10 members representing minorities; Senate has 87 members. The president, who is head of state, is elected for a 5-year term by a joint sitting of the federal legislature.

Main political parties Pakistan Muslim League, Pakistan People's Party

Climate and topography

Continental, with daily temperature ranges of 15°C (60°F); average 4°C (39°F) in Jan, over 40°C (105°F) in summer. Rainfall 750–900mm (30–35in) in the mountains, but less than 500mm (20in) elsewhere. The Himalayas in the far north feed rivers that run through a scrubby plateau to Pakistan's heartland: the flat alluvial flood plain of the Indus. In the west the mountainous border with Afghanistan gives way to the Baluchistan plateau and deserts.

People and society

Population m	129.8	% under 15	43.5
Pop. per sq km	169.0	% over 60	0.9
% urban	35.0	No. women per 100 men	92.0
% av. ann. growth 1980–95	3.0	Human Development Index	44.5
No. households m	18.7		

Life expectancy	yrs	Education	
Men	62	Spending as % of GDP	2.7
Women	64	Years of compulsory education	…
Crude birth rate	38	Adult literacy %	37.1
Crude death rate	8	Primary school enrolment %	65
Infant mortality		Secondary school enrolment %	…
per 1,000 live births	90	Tertiary education enrolment %	…

Workforce	% of total	Consumer goods ownership	
Services	30		per 1,000 people
Industry	19	Cars	4.0
Agriculture	52	Televisions	22.0
% of pop. over 15 in workforce	35	Mobile phones	0.3
		Personal computers	1.2

Ethnic groups	% of total	Religious groups	% of total
Punjabi	66	Muslim	97
Sindhi	13	Hindu	2
Pushtun	8	Christian	1

Tourism		Health	
Tourist arrivals m	0.2	Spending as % of GDP	0.8
Tourism receipts $bn	0.1	People per doctor	1,923.0

a Year ending June 30th 1995.
b 1995.

PAPUA NEW GUINEA

Papua New Guinea (PNG) has the potential to bring prosperity to its fast-growing population. But Papuans are divided from each other by ethnic conflicts, hundreds of different languages and rugged terrain. Many tribes are virtually in the Stone Age; violent crime is common in the cities; and corruption permeates politics.

History: forced evolution

Since Britain claimed the island in 1793, New Guinea's fate has been decided by the outside world. The Dutch colonised the western half of New Guinea (which in 1969 became Irian Jaya, a province of Indonesia); the British took the south-east, which in 1904 was passed over to Australia and renamed Papua; and the Germans, until they were dispossessed during the first world war, occupied the northeast. In 1942 the Japanese invaded, only to be replaced by the Australians, whose influence has remained even after independence on September 16th 1975.

Politics: a fractious democracy

As a member of the British Commonwealth, with Queen Elizabeth II (represented by a governor-general) as its head of state, PNG is a parliamentary monarchy. Despite the dominance of the prime minister, Michael Somare (followed by Paias Wingti, Rabbie Namaliu, Julius Chan and Bill Skate), in the decades after independence, the system is extremely fluid. The power of patronage is what counts for an electorate divided by tribe and race (four-fifths are Papuan, a sixth Melanesian, the rest Polynesian, Chinese and European).

The Free Papua Movement seeks the secession of Irian Jaya from Indonesia and stages attacks from bases in PNG. Meanwhile, the Melanesian population of Bougainville, which is part of the Solomon islands chain, has its own movement seeking secession from PNG (in 1997 South African mercenaries tried to quell the rebels).

The economy: promise unfulfilled

PNG's resources are huge: rich farmland and forests; minerals such as gold and copper (both found in the enormous Ok Tedi mine); oil and gas reserves; and great hydroelectric potential. Unhappily, because of the inhospitable terrain, the absence of efficient transport and the violence in Bougainville (which has large mineral deposits), PNG has yet to benefit greatly from these resources.

Total area	461,691 sq km	% agricultural area	1
Capital	Port Moresby	Highest point metres	Mt Wilhelm
Other cities	Wewak, Kikori		4,509
		Main rivers	Ramu, Sepik

The economy[a]

GDP $bn	5.0	GDP per head $	1,160
% av. ann. growth in		GDP per head in purchasing	
real GDP 1991–96	…	power parity $	2,420

Origins of GDP	% of total	Components of GDP	% of total
Agriculture	26	Private consumption	48
Industry	38	Public consumption	12
of which:		Investment	24
manufacturing	8	Exports	61
Services	34	Imports	45

Principal exports	$m fob	Principal imports	$m cif
Crude oil	814.1	Machinery & transport equip.	442.9
Gold	586.5	Manufactured goods	334.0
Logs	352.4	Food & live animals	204.2
Copper	293.4	Chemicals	85.9
Coffee	144.3	Mineral fuels & lubricants	40.8
Palm oil	138.3		

Government

System Parliamentary democracy, with the British sovereign as head of state, represented by a governor-general. Elections for the 109-member parliament are held every 5 years.

Main political parties Pangu Pati, People's Democratic Movement, People's Action Party, People's Progress Party, Melanesian Alliance

Climate and topography

Tropical, with temperatures of 23–32°C (73–90°F) year-round. Annual rainfall of at least 2,000mm (80in), rising to 7,000mm (276in) in highlands; driest May–Aug. The territory includes several smaller islands as well as the eastern half of the island of New Guinea, which has a mountainous interior covered by tropical rain forest. There are few towns.

People and society

Population m	4.1	% under 15	39.9
Pop. per sq km	9.0	% over 60	7.0
% urban	16.0	No. women per 100 men	94.0
% av. ann. growth 1980–95	2.2	Human Development Index	52.5

Ethnic groups	% of total	Religious groups	% of total
Papuan	83	Protestant	58
Melanesian	15	Roman Catholic	33
		Anglican	5

a 1995.

PHILIPPINES

Total area	300,000 sq km	Population	70.3m
GDP	$83.8bn	GDP per head	$1,190
Capital	Manila	Other cities	Davao, Cebu

The Republic of the Philippines is a country which fell from grace. One of Asia's richest countries in the 1950s, by the 1980s it had become one of the poorest. Yet the country's resources and potential remain enormous. Recovery is in essence a political and social challenge: to move from feudalism to stable democracy, and to establish an economic system less distorted by corruption and feudalism.

History: from the convent to Hollywood

The Filipinos had early contacts with India, Arabia and China, but it was the effects of Spanish colonisation, following Ferdinand Magellan's discovery of the Philippine islands in 1521, which defined the modern Philippines. By the end of the 16th century, most people of the northern and central Philippines had converted to Roman Catholicism.

For the Spanish, the Philippines was first an entrepot for the exchange of Chinese silks and Mexican silver, and then a source of sugar and abaca for export to Europe. But by the late 19th century the power and wealth of the Catholic friars led to several anti-clerical riots, ironically involving sons of the landowning elite: young men, such as Jose Rizal, Andres Bonifacio and Emilio Aguinaldo, who had absorbed nationalist ideals while being educated in Europe. In 1896 the unrest culminated in an insurrection which was put down by Spain's soldiers (Rizal was shot by firing squad).

The colonists' victory was temporary. In 1898 Spain lost its war with America, which had been helped by the Philippine nationalists. Spain then ceded the Philippines to America, which proceeded to turn on its nationalist allies, finally suppressing their independence struggle in 1902.

America soon boosted the Philippine economy by encouraging American investment and by allowing Philippine agricultural exports preferential access to the American market. However, America felt uncomfortable with its imperial role, and rationalised it by training what Civil Governor (later President) William Howard Taft once called America's "little brown brothers" for eventual independence. In 1935 this led to the establishment of the Commonwealth of the Philippines, with a semi-colonial status.

But the preparation for independence was interrupted

by the second world war and the Japanese invasion of 1941. In 1944 America's troops, as General MacArthur had promised, returned. Two years later, on July 4th 1946, the Philippines was granted full independence.

Independent hardships

The immediate need on independence was to remedy the devastation caused by the second world war (about 80% of Manila had been destroyed), but the corrupt administrations of first President Manuel Roxas (1946–48) and then Elpidio Quirino (1948–53) proved unequal to the challenge. Meanwhile, the task of successive administrations was made still more difficult by the Hukbalahap guerrillas, who had fought against the Japanese in the war and who now, inspired by Mao Zedong's victory in China, sought to achieve a peasant revolution in the Philippines.

The Huks were finally defeated by Ramon Magsaysay, a president unique in the Philippines for his humble origins and honesty. Unfortunately, Magsaysay was killed in an air crash in 1957. His era was followed by the corrupt administrations of Carlos Garcia (1957–61) and Diosdado Macapagal (1961–65).

The Marcos era

When Ferdinand Marcos narrowly won the presidential election of 1965, it seemed the country might be on the verge of greatness. Marcos was a brilliant lawyer who had entered the House of Representatives in 1949, at the age of 32, and the Senate in 1959. The Philippines possessed abundant agricultural resources and its manufacturing output had been growing during the 1950s by 12% a year. Marcos promised to cut corruption, increase tax revenues, get more rice grown, provide more roads, schools and hospitals, and eliminate feudalism with a programme of agrarian reform which would give land to the peasantry.

So much for good intentions. Marcos's brilliance was flawed by corruption; he was in any case the product of a violent political culture (at the age of 22 he had successfully defended himself before the Supreme Court against the charge of murdering a political rival of his father). By the time Marcos was re-elected in 1969, corruption and police brutality were provoking demonstrations and strikes, and the communist New People's Army – successors of the Huks – began their stubborn insurrection. In September 1972, using as his excuse a faked ambush on the car of defence secretary, Juan ("Johnny") Ponce Enrile, Marcos declared martial law and announced the "New Society".

Marcos's mischief

"The cornerstone of the New Society" was a programme to distribute rice and corn holdings to landless peasants. In addition, infrastructure projects were used to boost economic growth, and "non-traditional" export industries, such as shoes, processed foods, electrical components and garments, were developed.

But the fates conspired against Marcos in the shape of the OPEC price rises of the mid- and late-1970s. Foreign debt ballooned out of control, from $2.6 billion in 1975 to $10.5 billion in 1980 and $26 billion in 1984. Meanwhile, Marcos became extravagantly corrupt, awarding contracts and quasi-monopolies to his friends – "crony capitalism" as it was known – in return for a piece of the action.

The EDSA revolution

Marcos's downfall can be traced to the assassination as he stepped from his airliner at Manila airport of Benigno ("Ninoy") Aquino, on August 21st 1983. Aquino was returning from exile in America (he had gone there in 1980 after being imprisoned by Marcos for eight years). The killing provoked a massive flight of capital, which worsened the economic plight and forced the Philippines in October to declare a moratorium on its foreign debt.

This in turn led to an IMF-imposed austerity programme, with imports falling by 16% in 1984 and another 23% in 1985. As unemployment rose to more than a third of the workforce, so did popular discontent. To reassert his authority, and to appease criticism from America, Marcos called a "snap" presidential election in February 1986. After blatantly rigging the vote, Marcos declared himself the victor over the opposition candidate (and widow of Ninoy Aquino), Corazon Cojuangco Aquino.

Manila's masses gathered by the hundreds of thousands at EDSA – the capital's arterial highway, Epifanio De Los Santos Avenue – and dared the military to attack them. The military backed down; the deputy chief of staff, General Fidel Ramos, and Marcos's defence minister, Johnny Enrile, declared their support for Mrs Aquino. Four days later "People Power" triumphed: Marcos fled by helicopter to America's Clark air base, and then on to exile in Hawaii (where he died in September 1989).

Aquino's democracy

President Corazon ("Cory") Aquino's great achievement was to restore democracy. In 1973 a new constitution had been approved by referendum to provide a parliamentary system, but it was never fully implemented and the first elections to a unicameral legislature did not take place until 1978 (they were swept by Marcos's New Society Movement, KBL). In 1981 further amendments replaced the parliamentary form with a mixed presidential and parliamentary system, and it was under this constitution that Marcos was re-elected for another six-year term in June 1981.

But whatever the constitutional trappings, the Marcos era had been a dictatorship. Mrs Aquino was determined that it should not happen again. The constitution of February 1987, approved by a 76% vote in a referendum with an 87% turnout, limits the president to a single six-year term; the president cannot overrule a two-thirds vote by Congress; the president cannot abolish Congress; and the president cannot impose martial law for longer than 60 days. There is a 24-member senate, directly elected on a nationwide vote for six years (but just five initially, to coincide with the end of Mrs Aquino's mandate), and a 250-member House of Representatives (nearly 50 of whom are presidential appointees or party-list members) elected by constituency for a three-year term, although its first term was also timed to end with the end of Mrs Aquino's term.

Plots, and more plots
The democratic institutions during the Aquino era revealed the weakness of a presidential system in which the chief executive cannot be legally dismissed except through impeachment. The alternative is the illegal dismissal by a coup, and there were at least half-a-dozen coup attempts against Mrs Aquino during her term, the earliest of which was in July 1986.

One reason for the plots was that Mrs Aquino's initial administration was a coalition of rival interests: it included both "left-leaners", such as Jaime ("Jimmy") Arroyo, and Johnny Enrile, who had once administered martial law for Marcos. Another reason is that Mrs Aquino's whole term was marred by inefficiency. The result was that "Cory" was less able over time to rely on "People Power" to protect her from disaffected military plotters, notably Colonel Gregorio ("Gringo") Honasan, belonging either to the Reform the Armed Forces Movement (the "Ramboys") or the more right-wing Young Officers' Union.

The most dangerous coup attempt was in December 1989; the government survived only because American aircraft from their base at Clark overflew the rebels and prevented the capture of the presidential palace of Malacanang. In five days of fighting 113 were killed and over 600 wounded; Enrile, who had long ago been dismissed from the government, was accused of complicity.

Welcome Eddie

That Mrs Aquino completed her term may have been God's will (she is a devout believer, and had the support of the archbishop of Manila, Cardinal Jaime Sin); it was also because she retained the backing of General Fidel ("Eddie") Ramos, who was her chief of staff and then defence secretary. In an enthusiastic election on May 11th 1992 Ramos was elected president, with about a quarter of the vote, in a race of seven candidates; they included Marcos's widow Imelda and also Eduardo ("Danding") Cojuangco, who was both Mrs Aquino's first cousin and one of Marcos's biggest cronies. Ramos, a Protestant, had not been endorsed by Cardinal Sin, but was Mrs Aquino's favourite – and proved the better president.

Politics: families and film stars

Philippine democracy embraces a plethora of political parties: for example, the Liberal Party; the Nacionalista Party (to which Marcos once belonged); and the Kilusan Bagong Lipunan (New Society Movement, founded by Marcos in 1978). In 1982, a year after Marcos lifted martial law and was returned to office for another term, the opposition formed the United Nationalist Democratic Organisation (UNIDO), a coalition including Lakas ng Bayan (Laban, or the People's Power Movement, founded by Ninoy Aquino in 1978) and the Pilipino Democratic Party. These two merged in 1983 to form the PDP-Laban, a faction of which in 1988 joined with the Lakas ng Bansa (People's Struggle) to form the Laban ng Demokratikong Pilipino (LDP).

All parties are prone to internal squabbles based on personalities rather than policies. For example, because the pro-government LDP would not endorse Fidel Ramos as its presidential candidate in 1992, Ramos formed his own party, Lakas ng EDSA. The truth is that personalities matter more than ideology: politics, like the economy, is dominated by perhaps 60 families, whose politicians are called *"trapos"* or traditional politicians. Those politicians who are not backed by the vote-machine of a feudal family must find popularity by other means, which is how several film stars, such as Joseph Estrada, have become successful. One obvious drawback of the feudally based system is that an initiative such as the Comprehensive Agrarian Reform Programme (CARP) has become nullified – like previous land reform programmes – by the vested interests of Congress.

Ideological fervour belongs mainly to the pro-China Communist Party of the Philippines (which President Ramos legalised in 1992), and its armed wing, the New People's Army. Despite the economic mismanagement of the Aquino era, the NPA, which had grown rapidly under Marcos, lost ground, falling in number from over 25,000 fighters in the mid-1980s to under 18,000 at the start of the 1990s. Another low-key struggle is with the Moro National Liberation Front, a Muslim separatist movement in the southern islands. The constitution allows for autonomy in Muslim areas, but only four out of 13 relevant provinces in Mindanao voted for this in a referendum in November 1989 (they now constitute Muslim Mindanao). In 1996 a ceasefire was agreed with the MNLF, and the MNLF leader, Nur Misuari, became governor of the Autonomous Region of Muslim Mindanao.

Foreign policy: Uncle Sam's umbrella

The Philippines, which is a founder member of the Association of South-East Asian Nations (ASEAN), has occasional territorial disputes with its ASEAN colleague, Malaysia; it also claims the Spratly Islands, as do Malaysia, Brunei, China, Taiwan and Vietnam. But these issues rarely have any political effect in Manila. Instead, it is the relationship with America (Filipino soldiers fought for America in the Vietnam war) which obsesses all Filipinos.

One reason is that the relationship goes back a century; another is strong economic ties; the strongest, however, was the presence of American military "facilities" – the largest outside America – at the Clark air base and the Subic Bay naval base. These had existed in some form almost from the beginning of the American colonial era; after independence a succession of agreements gave sovereignty of the bases, and four smaller facilities, to the Philippines in return for a long lease to the Americans, who then contributed aid and military assistance to the Philippines.

But according to the 1987 constitution, when the bases' lease expired in September 1991, its renewal had to be ratified by a two-thirds vote of the Senate. Despite the economic importance of the bases (they were the biggest employer after the Philippine government), sentiment in the Senate was against them. Senators argued that there was no external security threat (indeed, the bases might attract an attack), and that the bases encouraged a dependent mentality which stopped the country achieving its potential. They added that the bases had spawned a huge sex industry, second in Asia only to Thailand's.

Given the popular support for the bases, enough money for the Philippines might have changed the senators' minds, but first the strategic importance of the bases lessened with the ending of the cold war, and then the eruption of the Pinatubo volcano in June 1991 buried the Clark base in ash. To keep just Subic for ten years America offered to pay $203m a year ($323m in the first year). Mrs Aquino's government accepted, but the Senate voted 12–11 against, and the following year America withdrew its forces.

Society: questions of family

Anthropologists say that among the 7,000 or so islands in the Philippines there are 111 different cultural and racial groups, speaking some 70 different languages. They range from Muslim Malays in the southern Sulu archipelago to Episcopalian Igorot aborigines in the mountains of Luzon. The national language is Pilipino, which is in essence Tagalog, but English is used in government documents and by most of the Manila press.

The predominant racial strain is Malay, with strong dashes of Chinese and Spanish blood. At the top of what remains a feudal society are the *mestizos,* those whose blood is mixed. Spanish *mestizos* rank socially above Chinese *mestizos,* although the line has blurred into a single aristocracy as the Chinese hispanicised their names (witness the syllables of the Aquino and Cojuangco clans). The top fifth of the population receives half the national income.

The influence of Spain has made the Philippines Asia's only Christian country. About 85% of the people are Roman Catholics, but there are also local Philippine churches, the Aglipayans and the Iglesia ni Kristo, and some Protestants (such as President Ramos). Muslims make up about 4% of the population. In recent years Christian fundamentalists from America have claimed many converts.

The economy: underachieving

The Philippines should be one of Asia's most prosperous economies: it has natural resources – timber, coconut, sugar, bananas, rubber and minerals – in abundance and a literate, hard-working labour force. Instead, it is one of the worst-performing economies in the ASEAN region (although GDP per head is above Indonesia's and prospects improved markedly with President Ramos).

Its relative failure has several causes. In the 1950s industrialisation concentrated on import-substitution, but in the 1960s there was no attempt to build export-oriented industries based on the import-substituting factories. By the end of the 1960s the Philippines was the slowest growing economy in non-communist South-East Asia. It compounded its problems by erecting high tariffs to protect its industries (and the profits of their owners) from foreign competition.

The consequence was a country living beyond its means. The rampant corruption of the Marcos era and the oil shocks of the 1970s made the situation still worse, counteracting the belated development of "non-traditional" exports (as a share of total exports they rose from less than 10% in 1970 to 23% in 1975 and 58% in 1983).

The remedy, imposed by the International Monetary Fund after the Philippines defaulted on its debt in 1983, was a harsh austerity programme: government spending was slashed; credit was tightened; and, in 1984, some 400,000 workers were laid off.

The cure is missed...

The world recovery in the late-1980s and the international welcome given to Mrs Aquino's administration gave the economy a boost of growth, which was then checked by the administration's incompetence and by the atmosphere of political instability. By the end of the 1980s Filipinos had managed to recover economically only to the point they had been at ten years earlier. Further shocks came at the start of the 1990s with a series of natural disasters – including the eruption of Pinatubo – and with the Gulf war against Iraq. This meant the loss of remittances from Filipinos in the Middle East (at least 2m Philippine citizens work overseas, mainly as seamen and domestic servants).

...but remains the same

Despite the Philippines' troubles, its potential can still be tapped, if political stability can be sustained (hence business pressure in 1997 to allow Ramos a second term) and if the government can translate words into action. This means improving agricultural productivity, not least by implementing agrarian reform; privatising state-owned enterprises; improving the savings rate in order to fund domestic investment; and continuing to liberalise the economy, especially by lowering tariffs. Above all, it means checking corruption and introducing accountability to a society used to forgiveness. That, of course, means changing the Philippines' culture as much as its economy.

Total area	300,000 sq km	% agricultural area	41
Capital	Manila	Highest point metres	Mt Apo 2,954
Other cities	Davao, Cebu	Main rivers	Cagayan, Agusan

The economy

GDP $bn	83.8	GDP per head $	1,190
% av. ann. growth in		GDP per head in purchasing	
real GDP 1991–96	3.4	power parity $	2,850

Origins of GDP	% of total	Components of GDP	% of total
Agriculture	22	Private consumption	74
Industry	32	Public consumption	11
of which:		Investment	23
manufacturing	23	Exports	36
Services	46	Imports	44

Structure of manufacturing

			% of total
Agric. & food processing	31	Other	44
Textiles & clothing	11	Av. ann. increase in industrial	
Machinery & transport	14	output 1991–96	...

Inflation and exchange rates

Consumer price 1996 av. ann. incr.	8.4%	Pesos per $ 1997 average	29.74
Av. ann. rate 1991–96	8.4%	Pesos per $ end-1997	39.98

Balance of payments, reserves and debt

			$bn
Exports, goods & services	26.8	Net capital account	...
Imports, goods & services	33.3	Net direct & portfolio investment	2.3
Net income	3.7	Other net investment	3.0
Net current transfers	0.9	Net errors & omissions	-2.1
Current-account balance	-2.0	Net change in reserves	-1.2
as % of GDP	-2.8	Level of reserves, end-Dec.	7.8
Foreign debt	39.4	Debt service	7.0
as % of GDP	49.4	as % of export earnings	16.0

Principal exports[a]	$bn fob	Principal imports[a]	$bn fob
Electrical & electronic equip.	7.4	Parts for manufacture	
Garments	2.6	of electrical equipment	3.8
Coconut oil	0.8	Semi-processed manufactures	3.6
Machinery & transport equip.	0.7	Telecommunication &	
Copper	0.5	electrical machinery	3.2
Fish	0.4	Power generation equipment	
		& specialised machinery	2.9
		Mineral fuels	2.5

Main export destinations[a]	% of total	Main origins of imports[a]	% of total
United States	35.3	Japan	22.4
Japan	15.7	United States	18.9
Singapore	5.7	Singapore	5.9
UK	5.3	Saudi Arabia	6.2
Hong Kong	4.7	Taiwan	5.4

Government

System Presidential democracy. President serves one 6-year term. Upper house of bicameral legislature is a 24-member Senate elected for 6-year terms. The House of Representatives has 250 members of which 204 are elected for 3-year terms.

Main political parties Lakas, Laban, NPC, PMP, CPP, MNLF, MILF

Climate and topography

Tropical marine with north-east monsoon (Nov–Apr) and south-west monsoon (May–Oct). Most of the islands in the archipelago are mountainous, with most ranges running north–south. Some of the islands are coral and some volcanic (there are 10 active volcanoes) and many have narrow coastal plains. Most of the population lives in intermontane plains on the larger islands, or on the coastal strips. Around 40% of the land is forested.

People and society

Population m	70.3	% under 15	38.8
Pop. per sq km	230.0	% over 60	5.0
% urban	53.0	No. women per 100 men	99.0
% av. ann. growth 1980–95	2.3	Human Development Index	67.2
No. households m	12.4		

Life expectancy	yrs	Education	
Men	64	Spending as % of GDP	2.4
Women	68	Years of compulsory education	6
Crude birth rate	29	Adult literacy %	94.4
Crude death rate	7	Primary school enrolment %	111
Infant mortality		Secondary school enrolment %	79
per 1,000 live births	39	Tertiary education enrolment %	26

Workforce	% of total	Consumer goods ownership	
Services	39		per 1,000 people
Industry	15	Cars	26.0
Agriculture	46	Televisions	121.0
% of pop. over 15 in workforce	40	Mobile phones	7.3
		Personal computers	11.4

Ethnic groups	% of total	Religious groups	% of total
Malay (predominantly)	90	Christian	93
Aborigines	6	(Roman Catholic 85, other 8)	
Chinese	1	Muslim	4

Tourism		Health	
Tourist arrivals m	1.8	Spending as % of GDP	2.4
Tourism receipts $bn	2.8	People per doctor	8,273.0

a 1995.

SINGAPORE

Total area	633 sq km	Population	3m
GDP	$94.1bn	GDP per head	$30,940
Capital	Singapore	Other cities	–

The Republic of Singapore is one of the world's great economic successes. A tiny, multiracial island state, dangling with some 50 islets from the toe of Malaysia, it offers its disciplined and hard-working citizens a standard of living unmatched in Asia. The question, constantly posed by the government, is how this standard can be maintained: does Singapore's future depend on adjusting the social and political formula which has produced today's miracle?

History: the "Lion City"

Malay tradition holds that the name Singapura – Lion City – was given by Sri Tri Buana, a Sumatran ruler of the 13th century who saw a lion when seeking shelter from a storm in the settlement of Temasek (Sea Town). During the successive centuries this settlement came under the influence of the Sumatrans, the Thais, the Javanese, the Portuguese and the Dutch. Then, in 1819, Sir Thomas Stamford Raffles, of Britain's East India Company, signed a treaty with the sultan of neighbouring Johore establishing Singapore as a British trading station on the sea-route between India and China. Seven years later Singapore was joined with Penang and Malacca, on the Malay peninsula, to form Britain's "Straits Settlements" (of which it became the centre of government in 1832). On April 1st 1867 the Straits Settlements formally became a colony of the British Crown.

From Raffles to Lee

The British changed Singapore from a sleepy fishing village into a thriving entrepot. In 1877 they introduced rubber seedlings to Singapore (and subsequently to the Malay states), and then introduced Chinese and Indians to work the rubber estates and man the port. In 1824 the population had numbered fewer than 11,000 people, almost all of them Malay; by 1860 the population had swelled through immigration to number 80,792, of whom the Chinese accounted for 61.9%, the Malays 13.5% and the Indians 16.05%. But this population was mainly male; only after May 1938, when free female immigration was allowed, did Singapore's population take proper root.

From February 15th 1942 until September 1945 British rule was interrupted by the Japanese. After their defeat the British, recognising Singapore's value as a naval base, in

March 1946 made the territory a crown colony separate from Penang and Malacca (which in 1948 became part of the Federation of Malaya). But the white man was no longer someone to be automatically obeyed. In 1948 the Communist Party of Malaya began its 12-year fight (the so-called "emergency") in Malaya and Singapore; in the election of 1955, the first proper political contest in the colony's history, conservative pro-British parties were soundly beaten by the Labour Front of David Marshall and the People's Action Party (PAP) of Lee Kuan Yew.

Marshall became Singapore's first chief minister on April 6th 1955, but resigned on June 6th following the breakdown of talks with Britain to secure for Singapore full internal self-government. The era of his successor, Lim Yew Hock, lasted until 1959 and was marked by violent riots instigated by the communists which Lim put down, at the cost of being labelled "anti-Chinese".

In 1959 Lim's talks with Britain finally produced full internal self-government. In May a general election for the first fully elected Legislative Council gave the PAP 43 of the 51 seats and on June 5th 1959 Lee Kuan Yew was sworn in as Singapore's first prime minister.

Merger with Malaysia

Lee's ambition was to merge Singapore with Malaya. At first, Malaya was opposed, not wanting an extra million Singaporean Chinese to alter its delicate racial balance. Singapore's underground communist movement – with which Lee, to win power, had co-operated – was also opposed, not wanting to come under the anti-communist rule of Kuala Lumpur. However, as Britain pressed for a Malaysian federation, including Malaya, Sabah, Sarawak and Brunei (which, in the end, did not join), Malaya's prime minister, Tunku Abdul Rahman, realised that Singapore, if excluded, might become a South-East Asian "Cuba". Accordingly, on September 16th 1963, Singapore broke its last ties with Britain and became a founding member of the Federation of Malaysia.

The membership was short-lived. Malaysia's politically dominant Malays became fearful of the success of the PAP among the Malays in Singapore; they worried that the PAP would attempt to usurp the United Malays National Organisation as the federation's ruling party. Race riots broke out in Singapore in July and September 1964. As the atmosphere worsened, the Tunku decided that Singapore must leave the federation.

On August 9th 1965 Singapore became a separate, fully

independent state; Lee later admitted to shedding tears at the failure of the merger.

Nation-building

Singapore's separate prospects were inauspicious: its energies had already been sapped by the three-year military "confrontation" with Indonesia, which was opposed to the concept of federal Malaysia, and by the need to eliminate the communists, whom Lee had cleverly exploited for his own ends. Then, in July 1967, Britain announced it intended to withdraw its troops, which was a devastating decision since they accounted for 15% of the island's GDP and provided employment for 40,000 Singaporeans.

The solution of Lee and his finance minister, Goh Keng Swee, was a daring strategy of job creation and economic growth: industrialisation was coupled with an educational programme so that Singapore could become both a light-manufacturing centre and also the provider of shipping and financial services for the Malaysian hinterland. Meanwhile, decent accommodation was provided by a huge public-housing programme. Helped by the growth in world trade, the strategy worked: in the years to 1973 the economy grew by 12.3% a year, laying the foundation for Singapore not only to absorb the oil shocks of the 1970s but also to become in the 1980s the region's most technically proficient base for manufacturing and services.

Politics: Lee's legacy

Modern Singapore is politically the creation of Lee Kuan Yew. The son of a Chinese clerk, "Harry" Lee had a brilliant academic career at Fitzwilliam College, Cambridge, and returned to Singapore to become a lawyer active in trade union affairs. This gave him his entrée into politics, and in 1954 he founded the PAP to lead the struggle for independence. In the following decades, until November 1990 when, at the age of 67, he stepped down as prime minister, Lee guided the party, which soon jettisoned its quasi-socialist rhetoric, and the country towards a ruthlessly competitive meritocracy, carefully combining government incentives with liberal trade.

The result is that Singapore often seems to be a giant, super-efficient company, offering high material rewards in return for effort and obedience. This bargain has kept the PAP continuously in government and with a monopoly on seats in the one-chamber parliament from 1968 until the 1981 by-election victory of Joshua Benjamin Jeyaretnam, leader of the Workers' Party. In the 1984 general election Jeyaretnam held his seat and was joined in opposition by Chiam See Tong, of the centrist Singapore Democratic Party.

Such opposition successes rattled the government. Jeyaretnam was banned from parliament for five years in October 1986, after being fined and imprisoned on charges of falsifying his party's accounts. This meant he could not fight the 1988 general election. Jeyaretnam was subsequently said by Britain's Privy Council, at the time Singapore's highest court of appeal, to have "suffered a grievous injustice", but the conviction stood.

What perturbs the PAP is the possibility, remote though it seems, that its grip on power will be broken, and that Singapore's electorate – for whom voting is compulsory – will negligently let the nation slip into unstable coalition government. This fear traditionally has been based on the PAP's declining share of the vote: from 84.4% in April 1968 to 61% in August 1991, when opposition members took four of the parliament's 83 seats. The fear persists, even though in the 1997 election the PAP vote rose to 65%.

Goh's false start

The 1991 election, with its lower vote for the PAP, was a personal setback for Goh Chok Tong, Lee's successor as prime minister. Goh, a pleasant if somewhat stolid technocrat, had promised a gentler, more liberal Singapore. However, his failure to change the voting trend increased speculation that he was merely a stop-gap until Lee's talented son, Brigadier-General ("B-G") Lee Hsien Loong, who was trade and industry minister, could – without charges of nepotism – become prime minister. Meanwhile, Lee himself remained powerful both as the PAP's secretary-general (until December 1992) and as the government's senior minister. Although many predicted he would at some point become an elected, executive president, following a law ending the appointed, ceremonial presidency in 1993, the post was first filled by Ong Teng Cheong.

With a rising PAP vote in the 1997 election, Goh finally seemed secure as government leader. One reason was his espousal of hard-line policies favoured by the old guard; another was the health problems that earlier had afflicted B-G Lee.

A problem of power

The underlying question is whether Singapore's politics need to be redefined. The PAP was conceived in an era of adversarial debate, but has assumed the one-party rule found also in Japan and Taiwan. Lee praised the theory of opposition politics but cracked down on its practice. What is offered instead is a system of checks on any abuse of power by the PAP: Singapore is divided into 9 constituencies electing single members of parliament, and 15 Group Representation Constituencies electing 74 MPs. Each of the group constituencies returns a set of MPs from the same party, one of whom must be from the Malay, Indian or other minority communities. There is also a provision for the opposition parties to nominate up to six "non-constituency MPs" and for another six to be nominated by a committee of parliament. The oppositon complains that the system favours the better-resourced PAP.

It is clear, however, that dissent has strict limits. The Internal Security Act, created by the British during the Malayan "emergency", allows indefinite detention without trial, and has been used to punish what elsewhere would be innocuous leftism. Similarly, in the late 1980s, some foreign publications – the *Far Eastern Economic Review, Asiaweek, Time* and the Asian edition of the *Wall Street Journal* – had their circulation restricted on the grounds that they had interfered in Singapore's domestic politics.

Foreign policy: being of value

Singapore – tiny, predominantly Chinese and surrounded by much larger Malay, Muslim neighbours – has an acute sense of vulnerability. It therefore strives to be on good terms with its neighbours, to be of value to them and to conclude alliances that go beyond the neighbours. This means membership of the Association of South-East Asian Nations (ASEAN), and also of wider organisations, such as the Five Power Defence Arrangements (with Australia, New Zealand, Britain and Malaysia) and the Asia-Pacific Economic Co-operation forum. For the various colleagues in these groups, Singapore acts as a discreet banker – in 1997 it pledged a $5 billion loan to financially troubled Indonesia – a font of ideas and a preacher of free trade.

The pragmatism goes still further. Although the government is intensely anti-communist, Singapore's traders do business in Indochina. Similarly, Singapore is on good terms with both Taiwan and mainland China, and with Israel and the Muslim world.

When America left its bases in the Philippines, Singapore readily provided facilities to help compensate. The idea is not that foreign countries should necessarily become friends, but that they should have an interest – often commercial – in not hurting Singapore.

Society: carefully engineered

Singapore's population is racially (give or take a decimal point) 75.9% Chinese, 15.2% Malay and 6.5% Indian, the rest being Eurasians and Europeans. The government associates these proportions with social harmony and economic success, and so tries to preserve them. This is easier said than done: a programme to stem population growth in the 1970s ("Stop at Two") proved too successful, leading to the risk in the future of too many old people and not enough young to support them. Accordingly, in the 1980s the programme became "Three or More", and tax incentives were used to encourage pregnancy.

But Lee was after quality as well as quantity. Educated Chinese Singaporeans, in particular, were marrying later (or not at all) and having fewer babies. Singapore, therefore, has possibly the world's only avowed policy of eugenics. In 1983, for example, the Social Development Unit was established to help graduates meet, marry and breed.

Many Singaporeans bitterly resent such ideas. The government's reply is that Singapore's society needs careful monitoring if it is not to fragment along racial lines. Over 80% of the population lives in public-housing estates, and three-quarters of them have bought their public-housing apartment. However, in order to prevent ghettos forming, Malay families are dispersed among Chinese and Indian ones. In addition, Malays, who tend to be at the bottom of the social ladder, benefit from scholarships and other forms of "affirmative action".

Different tongues

One brilliant way of bridging ethnic divides was Lee's decision after independence to close Chinese schools and impose English – foreign to all – as the language of government. It was also commercially clever, since Singaporeans now speak the language of international business. The country's other official languages are Tamil, Chinese and Malay (which all Singapore's diplomats must speak).

A controversial policy now aims to replace Chinese dialects such as Hokkien and Cantonese with Mandarin. Ostensibly, this will give different Chinese clans a sense of their common heritage and enhance Singapore's links with China's huge and growing economy. However, non-Chinese feel they will be left out.

Many Chinese are also resentful, since they fear that their children's educational future may be wrecked by a poor knowledge of Mandarin. Certainly the language issue is one reason for a rate of emigration proportionately equivalent to that of Hong Kong (which had its reversion to China in 1997 to worry about). It is ironic that in order to preserve the racial mix, Singapore in 1989 offered to take in 25,000 skilled workers from Hong Kong and their dependents (a total of about 100,000).

The economy: planned freedom

Singapore vies with Hong Kong to be Asia's most open and international economy. There are no restrictions on foreign ownership of Singaporean assets; there are tax incentives to attract foreign multinationals, especially those that offer to transfer knowledge and technology; and there are no exchange controls. In addition, there is a well-developed financial services sector: the Stock Exchange of Singapore and the smaller SESDAQ, which is the exchange for unlisted securities, are probably the best regulated markets in Asia; SIMEX, which is a financial futures market, is linked to the Chicago Mercantile Exchange, allowing contracts to be opened in Chicago and closed in Singapore, or vice versa; the foreign exchange market has now overtaken Hong Kong as the biggest in Asia after Tokyo; and there is a government securities market, started in 1987, which is somewhat artificially (the government has no need to borrow money) trying to deepen the capital market to attract international interest.

Clean and fair

Most important of all, Singapore offers an efficient environment remarkably free from the corruption that stains most of the region. The result is that dozens of foreign multinationals use Singapore as their regional headquarters; indeed, they now account for three-quarters of Singapore's manufactured exports, leading to occasional worries that the country has become over-dependent on investment that could well migrate elsewhere.

The worries are probably groundless. Singapore is small enough to correct mistakes before they become serious. In the first phase of independence the emphasis was on basic industrialisation as a way of creating jobs; the second phase, beginning with the oil shock of 1973–74, was to become more efficient and to move upmarket; the third phase, beginning with the second oil shock of 1978, was designed to make Singapore a "centre of excellence" in upgraded manufacturing, technology and services so that, as it became more prosperous, it would not be priced out of the market by low-cost competitors.

Easier planned than achieved: the government deliberately raised wages and costs to force manufacturers "upmarket", only to be caught out by the slowing of the world economy in the early 1980s and by the willingness of foreigners to invest elsewhere. In 1985 the economy shrank for the first time since 1965.

But the government's response was immediate and effective: labour costs were reduced by a cut in employers' contributions to the Central Provident Fund (the compulsory saving scheme which provides workers' pensions) and by pressure on the trade unions (which are a docile partner for the government's ambitions). In 1986 the economy resumed its upward path. Moreover, although the government retains important shareholdings in "strategic" economic sectors, it has embarked on a privatisation programme (usually, in fact, semi-privatisation), affecting, for example, the airline and shipping industries.

A liberal future?

Singapore's ambition is to become a developed economy by the end of the 1990s. The goal is certainly feasible: Singaporeans are well-educated; the industrial base is reasonably diverse, from ship-repairing and tourism to making disk-drives and writing computer software; the country is geographically at the hub of the world's most dynamic region; and competition from Hong Kong may wane with its transfer to Chinese sovereignty.

The only real doubt concerns Singapore's personality. The Lee Kuan Yew era instilled the virtues of discipline, honesty and hard work, but at the cost of over-regulation (especially in contrast to Hong Kong) and boredom. The challenge for the government of Goh and his successors is to create an environment that will encourage spontaneity and the entrepreneurial spirit. That means allowing a liberalism which runs counter to tradition.

Total area	633 sq km	% agricultural area	1.9
Capital	–	Highest point metres	Bukit Timali 177
Other cities	–	Main rivers	Kalang

The economy

GDP $bn	94.1	GDP per head $	30,940
% av. ann. growth in		GDP per head in purchasing	
real GDP 1991–96	8.6	power parity $	22,770

Origins of GDP	% of total	Components of GDP	% of total
Agriculture	–	Private consumption	40
Industry	36	Public consumption	9
of which:		Investment	33
manufacturing	27	Exports	186
Services	64	Imports	168

Structure of manufacturing

			% of total
Agric. & food processing	4	Other	37
Textiles & clothing	2	Av. ann. increase in industrial	
Machinery & transport	58	output 1991–96	7.8

Inflation and exchange rates

Consumer price 1996 av. ann. incr.	1.3%	S$ per $ 1997 average	1.48
Av. ann. rate 1991–96	2.1%	S$ per $ end-1997	1.68

Balance of payments, reserves and debt

			$bn
Exports, goods & services	148.4	Net capital account	...
Imports, goods & services	134.0	Net direct & portfolio investment	-4.1
Net income	1.6	Other net investment	-2.8
Net current transfers	-0.9	Net errors & omissions	0.4
Current-account balance	15.1	Net change in reserves	-8.6
as % of GDP	18.9	Level of reserves, end-Dec.	68.7
Foreign debt	...	Debt service	...
as % of GDP	...	as % of export earnings	...

Principal exports	$bn fob	Principal imports	$bn fob
Machinery & equipment	82.5	Machinery & equipment	76.0
Mineral fuels	11.9	Manufactured goods	12.9
Manufactured goods	7.1	Mineral fuels	12.3
Chemicals	7.0	Chemicals	7.8
Food	2.3	Food	3.7
Crude materials	1.7	Crude materials	1.5

Main export destinations	% of total	Main origins of imports	% of total
United States	18.4	Japan	18.2
Malaysia	18.0	United States	16.3
Hong Kong	8.9	Malaysia	15.0
Japan	8.2	Thailand	5.5
Thailand	5.7	Taiwan	4.1
Germany	3.1	Saudi Arabia	3.8
UK	2.8	Germany	3.6

Government
System Parliamentary republic. The president, who is directly elected for a 5-year term, appoints the prime minister and cabinet. Unicameral 83-member parliament.
Main political parties People's Action Party, Singapore Democratic Party, Workers' Party

Climate and topography
Tropical: hot, humid and rainy. There is no pronounced rainy or dry season; thunderstorms occur on 40% of all days (67% of days in April). The small island at the southern tip of the Malay peninsula, from which it is separated by the narrow Johore strait, has one of the largest ports in the world. The rugged granitic centre of the island gives way to sandy hills on the east and a series of scarps on the west. Much of the northern area is mangrove swamp.

People and society

Population m	3.0	% under 15	23.9
Pop. per sq km	4,896.0	% over 60	9.0
% urban	100.0	No. women per 100 men	9.8
% av. ann. growth 1980–95	1.8	Human Development Index	90.0
No. households m	0.8		

Life expectancy	yrs	Education	
Men	74	Spending as % of GDP	3.3
Women	79	Years of compulsory education	...
Crude birth rate	16	Adult literacy %	91.0
Crude death rate	5	Primary school enrolment %	107
Infant mortality		Secondary school enrolment %	78
per 1,000 live births	6	Tertiary education enrolment %	...

Workforce	% of total	Consumer goods ownership	
Services	64		per 1,000 people
Industry	36	Cars	35.0
Agriculture	–	Televisions	362.0
% of pop. over 15 in workforce	49	Mobile phones	9,737.0
		Personal computers	172.4

Ethnic groups	% of total	Religious groups	% of total
Chinese	75.9	Taoist	29
Malay	15.2	Buddhist	27
Indian	6.5	Christian	10
		Hindu	4

Tourism		Health	
Tourist arrivals m	7.1	Spending as % of GDP	3.5
Tourism receipts $bn	7.9	People per doctor	714.0

SOUTH KOREA

Total area	99,222 sq km	Population	45.5m
GDP	$484.8bn	GDP per head	$10,645
Capital	Seoul	Other cities	Pusan, Taegu

The Republic of Korea has already proved its economic dynamism. Its challenges now are to translate dynamism into stability; to consolidate democracy, after decades of military-influenced rule; and to accomplish a reunification with North Korea which will be difficult and expensive, but which is surely inevitable.

History: division and unity

A distinctly Korean identity goes back at least 2,000 years. Indeed, legend traces Korea back much further, to Tangun (of "divine origin"), who became the first king in 2333 BC. Firmer evidence dates Korea back to 57 BC and the start of the Three Kingdoms of Silla (in the south-east), Koguryo (in the north) and Paekche (in the south-west).

Political unity came in AD 668, when Silla, having already defeated Paekche, finally conquered Koguryo with the help of China. The Silla dynasty was in 936 followed by the Koryo dynasty (hence "Korea"). In 1259 the Mongols invaded and conquered Korea, but in 1392 Yi Song-gye, a former Koryo general, established the Yi or Chosun dynasty. A Japanese invasion in 1593 was defeated with China's help; from the 17th century onwards Korea, while paying tribute to China, deliberately kept itself in isolation as the "Hermit Kingdom".

The appearance of unity, however, did not eliminate the peninsula's geographical divisions. South Korea's rulers have come from the Kyongsang provinces in the south-east, while the North harkens after the glories of Koguryo.

Japan swallows the shrimp

By the end of the 19th century Korea's introversion had made it weak. Surrounded by China, Japan and Russia, it was "a shrimp among whales", and Japan – having defeated China in 1894–95 and Russia in 1904–05 – duly swallowed defenceless Korea, assuming de facto control in 1905 and formally annexing the peninsula in 1910.

Japanese colonialism improved Korea's agriculture and gave it the infrastructure for its subsequent economic success. These improvements, however, were for the benefit of Japan's own settlers; Koreans were often made landless. Their language was suppressed and they were forced to take Japanese names and worship at Shinto shrines. About

2m Koreans moved to Japan (many under duress); during the second world war hundreds of thousands of Koreans were used as slave labour or, in the case of Korean women, were forced to be prostitutes ("comfort women") for Japan's armed forces. Although Koreans now admire Japan's economic and industrial success, and seek to emulate it, they are also bitterly resentful towards their neighbour.

Freedom and division

Liberation came with Japan's defeat in 1945 but with no plan by the Allies for Korea's future. Under a proposal hastily drafted in Washington, and accepted by the Soviet Union, Japan's troops north of the 38th parallel surrendered to Soviet troops and those south of this line to the Americans. The 38th parallel thus became the border between, first, Soviet and American zones of occupation and then, in 1948, between the Republic of Korea, under Syngman Rhee, in the south and the Democratic People's Republic of Korea, under Kim Il Sung, in the north.

Civil war

On June 25th 1950 the North launched an unprovoked attack (probably at the initiative of Kim Il Sung rather than his Soviet mentor, Stalin) on the South, which was immediately supported by America and other non-communist countries under the auspices of the United Nations.

The North's troops advanced inexorably until General MacArthur landed UN troops behind their lines at Inchon, carrying the war up to the border with China, which then intervened on the side of the fellow-communist North. The peninsula's capital, Seoul, changed hands four times in nine months. Finally, after two years of military stalemate and with the death toll reaching perhaps 4m, an armistice agreement was signed on July 27th 1953, partitioning the peninsula along the line of battle, which was more or less along the 38th parallel.

From Rhee to Chun

The authoritarian regime of Syngman Rhee (the first Korean to be awarded a PhD from an American university) laid the foundation for South Korea's economic miracle: education was improved and expanded; land reform dispossessed the landlords (who then became industrialists) and improved agricultural productivity; and import-substituting industries were founded which later became the platform for South Korea's export boom.

Rhee's ambitions, however, stirred widespread resentment. He had himself re-elected for a fourth presidential term in March 1960, after which student demonstrations and generalised violence broke out. Rhee fled to exile in Hawaii (where he died in 1965, aged 90) and South Korea adopted a parliamentary system. It lasted only nine months, before being overthrown by a military coup on May 16th 1961, which brought into power the Supreme Council for National Reconstruction, led by Major-General Park Chung Hee, who was elected president on October 15th 1963.

Park's obsession was to overhaul the North (which, in its early years, was growing vigorously). His method was state-directed industrialisation, complete with subsidised credit; a mercantilist export drive; and the absolute suppression of political dissent. In 1972 he imposed a new constitution which permitted indefinite re-election of the president and gave the president (ie, Park himself) the right to appoint a third of the one-chamber legislature.

On October 26th 1979 Park was shot by the director of the Korean Central Intelligence Agency. He was succeeded by the prime minister, Choi Kyu-han, but in May 1980 the military reacted to student demonstrations for democracy by imposing martial law (during this period students took over the southern town of Kwangju, which was then recaptured by government troops who left some 200 dead). On August 27th 1980 Lieutenant-General Chun Doo Hwan was elected president.

In October 1980 a new constitution reduced the president's powers and limited him to one term of seven years. Under this constitution Chun's presidency was endorsed in indirect elections in February 1981. By the mid-1980s, and despite the freeing of thousands of political prisoners and a rapid rise in living standards, student demonstrators were ever more violently demanding an end to the military's domination of politics. In January 1985 the followers of Kim Young Sam and Kim Dae Jung (who was about to return from exile) launched the opposition New Korea Democratic Party and gained 67 seats in the 276-member National Assembly (later boosted to 102 by the absorption of the Democratic Korea Party).

One of the new party's main demands was that Chun's successor should be chosen by direct elections. The governing Democratic Justice Party (DJP) threw the opposition into confusion by proposing a prime ministerial, rather than presidential, system. Kim Young Sam split from Kim Dae Jung and formed his own opposition party, the Reunification Democratic Party.

From Chun To Roh

In April 1987 President Chun suddenly announced that all political reforms would be suspended until after the Olympic Games had taken place in Seoul in 1988; he confirmed that he would leave office in February 1988 but said his successor would be chosen, as before, by indirect elections. In June 1987 the DJP chose Roh Tae Woo, a retired general, as its presidential candidate.

Students, backed by the middle class, rose in furious protest at the prospect of seven more years of military rule. But Roh astounded everyone (including Chun) by announcing that he would be a candidate only if the choice were by direct elections. Chun agreed; a plebiscite in October approved a new constitution for a single, five-year, presidential term; and on December 16th the election took place. Roh, who had correctly calculated that the opposition vote would be split between the bickering Kim Dae Jung and Kim Young Sam, was sworn in as South Korea's first directly elected president on February 25th 1988.

Politics: turbulent currents

At the apex of government is the president, elected by universal suffrage for a single term of five years. He governs with the help of an appointed State Council, led by a prime minister. The legislature is the unicameral National Assembly (Kuk Hoe), which consists of a minimum of 200 members elected for a term of four years. The National Assembly elected in April 1996 had 299 members: 253 of them chosen by direct elections on a first-past-the-post basis, and the remaining 46 distributed between the rival parties according to their share of the national vote.

The theory is that this structure will prevent the military dictatorships which most now feel South Korea has outgrown. Instead, Japan is seen as the political model to be emulated, and to this end President Roh in January 1990 announced that the ruling DJP would merge with the Reunification Democratic Party of Kim Young Sam and with the New Democratic Republican Party of Kim Jong Pil to form the Democratic Liberal Party (DLP), self-consciously modelled on Japan's then-ruling LDP. One impetus for the merger was that in the 1988 election the DJP had failed to win a majority in the National Assembly. As a reward for the merger, Kim Young Sam was in 1992 chosen as the party's candidate for the 1993 presidential election – which he won.

However, the attempt to imitate Japan appears to have

backfired. In the 1992 National Assembly election the new DLP gained only 149 seats, just short of a majority. In December 1995 the DLP changed its name to the New Korea Party, and in the April 1996 election then won 139 of the 299 seats. The NKP managed to get the support of 12 others, mainly independents, and so obtain a working majority.

President Kim Young Sam's term was marked by a drive against corruption. At times this was self-serving, witness the hounding of Chung Ju Yung, the former head of Hyundai, when he entered politics in the early 1990s. In 1996 two of Kim's predecessors, Chun Doo Hwan and Ruh Tae Woo, were put on trial for corruption. In a gesture of reconciliation they were released from gaol when Kim Dae Jung was elected president in December 1997.

Foreign policy: making new friends

The South's foreign policy has always been dominated by the relationship with the North. This has meant the presence of up to 40,000 American troops in South Korean bases. Although the American presence has constantly inflamed student anger – since the Americans were seen to be protecting dictatorial military regimes – it is the South's ultimate security guarantee.

However, South Korea's economic rise through the 1980s and the failure of communism as an economic model have led to dramatic changes in the South's foreign policy. First, trade began with both the Soviet Union and China (to the fury of the North); in 1989 full diplomatic relations were opened with Hungary, Poland and Yugoslavia; in 1990 diplomatic relations were also established with Mongolia, Bulgaria, Czechoslovakia, Romania and – six months after a meeting in San Francisco between Presidents Roh and Gorbachev – with the Soviet Union. Finally, in August 1992, diplomatic relations were agreed with China.

Nordpolitik

Such events, coupled with the North's economic privations, had their impact on the regime of Kim Il Sung. In 1968 the North sent a commando team into Seoul in an attempt to assassinate President Park; in the late 1970s invasion tunnels were discovered running from the North beneath the De-Militarised Zone (DMZ); in 1983 a bomb planted by Northern agents killed 17 South Koreans, including four cabinet ministers, on a visit to Rangoon; and in 1987 agents from the North planted a bomb that killed all 115 people aboard a South Korean airliner.

But by the late 1980s the North appeared to abandon such tactics. The North boycotted the 1988 Olympics in Seoul but in the same year modest trading links were established across the DMZ. At the end of 1990 the two Korean prime ministers met three times, and in the following year unified Korean teams were sent to some sporting events. When China let it be known that it would not veto the South's unilateral application to join the United Nations, the North had no option but to apply too, and both countries became UN members in September 1991.

Finally, in December 1991 the two countries reached an "agreement on reconciliation, non-aggression, co-operation and exchange", helped by President Roh's announcement that there were no longer any nuclear weapons on the soil of the South. This, in turn, helped the North to reach an agreement in January 1992 to open its nuclear installations to inspection by the International Atomic Energy Agency. Two months later the North agreed that there should be mutual inspection with the South of nuclear installations.

Lingering doubts

However, many South Koreans (and Americans, too) were doubtful of the sincerity of a North which, according to the American CIA, was within months of producing a nuclear bomb. They argued that economic desperation was prompting the North to appear friendly, and that the South must beware giving too many concessions (for example, reducing the American presence). Such judgments aside, many pragmatic South Korean policy-makers, taking the unification of Germany as their example, argued that hasty reunification with the North would be too expensive. The counter-argument was that reconciliation was urgent, since if the Kim dynasty were to end suddenly, the North might collapse into political chaos, which would then affect the South.

Society: all one

South Korea is a homogeneous society – the only racial minority consists of some 50,000 Chinese – with a proud, sometimes aggressive character. The population has more than doubled since the Korean war, providing a disciplined workforce to power the economy, but also leading to a concentration of a quarter of the population in Seoul.

Economic progress has spread prosperity widely; the ostentatious display of wealth is frowned upon in a culture which prefers egalitarianism in material matters.

Some 37% of the population is Buddhist; another 17%

follow Confucianism; and about 4% subscribe to Chundo Kyo, a religion peculiar to Korea and containing elements of Shamanism, Buddhism and Christianity. The fastest growing religion, with some 30,000 churches, is Christianity, which claims about 30% of the population. Fundamentalist sects, in particular, have made great inroads.

The economy: export and thrive

Apart from some tungsten and coal, South Korea has precious few natural resources. Its wealth, therefore, has had to come from the sweat of its people; in particular through a relentless process of industrialisation which saw GDP increase by an average of almost 9% a year from the 1960s to the 1990s.

The foundation for this growth was laid by President Park; his strategy was to keep interest rates low (even negative in real terms) and to allocate the resulting scarce, but cheap, credit to export-oriented industries. At the same time, domestic industries were protected. This mercantilist strategy enabled the *chaebol* – big family-controlled conglomerates such as Samsung, Daewoo and Hyundai – to thrive. Between 1963 and 1978 world trade grew in volume by 9% a year, but South Korea's exports grew by 31% a year. By the end of the 1980s the country had moved from basic industries, such as cement, fertilisers and industrial chemicals, through automobiles, electronics, iron and steel and shipbuilding, to computer and other high-technology products. Foreign debt was allowed to balloon from $23 billion at the start of the 1980s to $47 billion in the mid-1980s on the (correct) assumption that export revenue would increase to service the debt easily.

The need to adapt

Economic success, however, breeds its own problems. One is the need to go ever more upmarket as South Korea loses the edge it once enjoyed with cheap labour. South Korean exports of textiles and footwear are already in decline, as cheaper producers such as the Philippines, Indonesia, Bangladesh and Sri Lanka seek export markets.

A corollary of the need to go upmarket is the development of the financial sector in order to allow the *chaebol* and other companies to raise equity finance to lessen their traditional reliance on bank credit.

This need was dramatically highlighted in late 1997 with a full-blown financial crisis which triggered a $57bn rescue package from the IMF. The underlying problem was that too much of the cheap credit to the *chaebol* had turned into bad loans, with the banks' weakness made all the worse by similar, confidence-eroding developments in Thailand and Indonesia.

Another problem (especially when the national currency, the won, is weak) is that export success leads to foreign policy tensions if not matched by increased imports. South Korea runs a trade deficit with Japan but a big surplus with America. Government policy since the late 1980s has been to assuage American anger by diversifying Korea's export markets and by eliminating licences and reducing tariffs on Korea's imports (travel restrictions were also eased, allowing Koreans to spend money on holiday abroad). Even so, many trade barriers remain, with the government unwilling, in particular, to expose South Korea's rice farmers to world prices. One difficulty for the government is a national sense of economic vulnerability: when the trade balance switched into deficit at the start of the 1990s it was widely seen as a crisis, despite ample foreign exchange reserves.

Perhaps the most sensitive problem, however, is that of labour. Historically, the workforce's conditions and pay have failed to match its productivity. Moreover, the average Korean worker was working a 54-hour week, compared with 41 hours in Japan and 40 in America. By the late 1980s the labour force had become militant, staging massive strikes. These were eventually bought off with settlements which lifted average earnings in the manufacturing sector by 11.6% in 1987, 19.6% in 1988 and 21.1% in 1989. The message, however, was clear: in future the workforce would demand a greater reward for its efforts and employers would ignore the demand at their peril. Unfortunately the hopes of both sides were dealt a severe blow by the 1997 currency crisis, which threatened even the biggest companies.

Future promises

Whatever the gloom some South Koreans feel about the slowing of their economy, optimism remains more warranted than pessimism. South Korea's *chaebol* are now world-scale companies with global ambitions. The real question concerns reunification with the North. Will the North prove a financial burden, rather as the East has for West Germany, or will its cheap labour give Korea a timely boost, and so make Korea an ever stronger competitor to its old colonial master, Japan?

Total area	99,222 sq km	% agricultural area	23
Capital	Seoul	Highest point metres Halla San	1,950
Other cities	Pusan, Taegu	Main rivers Naktong, Hang Ang	

The economy

GDP $bn	484.8	GDP per head $	10,645
% av. ann. growth in		GDP per head in purchasing	
real GDP 1991–96	7.1	power parity $	11,450

Origins of GDP	% of total	Components of GDP	% of total
Agriculture	7	Private consumption	54
Industry	43	Public consumption	10
of which:		Investment	37
manufacturing	27	Exports	33
Services	50	Imports	34

Structure of manufacturing

			% of total
Agric. & food processing	10	Other	45
Textiles & clothing	12	Av. ann. increase in industrial	
Machinery & transport	24	output 1991–96	8.3

Inflation and exchange rates

Consumer price 1996 av. ann. incr.	5.0%	Won per $ 1997 average	951.29
Av. ann. rate 1991–96	5.3%	Won per $ end-1997	1,695.8

Balance of payments, reserves and debt

			$bn
Exports, goods & services	149.4	Net capital account	-0.5
Imports, goods & services	155.8	Net direct & portfolio investment	9.1
Net income	-2.3	Other net investment	8.1
Net current transfers	0.4	Net errors & omissions	-1.4
Current-account balance	-8.3	Net change in reserves	-7.0
as % of GDP	-1.9	Level of reserves, end-Dec.	32.8
Foreign debt	...	Debt service	...
as % of GDP	...	as % of export earnings	...

Principal exports	$bn fob	Principal imports	$bn cif
Transistors, semiconductors etc	17.3	Machinery & transport equip.	54.7
Textiles & fabrics	10.2	Mineral fuels & lubricants	24.3
Passenger cars	9.1	Chemicals	13.2
Ships & floating structures	7.1	Raw materials	11.0
Clothing & accessories	4.2	Food & live animals	7.3

Main export destinations	% of total	Main origins of imports	% of total
United States	16.7	United States	22.2
Japan	12.2	Japan	20.9
Hong Kong	8.6	Germany	4.8
Singapore	5.0	Saudi Arabia	4.4
Germany	3.6	Australia	4.2

Government
System Parliamentary democracy with legislative power exercised by 299-member National Assembly elected for 4 years. Most members are elected by a simple majority but 46 seats are allocated among the parties proportionally to the votes they receive. Executive power is exercised by an elected president who serves a 5-year term.

Main political parties New Korea Party, National Congress for New Politics, United Liberal Democrats

Climate and topography
Continental, with an average temperature range from -5°C (23°F) in winter to 27°C (81°F) in summer, more extreme in the interior. Annual rainfall is 1,000–1,400mm (40–55in). Basically mountainous, the population is concentrated in the arable river valleys and along the coastal plain. The plain is wider on the west coast, where there are many rias and offshore islands, than on the east, where the Taebaek range often falls sheer into the sea.

People and society

Population m	45.5	% under 15	23.3
Pop. per sq km	454.0	% over 60	9.0
% urban	81.0	No. women per 100 men	99
% av. ann. growth 1980–95	1.1	Human Development Index	89.0
No. households m	13.1		

Life expectancy	yrs	Education	
Men	68	Spending as % of GDP	4.5
Women	75	Years of compulsory education	9
Crude birth rate	16	Adult literacy %	97.9
Crude death rate	6	Primary school enrolment %	101
Infant mortality		Secondary school enrolment %	93
per 1,000 live births	10	Tertiary education enrolment %	48

Workforce	% of total	Consumer goods ownership	
Services	47		per 1,000 people
Industry	35	Cars	48.0
Agriculture	18	Television	115.0
% of pop. over 15 in workforce	46	Mobile phones	36.6
		Personal computers	120.6

Ethnic groups	% of total	Religious groups	% of total
Korean	99	Buddhist	37
		Christian	30
		Confucian	17
		Chundo Kyo	4

Tourism		Health	
Tourist arrivals m	3.3	Spending as % of GDP	5.4
Tourism receipts $bn	5.4	People per doctor	951

SRI LANKA

Total area	65,610 sq km	Population	18.4m
GDP	$13.9bn	GDP per head	$760
Capital	Colombo	Other cities	Dehiwala-Mount Lavinia, Moratuwa, Jaffna

The Democratic Socialist Republic of Sri Lanka may yet become an Asian success to rival Malaysia, Thailand and Singapore. Its people are well-educated; its soil is fertile; its sunshine attracts tourists. But the island's potential will be fully realised only if Sri Lanka can first overcome the ethnic tensions that have provoked years of bloody civil war.

History: the land of serendip

Sri Lanka, a name which caused Horace Walpole in 1754 to coin the word "serendipitous", is dominated by the Sinhalese, an Indo-European group who arrived from northern India around the 5th century BC. From the early centuries AD until about 1200, the Sinhalese were joined by Tamils from Dravidian southern India. The tensions between the two races have bedevilled the island ever since. By the 14th century, the Tamils had established a kingdom in the north of Ceylon, as Sri Lanka was known.

Conflicts between rival kingdoms made the island vulnerable. From the 13th century there were Indian, Chinese and Malay invasions. In the early 16th century Portugal began to extract trade concessions. By 1619 most of the island was under Portugal's control, which prompted the Sinhalese kingdom of Kandy to invite in the Dutch East India Company. From the middle of the century control rested with the Dutch, ousted in turn in 1796 by the British, who in 1802 made Ceylon a crown colony.

The British, who planted first coffee (the plantations were destroyed by disease) and then tea, did well from Ceylon and, arguably, for Ceylon. But early this century nationalism took root: in 1919 the Ceylon National Congress united Sinhalese and Tamils. In February 1948 Ceylon became independent within the Commonwealth.

Politics: from Ceylon to Sri Lanka

Political power since independence has rested with the United National Party (UNP), which has traditionally tried to protect the rights of the mainly Hindu Tamils, and the Sri Lanka Freedom Party (SLFP), formed in 1951 by Solomon Bandaranaike and emphasising the heritage of the Buddhist Sinhalese. Apart from a three-month interlude in 1960, the

SLFP was the dominant party from the 1956 elections until 1965, despite the assassination of its founder in 1959 (he was succeeded by his widow, Sirimavo Bandaranaike). In the process it became increasingly left-wing and in 1970 led a United Front coalition government with both a Trotskyite and a pro-Moscow party. In 1972 the country became a republic, changed its name from Ceylon to Sri Lanka, but stayed within the Commonwealth.

Turmoil, terrorism and Tamil Tigers

What's in a name? The 1970s began the country's slide into violence, with an uprising in 1971 by the leftist Sinhalese Janatha Vimukthi Peramuna (JVP, or People's Liberation Front). By 1976 the Tamil parties had formed the Tamil United Liberation Front, which called for an independent Tamil state, Eelam, to be set up in the north and east. By 1977 the electorate, tired of scarcity and Mrs Bandaranaike's harsh brand of socialism, had swept the SFLP from power and installed the UNP under a new prime minister, Junius Jayawardene. He proceeded to establish a presidential system of government, becoming in February 1978 the country's first executive president, directly elected and not accountable to the unicameral parliament.

Mr Jayawardene's tenure in power, lengthened by a December 1982 referendum to prolong the life of parliament until 1989, was marred by constant ethnic terrorism and repeated states of emergency (from 1980 to 1986 Mrs Bandaranaike was deprived of most of her civil rights). An All-Party Conference, encouraged by India, met throughout 1984 but failed to break the impasse between the Sinhalese and the Tamils. By 1986, after internecine Tamil fighting, the Liberation Tigers of Tamil Eelam, otherwise known as the Tamil Tigers, had emerged as the dominant Tamil secessionist group, adept at terror and militarily capable.

The president's strategy was to involve India, which has its own large Tamil population in the south, in the search for a solution. In June 1985 India's then prime minister, Rajiv Gandhi, promised to press the Tamils to accept devolution rather than independence. But the violence continued, reaching all-out war in early 1987 between the army and the Tigers (with India's air force dropping supplies to the Tamil population besieged in Jaffna).

A role for India

On July 29th 1987 Mr Jayawardene and Mr Gandhi signed what appeared to be a breakthrough agreement: India would provide a peacekeeping force; the Tamils would surrender their arms; the northern and eastern provinces would become a single unit subject to a referendum of the mixed population in the east; there would be an amnesty for Tamil militants; Tamil refugees would be repatriated from India; and Tamil would become an official language alongside Sinhala.

The accord failed: the Tamils fought among themselves; many Sinhalese were furious at the concessions; and the JVP emerged once more. By mid-1988 there were 50,000 Indian troops in Sri Lanka, acting almost as an army of occupation and, ironically, pitted against the Tamil Tigers. Almost the only gain was a constitutional amendment in late 1988 making Tamil an official language.

Premadasa's presidency

In the presidential election at the end of 1988 the UNP's Ranasinghe Premadasa, ill-educated and from an undistinguished family, succeeded the aristocratic Mr Jayawardene. The new president was determined that India's troops should leave; he wanted to negotiate with the Tigers, and indeed he offered an unconditional (and unaccepted) amnesty to both the Tigers and the JVP.

However, it was not until March 1990 that India reluctantly withdrew. Although the JVP has been more or less crushed, the Tigers remained undefeated, capable of holding much of the north and east and of committing atrocities even in the heart of Colombo – including, it seemed, the assassination of Mr Premadasa in May 1993. In November 1994 Chandrika Kumaratunga became president, and immediately installed her mother, Mrs Bandaranaike, as prime minister of a minority SLFP-led government.

Foreign policy: in India's shadow

As a member of the Non-Aligned Movement Sri Lanka officially pursues an independent foreign policy. In 1990 Mr Premadasa was willing to upset the West (and his own foreign ministry and army) by closing the Israeli interests section at the American embassy, apparently to gain favour with Sri Lanka's Muslim minority. Meanwhile, there is frequent western criticism that Sri Lanka is abusing human rights in its fight against terrorism.

More pressing, however, is Sri Lanka's relationship with India, which dominates the South Asian Association for Regional Co-operation (SAARC). India feels it has a responsibility for Sri Lanka's Tamils (even though the Tigers are said to have killed Rajiv Gandhi in 1991), which implies a role for India in Sri Lankan affairs. In late 1991 India snubbed Sri

Lanka's attempt to hold a SAARC summit in Colombo.

Society: divisions and distrust

Sri Lanka's ethnic tensions are rooted in history. Roughly 75% of the population are Sinhalese, speaking Sinhala and for the most part Buddhist. These are divided into the "Kandyan" Sinhalese, who were the last to accept British rule, and the more educated "low country" Sinhalese.

The next biggest group, about 18% of the population, are the Sri Lankan Tamils, mostly Tamil-speaking Hindus, but with a Christian minority, who migrated from India several centuries ago and were disproportionately powerful (and well-educated) under the British. The "up-country" or "Indian" Tamils, who make up 5% or so of the population, were brought from India by the British to work the tea plantations; some did not become citizens until 1988. Other minorities are the Tamil-speaking Muslims, or Moors, who make up about 7% of the nation, and tiny Malay and "Burgher" (Eurasian) communities.

The economy: prosperity despite all

The years of strife have clearly damaged Sri Lanka's fortunes, especially in tourism, an important source of foreign exchange. Even so, per person incomes are comfortably above those elsewhere in the Indian subcontinent.

One explanation is the diversity of the economy. Agriculture, which accounts for almost half of the workforce and a quarter of GDP, includes tea, rubber, spices and coconut, all of which earn export revenue (and would earn more with increased investment). Agriculture is balanced not just by tourism but also by gem stones and by textiles and clothing (now the biggest earner of foreign exchange). Tourism, which was beginning to boom in the mid- to late-1970s, has been hit by the persistent violence.

But another explanation is the liberalisation of the economy after the early years of doctrinaire socialism. Although liberal reform began with the Jayawardene government, it was Mr Premadasa who, in 1989, pushed through the most radical reforms: removing import controls; lifting foreign exchange restrictions; opening the stock exchange to foreigners; privatising state enterprises; curbing the public sector; and liberalising the tax regime.

The need is to marry such sensible economic measures with political stability and social harmony. Unhappily, that is easier said than achieved.

Total area	65,610 sq km	% agricultural area	40
Capital	Colombo	Highest point metres	
Other cities	Dehiwala-Mount Lavinia,		Pidurutalagala 2,524
	Moratuwa, Jaffna	Main rivers	Mahaweli

The economy

GDP $bn	13.9	GDP per head $	760
% av. ann. growth in		GDP per head in purchasing	
real GDP 1991–96	5.2	power parity $	3,250

Origins of GDP	% of total	Components of GDP	% of total
Agriculture	23	Private consumption	74
Industry	25	Public consumption	12
of which:		Investment	25
manufacturing	16	Exports	36
Services	52	Imports	47

Structure of manufacturing

			% of total
Agric. & food processing	48	Other	27
Textiles & clothing	23	Av. ann. increase in industrial	
Machinery & transport	2	output 1991–96	...

Inflation and exchange rates

Consumer price 1996 av. ann. incr.	15.9%	Rupees per $ 1997 average	58.99
Av. ann. rate 1991–96	11.0%	Rupees per $ end-1997	61.29

Balance of payments, reserves and debt

			$bn
Exports, goods & services	4.6	Net capital account	...
Imports, goods & services	5.7	Net direct & portfolio investment	0.2
Net income	-0.1	Other net investment	0.7
Net current transfers	0.8	Net errors & omissions	-0.0
Current-account balance	-0.5	Net change in reserves	-0.3
as % of GDP	-4.3	Level of reserves, end-Dec.	2.1
Foreign debt	8.2	Debt service	3.2
as % of GDP	43.6	as % of export earnings	7.3

Principal exports	$m fob	Principal imports	$m fob
Textiles & garments	1,697	Textiles	1,169
Tea	616	Machinery & equipment	651
Diamonds	157	Petroleum	480
Rubber	110	Building materials	263
Petroleum products	104	Wheat	204
Gems	86	Transport equipment	179

Main export destinations	% of total	Main origins of imports	% of total
United States	34.1	India	11.2
UK	9.5	Japan	9.9
Japan	6.2	Hong Kong	7.0
Germany	5.8	South Korea	7.0
Belgium-Luxembourg	5.3	Singapore	7.0
Russia	2.8	Taiwan	5.7

Government

System Presidential democracy. Unicameral parliament of 225 members directly elected by proportional representation (since 1989) for 6-year terms. The president is elected directly.

Main political parties People's Alliance, United National Party

Climate and topography

Tropical monsoon; monthly temperatures 25–29°C (77–84°F). Main rainy season, May–Oct; secondary season, Dec–Mar. From the south-central highlands the land falls by steppes to a rolling coastal plain, narrow in the south and west and broad in the north. Rivers are generally short, and rainfall heaviest in the south. The uplands and wet zone are most densely populated.

People and society

Population m	18.4	% under 15	29.9
Pop. per sq km	280.0	% over 60	8.0
% urban	22.0	No. women per 100 men	100.0
% av. ann. growth 1980–95	1.4	Human Development Index	71.1
No. households m	...		

Life expectancy	*yrs*	**Education**	
Men	70	Spending as % of GDP	3.2
Women	75	Years of compulsory education	11
Crude birth rate	19	Adult literacy %	90.1
Crude death rate	6	Primary school enrolment %	106
Infant mortality		Secondary school enrolment %	74
per 1,000 live births	16	Tertiary education enrolment %	6

Workforce	*% of total*	**Consumer goods ownership**	
Services	31		*per 1,000 people*
Industry	21	Cars	9.0
Agriculture	48	Televisions	66.0
% of pop. over 15 in workforce	40	Mobile phones	2.8
		Personal computers	1.1

Ethnic groups	*% of total*	**Religious groups**	*% of total*
Sinhalese	74	Buddhist	70
Tamil	18	Hindu	15
Moor	7	Christian	8
		Muslim	7

Tourism		**Health**	
Tourist arrivals m	0.3	Spending as % of GDP	1.9
Tourism receipts $bn	0.2	People per doctor	6,843.0

TAIWAN

Total area	36,000 sq km	Population	21.1m
GDP	$272.3bn	GDP per head	$12,740
Capital	Taipei	Other cities	Kaohsiung, Taichung, Tainan

Taiwan – or the Republic of China, as it calls itself – is one of the world's most dynamic economies. Its long-term need, however, is to establish a harmonious relationship with mainland China, from which Taiwan's government was expelled in 1949 by Mao's victorious communists. The question is whether this will mean a reunification of China, to which the governments in both Beijing and Taipei are formally committed, or the acceptance of Taiwanese independence.

History: under others' control

Taiwan's original population was of immigrants from what is now Indonesia. Sizeable Chinese immigration did not come until the 17th century. Before that, Taiwan had already been discovered by the European powers. The Portuguese came in 1590, and called it Ilha Formosa (Beautiful Island), but did not settle. The Dutch and Spanish then came, and established fortified settlements on the west coast. In 1646 the Dutch took the whole island by seizing the Spanish settlement, only to be ousted in turn by refugees, led by Cheng Cheng-kung (normally known as Koxinga), from China's deposed Ming dynasty. Then, in 1683, China's Manchu dynasty incorporated the island into Fukien province, before making it a separate province in 1886.

The Manchus' defeat in war with Japan led in 1895 to the ceding of Taiwan to the Japanese, who looked to the the island to be a major supplier of rice and sugar. For the next 50 years Taiwan was a Japanese colony, until, on Japan's defeat at the end of the second world war, the allies handed Taiwan over to the Kuomintang (KMT), or Nationalist, government of General Chiang Kai-shek in China.

Mainland arrivals

The transfer was not universally popular. Chiang's government plundered Taiwan to help the war against the communist forces of Mao Zedong. A small incident on February 28th 1947 involving a woman selling cigarettes on the black market led to an uprising of local Taiwanese. On May 8th some 10,000 troops arrived from the mainland and went on a two-week rampage of killing, rape and looting.

The birth of modern Taiwan, however, came with the defeat of the KMT government in 1949 by Mao's communists.

Chiang fled with his army to Taiwan, which became the "temporary" site of the Republic of China's government pending the end of the communist "rebellion" on the mainland.

From CKS to CKK

For almost the next four decades Taiwan was governed with severe authoritarianism, not least because the danger of a communist invasion was initially very real. Support for Taiwan's independence was illegal, since it contradicted the notion that China was only temporarily divided. Chiang Kai-shek's iron rule as president lasted until his death in 1975. He was succeeded briefly by Yen Chia-kan and then, in 1978, Chiang's son, Chiang Ching-kuo, became president.

To general surprise, Chiang Ching-kuo in the mid-1980s set Taiwan on the tide of liberalisation that had just swept the Philippines and South Korea. In July 1987 martial law was lifted after 38 years; in October mainlanders and their descendants (and, in practice, anyone who cared to invent a relative in China) were allowed to travel, via Hong Kong or Japan, to visit the families they had left behind; from January 1988 newspapers were allowed to double in size (and be joined by competing papers).

Lee's liberalism

Chiang's liberalism survived his death in January 1988. The vice-president, Lee Teng-hui, assumed the presidency and became the island's first president to be Taiwan-born and bred. Lee quickly rebuffed the KMT's conservatives. In late 1988 Chinese from the mainland were allowed to visit Taiwan for humanitarian purposes; in December 1989 opposition parties were allowed to campaign openly; in 1990 Taiwanese were allowed – through intermediate points like Hong Kong – to invest and trade with the mainland; and, on April 30th 1991, the "period of mobilisation for the suppression of the Communist rebellion" was terminated, so allowing the lifting of the "Temporary Provisions", which had been in place since 1948 to limit constitutional freedoms during the state of war with the mainland. By the early 1990s President Lee, confirmed in office unopposed in March 1990 for a six-year term and re-elected in March 1996, had more or less completed the path of reform begun by Chiang Ching-kuo.

Politics: a question of China

Taiwan's political structure consists of five Yuans (governing bodies). The Executive Yuan (or council of ministers) is responsible to the Legislative Yuan. The Control, Judicial and Examination Yuans respectively scrutinise the work of the executive; interpret the constitution and laws; and supervise examinations for public office. In addition, the National Assembly, which normally meets once every six years, amends the constitution and – until 1996 – elected the president and vice-president for six-year terms.

Until recently this structure was dominated by aged, often senile, politicians elected on the mainland in 1947. They stayed in office because of the fiction that the government represented all of China, but elections were possible only for constituencies in Taiwan. Although the numbers shrank because of deaths (the National Assembly had begun with 2,961 members in 1947 and was down to 972 by the 1986 elections), the presence of the mainlanders was a constant cause of resentment among the Taiwanese.

Reform

After reforms begun in April 1991, the National Assembly was reduced to a normal membership of 325 members (although this was not to be achieved until 1993), with all the mainland-elected members having retired by the end of 1991. The same retirements happened with the Legislative Yuan, which in December 1992 began a new three-year term with 160 seats: 118 through open elections; 6 from aboriginal Taiwanese; 6 overseas Chinese appointed by the president; and 30 allocated to the various political parties on a proportional basis. The only remaining reform, finally achieved in 1994, was to have the electorate, rather than the National Assembly, choose future presidents – hence a 54% popular vote for Lee Teng-hui in 1996.

The KMT still rules

The process of democratisation offended many of the Kuomintang's traditionalists. Yet, ironically, it may have helped guarantee the KMT's survival as the ruling party by meeting the demands of its Taiwanese "Young Turks" for greater influence. The Democratic Progressive Party, formed (at the time illegally) in September 1986, is the only credible opposition. Although in the December 1991 elections for the National Assembly the KMT won 71.2% of the vote and the DPP only 23.9%, a significant drop from its 28.3% share in the 1989 Legislative Yuan election, the DPP bounced back a year later by taking 31% of the votes for the new Legislative Yuan. In the 1995 election for the Legislative Yuan the DPP's share rose to 33.2%, and in elections in 1997 for 23 city mayors and district magistrates the DPP won 12 seats and the KMT lost seven. One problem for the DPP, however, is that its bias towards Taiwan's independence unnerves many voters, since a declaration of independence might provoke a Chinese invasion.

Foreign policy: pragmatic

Taiwan's pretension to represent all of China has led it into diplomatic isolation. Most countries recognised Communist China, and so cut their diplomatic links with Taiwan. In 1971 the Beijing regime took China's seat in the United Nations, which meant Taiwan had to leave.

The worst blow was the decision by America on January 1st 1979 to recognise China and abrogate the mutual defence treaty with Taiwan (although in the Taiwan Relations Act of April 1979 this was softened by an American promise to provide "the governing authorities on Taiwan" with arms "of a defensive character"). With the defection of Saudi Arabia in 1990 and South Korea in 1992 almost all of the nations that maintain diplomatic relations with Taiwan are poor countries from Latin America and Africa.

Even so, with "flexible diplomacy" Taiwan has forged good, albeit unofficial, relations with most of the world. Quite simply, Taiwan's financial clout is too great to be ignored. Under the title "Chinese Taipei", Taiwan in 1991 joined the Asia-Pacific Economic Co-operation forum; the same title allows participation in the Olympics. Although Taiwan is a member of the Asian Development Bank (known as "Taipei, China"), its ambitions go further: to being a member of the World Trade Organisation.

Mainland relations

Officially Taiwan's policy towards mainland China consists of the "Three Noes": no contact, no negotiation and no compromise. In practice, indirect links have been allowed for trade, investment, mail and family visits. In 1991 the National Unification Council, chaired by President Lee, suggested that Taiwan and the mainland might recognise each other as separate political entities: "one country, two governments", to counter the idea from China (used for Hong Kong and Macau) of "one country, two systems".

Society: middle class and prospering

At least 98% of Taiwan's 21m people are Han Chinese, the rest being aborigines with Malay ethnic roots. About 2m of Taiwan's people came from the mainland in 1947–49; the remaining "Taiwanese" are descendants of immigrants, mainly from Fujian province across the Taiwan Strait, who came from the 17th century onwards.

Although Mandarin is the official language (as on the mainland), the Taiwanese (Hokkien) dialect is very common; many older people are still fluent in Japanese. The main religions are Buddhism and Taoism, but about 7% are Christians. Confucianism has a pervasive influence.

The benefits of dramatic economic growth have been carefully spread: the richest fifth of the population is only five times richer than the poorest fifth. One by-product of wealth, however, has been the desire or the need to use immigrant labour – most of it illegal – from poorer countries in Asia, such as the Philippines and Malaysia.

The economy: ever-booming

Despite a lack of natural resources Taiwan – because of the hard work and entrepreneurial talent of its people – is arguably Asia's most dynamic economy. From the 1950s to the 1990s, the island's GDP has grown by an average of about 9% a year.

This economic surge, taking Taiwan from desperate poverty to middle-class comfort, has had three distinct phases: in the 1950s agricultural productivity was raised and import-substituting industries were built on the base of the infrastructure left by the Japanese; in the 1960s export industries were developed for cheap, low-technology goods; finally, since the mid-1980s the government's planners have encouraged industry to move upmarket, so that rising labour costs will not price the island out of its export markets. This ambition may be more easily envisaged than achieved: Taiwan's manufacturing sector is based on small businesses for whom it is cheaper to move offshore than to invest in more sophisticated production.

The result is that where agriculture accounted for a quarter of the economy at the start of the 1960s, by the start of the 1990s it accounted for less than 4%, having long ceded its place to manufacturing. Taiwan's manufactured exports range from sports shoes to personal computers; but increasingly the handbags and shoes are being made abroad, as Taiwan's manufacturers look for cheaper labour, especially in mainland China.

Ecological problems

Another result of rapid development has been severe pollution. Public outrage has acted as a cramp on the development of the huge petrochemical sector, but has also acted as a stimulus for the building in the 1990s of a new infra-structure for Taiwan, a programme that formed the basis of the NT$8.2 trillion ($300 billion and more) Six-Year National Development Plan, from 1991 to 1996.

Trading problems

One purpose of this programme was to stimulate domestic demand and imports. Taiwan, which has lingering protec-tionist tendencies, is under pressure from its trading part-ners – especially America – to reduce its perennial trade surplus. Taiwan is trying to comply by diversifying its export markets (America's share of Taiwan's exports fell from 48% in 1985 to 29% in 1991 and less than 24% in 1995).

Taiwan's export drive has meanwhile amassed what are often the world's largest foreign-exchange reserves ($90 bil-lion in mid-1997). Since there are doubts about the govern-ment's ability to finance its grand schemes, the reserves will be useful. So too will be a programme of privatisation and a growing bond market.

One weakness of Taiwan is its financial sector, which has been far too regulated and conservative to cope with a high savings rate and dynamic economic growth. The result in the 1980s was to drive the stockmarket to dizzy heights of speculation, only for it to lose 80% of its value within seven months of its peak in February 1989. An ambition for the 1990s is to liberalise the whole financial sector: some state banks have been privatised; licences have been granted to new banks; the Central Bank's control over inter-est rates and foreign exchange rates has been loosened; and foreigners have been allowed to invest directly in the stock-market and to take small shares in Taiwanese companies. Yet a stockmarket slide and a falling currency in late 1997 showed that structural problems remain.

Plotting the future

The question is where Taiwan can go next. One answer is to invest abroad. Taiwan's businessmen can be found all over South-East Asia, as well as in Vietnam and, since the collapse of communism, eastern Europe. But their closest links are with mainland China, especially Fujian province. By the early 1990s perhaps 4,000 Taiwanese companies had invested in the mainland. But such economic ties need political protection. The big challenge for Taiwan's govern-ment is to integrate the island into the world's political sys-tem. Ultimately, that must involve some form of reconciliation with the mainland.

Total area	36,000 sq km	% agricultural area	30
Capital	Taipei	Highest point metres	Hsin-Kao
Other cities	Kaohsiung,		Shan 3,997
	Taichung, Tainan	Main rivers	–

The economy

GDP $bn	272.3	GDP per head $	12,740
% av. ann. growth in		GDP per head in purchasing	
real GDP 1991–96	6.3	power parity $	16,520

Origins of GDP	% of total	Components of GDP	% of total
Agriculture	3	Private consumption	60
Industry	36	Public consumption	15
of which:		Investment	21
manufacturing	28	Exports	49
Services	61	Imports	45

Structure of manufacturing

	% of total		
Agric. & food processing	...	Other	...
Textiles & clothing	...	Av. ann. increase in industrial	
Machinery & transport	...	output 1991–96	4.6

Inflation and exchange rates

Consumer price 1996 av. ann. incr.	3.0%	NT$ per $ 1997 average	28.43
Av. ann. rate 1991–96	3.6%	NT$ per $ end-1997	30.20

Balance of payments, reserves and debt

			$bn
Exports, goods & services	126.1	Net capital account	...
Imports, goods & services	121.1	Net current account	...
Net income	2.8	Other net investment	...
Net current transfers	-2.2	Net errors & omissions	...
Current-account balance	5.7	Net change in reserves	...
as % of GDP	2.1	Level of reserves, end-Dec.	95.6
Foreign debt	27.0	Debt service	1.7
as % of GDP	10.4	as % of export earnings	...

Principal exports	$bn fob	Principal imports	$bn fob
Machinery & electrical equip.	53.7	Machinery & electrical equip.	36.0
Textiles & clothing	15.7	Chemicals	10.9
Base metals & metal		Base metals & products	10.4
manufactures	10.3	Precision instruments,	
Plastic & rubber articles	7.7	clocks & watches	5.3
Vehicles, aircraft & ships	5.2	Crude petroleum	4.9
Chemicals	3.3	Vehicles, aircraft & ships	4.6
Animals & animal products	2.9	Textile products	3.6

Main export destinations	% of total	Main origins of imports	% of total
United States	23.2	Japan	26.9
Hong Kong	23.1	United States	19.5
Japan	11.8	Germany	4.9
Singapore	3.9	South Korea	4.1

Government

System Republic. The president is head of state and executive head of government. The National Assembly, which is a forum for debate and the development of policy, has 325 members; the Legislative Yuan, which decides on constitutional changes, has 160 members.

Main political parties Kuomintang (KMT, Nationalist Party), Democratic Progressive Party

Climate and topography

Subtropical, moderated by the Kuroshio Current, resulting in long warm summers (25–30°C, 77–86°F) and mild winters (15°C, 59°F). The island is divided by a mountain range running north-south. Steep mountains on east side; west is terraced with alluvial plains.

People and society

Population m	21.1	% under 15	25.1
Pop. per sq km	571.2	% over 60	7.8
% urban	...	No. women per 100 men	95.0
% av. ann. growth 1980–95	0.8	Human Development Index	...
No. households m	5.5		

Life expectancy	yrs	Education	
Men	72	Spending as % of GDP	6.5
Women	77	Years of compulsory education	...
Crude birth rate	14.3	Adult literacy %	92.0
Crude death rate	5.8	Primary school enrolment %	93
Infant mortality		Secondary school enrolment %	59
per 1,000 live births	5.0	Tertiary education enrolment %	12

Workforce	% of total	Consumer goods ownership	
Services	...		per 1,000 people
Industry	...	Cars	63.0
Agriculture	...	Televisions	312.0
% of pop. over 15 in workforce	...	Mobile telephones	...
		Personal computers	...

Ethnic groups	% of total	Religious groups	% of total
Han Chinese	98	Buddhist	43
Indonesian	2	Taoist	21
		Christian	7

Tourism		Health	
Tourist arrivals m	2.3	Spending as % of GDP	...
Tourism receipts $bn	3.1	People per doctor	961.0

TAJIKISTAN

Of all the former Soviet republics in Central Asia, Tajikistan has had the most troubled period of independence. Unhappily, its problems are likely to continue.

History: first the people, then the country

The Persian-speaking Tajiks were once part of the Bukharan emirate (a protectorate of Tsarist Russia since 1876), but in 1924 the victorious Russian Bolsheviks annexed the area and made it an autonomous republic within the Uzbek Soviet Socialist Republic. Five years later Tajikistan became a full republic within the Soviet Union. In retrospect the 1924 decision may have been a mistake, creating lasting tensions between Tajikistan and Uzbekistan. Equally mistaken was the notion that communism, imposed with repressive force, could supplant Islam as the main influence for most Tajiks.

After August 1991, when Tajikistan became independent following the dissolution of the Soviet Union, an anti-communist opposition emerged which combined supporters of Islam, secularism and minority rights. In November 1991, Rakhmon Nabiev was elected president, interpreting as his mandate the restoration of old-style communism.

The result was civil war, with Mr Nabiev forced out of office by Islamists and secularists in September 1992. The presidency was abolished and Imamali Rakhmonov, the parliamentary speaker, became the de facto head of state. But he was unacceptable to the Islamic-democratic alliance and the civil war resumed. The presidential system was restored in November 1994, and by June 1997 President Rakhmonov, prodded by Russian mediators, had signed a peace agreement with the Islamic Renaissance Party by which the opposition would take part in a coalition government. Prospects for stability were hardly promising, however, not least because of the rise of the fundamentalist Muslim Taliban in neighbouring Afghanistan.

The economy: hostage to circumstances

Tajikistan, on a per head basis, was the poorest republic within the Soviet Union – and the loss of captive Soviet markets for its cotton crop has not improved matters. Neither have the years of civil war: laws passed in 1992 to liberalise the economy were nullified, and the same may prove true of the government's 1995 commitment largely to privatise agriculture and industry by 2000.

Total area	143,100 sq km	% agricultural area	6
Capital	Dushanbe	Highest point metres	Qullai
Other cities	Khuzande,		Kommunizm 7,495
	Kurgan-Tyube	Main rivers	Sydaryn, Amu Darya

The economy[a]

GDP $bn	2.0	GDP per head $	340
% av. ann. growth in		GDP per head in purchasing	
real GDP 1991–96	...	power parity $	920

Origins of GDP	% of total	Components of GDP	% of total
Agriculture	...	Private consumption	71
Industry	...	Public consumption	11
of which:		Investment	17
manufacturing	...	Exports	114
Services	...	Imports	114

Principal exports	% of total	Principal imports	% of total
Base metals	52.7	Mineral products	74.6
Textiles	29.2	Machinery & equipment	10.9
Mineral products	16.5	Food & agricultural produce	7.0

Government

System Republic with unicameral national legislature. Universal suffrage over age 18. The prime minister is appointed by the president.
Main political parties Communist Party, Party of National Unity, People's Party

Climate and topography

Continental, with mild winters and hot summers; semi-arid to polar in Pamir mountains. The Pamir and Altay mountains dominate the landscape; the Fergana valley is in the north, and the Kofarnihon and Vakhsh valleys in the south-west.

People and society

Population m	6.0	% under 15	...
Pop. per sq km	42.0	% over 60	7.0
% urban	32.0	No. women per 100 women	100.0
% av. ann. growth 1980–95	2.6	No. households m	...
Human Development Index	58.0		

Ethnic groups	% of total	Religious groups	% of total
Tajik	65	Sunni Muslim	80
Uzbek	25	Shia Muslim	5
Russian	4		

a 1995.

THAILAND

Total area	514,000 sq km	Population	59.4m
GDP	$159.6bn	GDP per head	$2,740
Capital	Bangkok	Other cities	Songkhla, Chon Buri, Nakhon Si Thammarat, Chiang Mai

The Kingdom of Thailand dreams of maturing into the next Asian economic "dragon" (after Singapore, Hong Kong, Taiwan and South Korea) and becoming the leading power in its region. And why not? It can point to abundant natural resources; well-equipped armed forces; a sizeable population; and a record of strong economic growth. The process is, however, threatened by an uneven distribution of wealth, especially between the capital, Bangkok, and the deprived countryside; pervasive corruption; and a continuing tradition of political uncertainty.

History: "Land of the Free"

Thailand can – and does – boast that it is the only nation in South-East Asia never to have fallen under colonial rule. Indeed, its official name, Prathet Thai, means "Land of the Free". The Thai people, who arrived from China around 1,000 years ago, rebelled against the ruling Khmers and formed the Sukhothai kingdom in about 1220. This gave way in 1350 to the kingdom of Ayutthaya, which spent the next two centuries in constant conflict with the neighbouring (and at times victorious) Burmese.

But the foundations of modern Thailand were really laid by the Chakkri dynasty that came to power in 1782, established its capital in Bangkok and progressively extended the rule of Siam – as the nation was known until 1939 – south along the Malay peninsula, north into Laos and east into Cambodia. Thai ambitions, however, had to be reconciled with imperial Europe. In 1867 the kingdom ceded its claim on Cambodia to France and later recognised French control over Laos. Meanwhile, King Chulalongkorn (whose father, Mongkut, was the model for the musical "The King and I") began to westernise the institutions of the state. In particular, he introduced cabinet government and created a standing army and modern civil service.

Those reforms have helped preserve Thai independence, as has the country's pragmatism: in 1917 the kingdom entered the first world war on the side of the Allies; in the second world war it sided with Japan. From the mid-1960s onwards, however, it has allied itself with America, initially as a defence against communist Indochina and now because it is the largest market for Thai exports.

Politics: bedevilled by coups

In form, Thailand has been a constitutional monarchy with a parliamentary government ever since a bloodless coup in 1932 revoked the absolute powers of King Prajadhipok. In substance, however, the monarch holds an almost divine status for most Thais (*lèse majesté* is a very serious offence) and the elected government can operate only with the consent of the armed forces. In a bicameral National Assembly, the Senate is appointed by the king for a term of six years; the House of Representatives is directly elected by universal suffrage for a four-year term. The king appoints the prime minister on the advice of the National Assembly, and appoints the Council of Ministers on the advice of the prime minister.

Volatile mixture

This formula has proved inherently unstable, with at least 17 coups or attempted coups from the abolition of the absolute monarchy to the military putsch on February 23rd 1991 by the National Peace-Keeping Council (NPKC). Not surprisingly, perhaps, there have been long periods of martial law and numerous constitutions. The political debate is dominated not by issues but by personalities and patronage. Retired soldiers and business chieftains dominate most of the 15 or so political parties (the strongest of which are the Chart Thai, the New Aspiration Party, Social Action and the Democrats). Corruption is pervasive and was cited by the NPKC as one reason for the coup against the civilian government of (ex-General) Chatichai Choonhavan.

Nonetheless, Thailand's politics have matured. Until the 1980s civilian governments were a rarity. The strongman for most of the 1950s was Field Marshal Pibul Songgram, an admirer of German fascism who had been prime minister in 1939. Subsequent military dictators included Field Marshal Sarit Thanarat in the 1960s and General Thanom Kittikachorn in the 1970s. Although student protests ousted Thanom's government in 1973, their repetition in late 1976 was an excuse for the military to resume control until the 1979 elections promised by General Kriangsak.

The 1980s: an open verdict on democracy

After such turbulence, the 1980s was a decade in which civilian government, under the appointed prime minister, (ex-General) Prem Tinsulanonda, appeared to have established itself despite attempted coups in 1981 and 1985. The Prem governments coincided with rapid economic development. Although the apparent excesses after 1988 of the

Chatichai government meant that the 1991 coup was well received, most Thais – including much of the military – now associate prosperity with civilian democracy. Indeed, one of the first actions of the NPKC was to set up a government of civilian technocrats; another was to promise a new constitution and fully democratic elections within a year. However, those elections, held in March 1992, led to a crisis when the unelected General Suchinda Kraprayoon, leader of the 1991 coup, emerged as prime minister. Massive street protests followed. After the military killed scores of demonstrators, Suchinda resigned in June and the king appointed the civilian, Anand Panyarachun, as interim prime minister. After a constitutional amendment requiring an elected prime minister, elections in September returned an anti-military government under Chuan Leekpai, who was succeeded in 1995 by Banharn Silapa-arch. Two years later Chuan was back as prime minister, seen as a stabilising factor in a period of financial crisis.

The challenges ahead

If civilian democracy is to become permanent it must deal with the problems of economic growth. Just as the military governments of earlier, poorer decades were challenged by communism, so future governments will have to reduce corruption and narrow the now-widening economic gap between the capital and the rest of the country. This is the need first outlined in early 1987 by the armed forces commander, General Chaovalit Yongchaiyudh. The general, who later formed the New Aspiration Party and became prime minister in 1996, defined the need as a "*patiwat*", or peaceful revolution.

For this to happen, the monarchy must remain the stable base of the nation. There are, however, fears that Crown Prince Vajiralongkorn will fail to achieve the stature and popularity of his father, King Bhumibol Adulyadej, who became the ninth Chakkri king in 1946 after his older brother was found shot dead. Some believe that, if the tradition of male rule could be set aside, Princess Mahachakri Sirindhorn would make a better successor to her father.

Foreign policy: against communism

Thailand's foreign policy has always been conditioned by its fear of Vietnam. In modern times, this fear was justified by the victorious progress from the 1950s to the 1970s of Vietnam's communists against first the colonial French and then the Americans and the American-backed government of South Vietnam. What worsened Thai fears was the spread of communism into neighbouring Laos and Cambodia, the activity of a vigorous communist insurgency within Thailand itself and the invasion of Cambodia by Vietnamese troops in December 1978.

Uncle Sam and ASEAN

The Thai response has been twofold: it has allied itself firmly with America (and has allowed American weaponry to be stored on Thai soil); and it has been a committed founder member of the Association of South-East Asian Nations (ASEAN), which was determined to halt Vietnam's communism (even by supporting, in effect, the Cambodian Khmer Rouge guerrillas of the genocidal Pol Pot).

Ironically, however, Thailand's best defence has probably been its economic dynamism and communist Indochina's economic incompetence. By the 1980s Thailand's own communists had virtually disappeared.

Pointers to the future

These developments gave Chatichai Choonhavan, prime minister from August 1988 to February 1991, the opportunity for a sudden change in foreign policy. Breaking with the ASEAN position, he invited Hun Sen, prime minister of the Vietnamese-backed government in Cambodia, to Bangkok in January 1989 for talks. This was part of Chatichai's desire to turn Indochina from a "battlefield into a marketplace", with Thailand as the most powerful market-maker. Similar self-interest led, after three months of border fighting, to a rapprochement with Laos in early 1988 and, at the end of that year, to closer relations with the military regime in Myanmar. Thai officials envisage a "Golden Pentagon" – Thailand, Myanmar, Laos, Vietnam and Cambodia – complete with tremendous natural resources and a market of over 120m people.

Society: consensus and harmony

Thai culture prefers consensus to conflict, harmony to argument. In consequence, Thais have a keen sense of social hierarchy: the king is at the apex of a pyramid whose steps are defined by myriad nuances of language and gesture. Although Chinese blood runs in the veins of probably a third of the population (some of the biggest business families are ethnically Chinese), the Thais regard themselves as an ethnically homogeneous society. Some 95% are Buddhist; the small Muslim population (4% of the total population) along the southern border is ethnically Malay and, indeed, speaks Malay as its first language. In the past, the Muslims have demanded independence from Thailand, but their armed struggle has now fizzled out.

A potentially more serious social divide is between the investment-favoured area around Bangkok and the poor north, where the main city, Chiang Mai, has a population of only 102,000. The hill tribes are reduced to subsistence agriculture, or often smuggling and opium-growing.

The economy: aspiring to dragon status

In each of the past two decades Thailand's economy has doubled in size and Thai officials predict a similar doubling of GDP during the 1990s. Since this implies average economic growth of over 7% a year, while the population is growing by only 1.5% a year (thanks, in part, to a well-organised family planning programme), individual Thais are clearly enjoying an ever-improving standard of living.

This is especially so in the industrial region in and around Bangkok, which is home for over a tenth of the country's population. Whereas in the mid-1960s agriculture accounted for a third of GDP, by the mid-1990s its share was down to less than 12% (although it still employed two-thirds of the workforce). By contrast, the share held by manufacturing rose from 14% to more than 28%. The services sector – with tourism having been the country's leading source of foreign exchange since 1982 – doubled in size during the 1980s and now provides about half of Thailand's GDP.

The virtues of prudence

Such economic well-being is evidence in part of prudent economic management. Until the currency crisis of 1997 Thailand had avoided "boom-bust" cycles and had carefully limited its foreign borrowings (the debt-service ratio to export earnings at the end of 1996 was only just over 10%). It is also proof of the country's natural advantages: a fertile central plain that allows Thailand to be the world's largest rice exporter; valuable deposits of precious stones, as well as tin and other minerals; and tourist attractions that include ubiquitous night-life (some estimates put the number of prostitutes at well over 500,000), Buddhist temples in Bangkok, opium-growing hill tribes in the north and beautiful beaches and islands in the south. In addition, the Thai population provides both cheap labour and a sizeable domestic market.

Not surprisingly, therefore, Thailand during the 1980s

was the favourite South-East Asian destination for direct foreign investment, especially from Japan and latterly Taiwan. This has generated manufactured exports from garments and toys to integrated circuits and computer disk drives, more than compensating for the falling prices of traditional exports such as rice, rubber and tapioca.

Growing problems

But pell-mell economic growth sustained over such a long period is bound to carry a cost. One sign has been a growing current-account deficit, because of the imports of capital goods and other manufacturing inputs. Other costs have been lax banking standards. In mid-1997 these led to a full-blown currency crisis, IMF intervention and the closing of more than 50 financial institutions. Environmental damage is equally worrying. Increased cultivation, some of it by hill tribes using slash-and-burn methods to clear ground, and irresponsible logging combined to reduce Thailand's forests by 2.5% a year in the period 1980–88. After deforestation had allowed devastating floods in the south, a royal decree in January 1989 banned all commercial logging (hence the rush to make logging deals with Myanmar). Meanwhile, the tourism industry (which handles over 5m arrivals a year) complains of inadequate water supplies and sewerage, and in Bangkok, whose traffic congestion is worsened by 400 new cars on the streets a week, the quality of air and water is frequently appalling.

Facing up to the challenges

The challenge for Thailand, therefore, is to put in place an adequate infrastructure before the country is poisoned by its own economic progress. But if that progress is to continue, it must also upgrade its industries to avoid being undercut by cheaper labour from competitors such as India, Sri Lanka or, indeed, Vietnam.

The government is certainly aware of the challenge, and of the need to increase the savings rate in order to finance the necessary investment (the country has suffered a persistent resource gap between savings and investment). Official policies are geared to favour the private sector and to attract foreign capital and expertise; an infrastructure programme has been launched to provide Bangkok with a mass transit system and 6m new telephone lines; and a deep-water port and associated industries are being developed around Laem Chabang east of Bangkok. Add financial self-discipline and Thailand may grow into a proper "dragon".

Total area	514,000 sq km	% agricultural area	58
Capital	Bangkok	Highest point metres	Doi Inthanan
Other cities	Songkhla, Chon Buri,		2,595
Nakhon Si Thammarat, Chiang Mai		Main rivers	Mekong, Chao Phraya

The economy[a]

GDP $bn	159.6	GDP per head $	2,740
% av. ann. growth in		GDP per head in purchasing	
real GDP 1991–96	...	power parity $	7,540

Origins of GDP	% of total	Components of GDP	% of total
Agriculture	11	Private consumption	54
Industry	40	Public consumption	10
of which:		Investment	43
manufacturing	29	Exports	42
Services	49	Imports	48

Structure of manufacturing

			% of total
Agric. & food processing	55	Other	26
Textiles & clothing	8	Av. ann. increase in industrial	
Machinery & transport	9	output 1991–96	...

Inflation and exchange rates

Consumer price 1996 av. ann. incr.	5.9%	Baht per $ 1997 average	31.36
Av. ann. rate 1991–96	4.8%	Baht per $ end-1997	47.25

Balance of payments, reserves and debt

			$bn
Exports, goods & services	70.3	Net capital account	...
Imports, goods & services	82.2	Net direct & portfolio investment	5.3
Net income	-2.1	Other net investment	16.7
Net current transfers	0.5	Net errors & omissions	-1.2
Current-account balance	-13.6	Net change in reserves	-7.2
as % of GDP	-8.5	Level of reserves, end-Dec.	36.9
Foreign debt	56.8	Debt service	4.6
as % of GDP	35.3	as % of export earnings	10.2

Principal exports	$bn fob	Principal imports	$bn cif
Computers & parts	6.5	Capital goods	33.3
Textiles	5.4	Raw materials & intermediates	18.7
Integrated circuits	2.3	Consumer goods	7.6
Rice	2.0	Fuel & lubricants	6.2
Footwear	1.3		

Main export destinations	% of total	Main origins of imports	% of total
United States	18.0	Japan	28.3
Japan	16.8	United States	12.5
Singapore	12.9	Singapore	5.5
Hong Kong	5.8	Germany	5.1
China	3.6	Taiwan	5.0

Government

System Constitutional monarchy. The king is head of state and appoints a prime minister on the advice of a bicameral national assembly. The 268 members of the non-party senate are appointed by the king for 6 years, and the 357 members of the house of representatives are elected for a 4-year term.

Main political parties New Aspiration, Democrat Party, Chart Pattana, Chart Thai, Social Action Party, Prachakorn Thai, Solidarity Party, Seritham, Muan Chon

Climate and topography

Tropical and humid, with an average annual temperature of 29°C (85°F). There are 3 main seasons: hot, rainy and cool. The country has a short coastline on the Indian Ocean and a long Pacific coastline.

People and society

Population m	59.4	% under 15	29.8
Pop. per sq km	114.0	% over 60	7.0
% urban	36.0	No. women per 100 men	100.0
% av. ann. growth 1980–95	1.5	Human Development Index	83.3
No. households m	12.7		

Life expectancy	*yrs*	**Education**	
Men	67	Spending as % of GDP	3.8
Women	72	Years of compulsory education	6
Crude birth rate	17	Adult literacy %	93.5
Crude death rate	6	Primary school enrolment %	98
Infant mortality		Secondary school enrolment %	37
per 1,000 live births	35	Tertiary education enrolment %	19

Workforce	*% of total*	**Consumer goods ownership**	
Services	22		*per 1,000 people*
Industry	14	Cars	178.5
Agriculture	64	Televisions	221.0
% of pop. over 15 in workforce	57	Mobile phones	18.5
		Personal computers	15.3

Ethnic groups	*% of total*	**Religious groups**	*% of total*
Thai	54	Buddhist	95
Lao	28	Muslim	4
Chinese	11		
Malay	4		

Tourism		**Health**	
Tourist arrivals m	5.2	Spending as % of GDP	5.3
Tourism receipts $bn	8.5	People per doctor	4,416.0

a 1995.

TURKMENISTAN

Of all the former Soviet republics in Central Asia Turkmenistan has done the least to reform its politics and economy. Whether that will make for an easier future is doubtful.

History: a matter of geography

The region of what is now Turkmenistan was always bound to tempt Russia – as a friendly bridge to Iran and as a buffer in the days of colonial India against the British. Accordingly, Tsarist Russia bloodily conquered the area in 1881 and established the Tsarist province of Transcaspia.

When the Bolsheviks overthrew the Tsar in 1917, Transcaspia was seized by their opponents, supported by a small British force sent from Iran and India. However, the British withdrew in 1919 and the anti-Bolshevik resistance gradually faded. In 1924, in their national delimitation of Central Asia, the Bolsheviks established the Turkmen Soviet Socialist Republic. Bolshevik rule brought education and some female emancipation, but no fundamental shift to communism: while the political leadership was dominated by ethnic Russians, the republic remained a confederation of Turkmen tribes, allowed considerable autonomy (and a thriving black market) in return for loyalty to Moscow.

That recipe had widespread support: in March 1991 some 95% of the population voted to keep the Soviet Union intact. Within months the USSR was dissolved and Turkmenistan (following a 95% vote in favour) declared independence in December 1991 with Saparmurad Niyazov continuing as president. A May 1992 constitution strengthened his powers, and in June 1992 he was the sole candidate for the presidency and then appointed himself as prime minister. In January 1994 a referendum, with a turn-out of 99.9%, approved by a 99.9% vote the cancellation of the 1997 election, so allowing Mr Niyazov to remain in office until 2002.

The economy: a need for action

Before independence Turkmenistan exported its cotton and oil and gas to the rest of the Soviet Union at prices well below world levels. Now it says that former Soviet republics should pay higher prices, ignoring the inability of countries such as Ukraine to do so. Nonetheless, in 1993 Mr Niyazov announced a ten-year programme of prosperity and welfare, with free bread and basic utilities apparently to come. Reforms, such as full property rights and the partial privatisation of key sectors, will surely come, but through necessity rather than instinct.

Total area	488,100 sq km	% agricultural area	2
Capital	Ashgabat	Highest point metres	Ayrybaba 3,139
Other cities	Chardzhou, Mary, Nebit-Dag	Main rivers	–

The economy[a]

GDP $bn	4.1	GDP per head $	920
% av. ann. growth in real GDP 1991–96	...	GDP per head in purchasing power parity $	...

Origins of GDP	% of total	Components of GDP	% of total
Agriculture	...	Private consumption	...
Industry	...	Public consumption	...
of which:		Investment	...
manufacturing	...	Exports	...
Services	...	Imports	...

Principal exports	% of total	Principal imports	% of total
Oil & gas	72.6	Agricultural & food products	25.1
Textiles	24.7	Misc manufactured goods	13.3
Food & agricultural products	0.6	Machinery & equipment	13.0
Chemicals	0.6	Base metals	11.4
Base metals	0.2	Chemical products	7.5

Government
System Republic with universal suffrage over age 18. The People's Council is the ultimate representative body. The smaller Assembly is the main legislature.
Main political parties Democratic Party of Turkmenistan, Peasant Justice Party

Climate and topography
Subtropical desert, rising to mountains in the south along the Iranian border.

People and society

Population m	5.0	% under 15	...
Pop. per sq km	10.0	% over 60	...
% urban	45.0	No. women per 100 men	102.0
% av. ann. growth 1980–95	3.0	No. households m	...
Human Development Index	72.3		

Ethnic groups	% of total	Religious groups	% of total
Turkmen	73	Muslim	87
Russian	10	Eastern Orthodox	11
Uzbek	9		

a 1995.

UZBEKISTAN

The most populous of the ex-Soviet republics of Central Asia, the Republic of Uzbekistan has controversial ambitions to play a defining role in Central Asia.

History: a question of identity

Uzbekistan has its origins in the medieval khanates of Transoxania which, in the 1860s and 1870s, came under the sway of Tsarist Russia and became the protected khanates of Bukhara and Khiva. In 1923 Russia's Bolsheviks annexed the protectorates – overriding the Basmachi guerrilla resistance – and in 1924 proclaimed the Uzbek Soviet Socialist Republic (which included most of what is now Tajikistan). The population consisted of Turkic-speakers, who came to be known as Uzbeks, and Persian-speakers later known as Tajiks, with the usually bilingual town-dwellers being known as the Sart. One lasting consequence of the establishment of the republic was the creation of rival Uzbek and Tajik nationalism in the region.

Initially, control of the country was in the hands of ethnic Russians, but after the second world war local Uzbek communists began to take over. The dominant figure was Sharaf Rashidov, the ruthless head of the republic's Communist Party from 1961 to 1983. Attempts by the Soviet leader, Mikhail Gorbachev, in the late 1980s to eliminate corruption and to introduce political and economic liberalisation were successfully resisted by the local communists, who regarded the old-style USSR as a political and economic life-line.

Following the collapse of the Soviet Union Uzbekistan became independent in September 1991, since when it has in practice been run as a quasi-dictatorship, with President Islam Karimov having inherited the Rashidov mantle. Partly out of fear that Afghanistan's unrest will spread north, Mr Karimov is keen to promote Turkic solidarity, with Uzbekistan as the leader of a Central Asian "Turkestan".

The economy: in need of help

Uzbekistan remains a mostly agricultural economy, with cotton – introduced a century ago by the Russians – as the dominant crop. Unfortunately, three-fifths of the country is desert. Of the country's oil and gas output, most is consumed domestically. The Karimov government has received help from the European Union, the EBRD and the IMF, but foreign donors are unimpressed by the Uzbek record on human rights and economic reform.

Total area	447,400 sq km	% agricultural area	10
Capital	Tashkent	Highest point metres	Adelunga Toghi
Other cities	Samarkand,		3,301
	Andizhan, Namangan	Main rivers	Amu Darya, Sirdaryo

The economy[a]

GDP $bn	22.0	GDP per head $	970
% av. ann. growth in		GDP per head in purchasing	
real GDP 1991–96	...	power parity $	2,370

Origins of GDP	% of total	Components of GDP	% of total
Agriculture	33	Private consumption	59
Industry	34	Public consumption	25
of which:		Investment	23
manufacturing	18	Exports	63
Services	34	Imports	62

Principal exports	% of total	Principal imports	% of total
Cotton fibre	48.4	Machinery & equipment	35.8
Energy	11.7	Foodstuffs	29.5
Metals	4.6	Chemicals & related products	12.5
Chemicals & related products	2.5	Metals	6.7

Government

System Republic with universal suffrage over age 18. The unicameral legislature has little power.

Main political parties People's Democratic Party, Homeland Progress, Justice, National Revival

Climate and topography

Desert with long, hot summers and mild winters. Mostly flat with rolling sandy desert. Mountainous borders with Tajikistan and Kirgizstan.

People and society

Population m	23.0	% under 15	...
Pop. per sq km	55.0	% over 60	7.0
% urban	42.0	No. women per 100 men	102.0
% av. ann. growth 1980–95	2.4	No. households m	...
Human Development Index	66.2		

Ethnic groups	% of total	Religious groups	% of total
Uzbek	71	Muslim	88
Russian	8	Eastern Orthodox	9
Tajik	5		
Kazakh	4		

a 1995.

VIETNAM

Total area	329,566 sq km	Population	73m
GDP	$17.6bn	GDP per head	$240
Capital	Hanoi	Other cities	Ho Chi Minh, Hue

The Socialist Republic of Vietnam could become Asia's most dynamic economy: its growth starts from a low base; it has a large, disciplined, literate and cheap workforce; and it is in the centre of a prospering region which has capital to invest. To exploit this potential, however, will demand the continued restructuring of Vietnam's politics.

History: defeating the foreigner

Vietnam emerged as an ethnically distinct country in about 200 BC, but in 111 BC it was conquered by the Chinese. It broke free in AD 939, but in subsequent eras, despite repelling three Mongol invasions in the 13th century, frequently came under China's effective control.

By the 19th century China's influence had given way to France's. In 1867 Cochin-China (the southern part of Vietnam) became a French colony; in 1883 Annam and Tonkin (central and northern Vietnam) became French protectorates. Soon, all three regions were joined with Laos and Cambodia to form French Indochina.

In September 1940 the Japanese occupied Vietnam, with the co-operation of the French authorities. In March 1945 the Japanese formally ended French rule, only to surrender to the allies the following August. This, in turn, allowed the Vietnamese nationalist, Ho Chi Minh, to lead his independence fighters into Hanoi; on September 2nd 1945 Ho proclaimed himself president of the independent Democratic Republic of Vietnam.

Ho's struggle

The declaration was premature. In March 1946 French forces re-entered Vietnam, which was then recognised as a "free" state within the French Union. War broke out in December. Finally, in May 1954, Ho's guerrillas defeated the French at Dien Bien Phu. Two months later the Geneva Agreements partitioned Vietnam into the French-controlled South and the communist North along the 17th parallel. Later in 1954 the French withdrew from the South, whose prime minister, Ngo Dinh Diem, the following year proclaimed himself president of the Republic of Vietnam.

Diem refused to hold elections and guerrilla pressure, supported by the North, worsened. In 1961, during the Kennedy administration, American military advisers arrived to help Diem against the National Front for the Liberation of Vietnam. By the end of the year their number had increased from 800 to 18,000 and they were authorised to take part in combat.

America's role

The American presence increased rapidly, especially after the assassination (perhaps with CIA involvement) of the unpopular Diem in 1963. After a reported attack on an American destroyer in the Gulf of Tonkin in August 1964, President Johnson authorised the bombing of the North. By 1967 there were 389,000 American troops in Vietnam.

Ho's Viet Cong forces launched a Tet (lunar new year) offensive on January 30th 1968. The following year, as the war became increasingly unpopular within America, President Nixon withdrew some forces – by now numbering over 500,000 – and encouraged the "Vietnamisation" of the South's military struggle.

The policy was as ineffectual as the Paris peace talks, begun a year earlier. Despite the death of Ho in 1969, the war expanded, with America in 1970 attacking Viet Cong bases in Cambodia and bombing Viet Cong forces in Laos. Then in July 1972 America's Secretary of State, Henry Kissinger, began new peace talks in Paris. The following January an accord was signed under which the Americans withdrew, leaving the 17th parallel to divide the country pending reunification by "peaceful means".

So much for good intentions. At the end of 1974 the communists launched a big offensive and on April 30th 1975 Saigon surrendered. On July 2nd 1976 the country was officially reunited as the Socialist Republic of Vietnam.

Politics: party rule

Vietnam's legislative power is vested in a National Assembly elected every five years with a maximum of 400 members. It elects from them the Council of State and the Council of Ministers. There are two puppet parties, the Democratic Party (founded in 1944) and the Socialist Party (founded in 1946). Real power rests with the 2m-strong Communist Party of Vietnam.

The party's leadership won many wars, but then lost the peace so disastrously that Vietnam is now one of the world's poorest countries. However, the leadership is changing. The Seventh Party Congress in June 1991 decided to retire seven of the 12-man politburo, so reducing the average age from 71 to 64. The new politburo contained five southerners – who have a more liberal tradition than northerners – compared with one previously. In addition, Vo Van Kiet, a southerner and liberal, was made prime minister (chairman of the Council of Ministers).

The consequences became clear in April 1992, when the National Assembly adopted a new constitution. The 1980 constitution had declared Vietnam a "proletarian dictatorship ... run on the principles of socialism"; the new constitution preserved the "leadership" of the Communist Party but guaranteed several economic freedoms, decreeing, for example, that property cannot be nationalised. In 1997 the liberal Phan Van Khai became prime minister – but the less liberal General Le Kha Phieu became party leader.

Foreign policy: desperately making friends

The new constitution also dropped all references to Vietnam's wars against France, America and China (which made a brief, abortive attack in February 1979 to punish Vietnam for its occupation in December 1978 of Cambodia).

This represents a complete reassessment of the country's place in the world. After the fall of Saigon in April 1975 (it was then renamed Ho Chi Minh City), Vietnam saw itself as a regional power, with the Soviet Union as its superpower sponsor. This showed in the conquest of Cambodia, whose Khmer Rouge government under Pol Pot Vietnam was considered both too nasty and too aggressive. This, in turn, provoked the attack by China, which was both a traditional enemy of Vietnam (although an ally in its war of liberation) and at odds with the Soviet Union. In addition, China and Vietnam had clashed in 1974 over their rival claims to the Spratly Islands (another clash took place in 1988).

The reassessment was forced by two things: America's refusal to allow communism to spread; and the economic strain of an American trade and investment embargo.

The Cambodian catalyst

As early as 1984 Vietnam had agreed in principle to withdraw its 100,000 troops from Cambodia. The pressure was stepped up in the late 1980s by the Soviet president, Mikhail Gorbachev, who was keen to reduce the aid that kept Vietnam economically afloat. In April 1989 Vietnam and its puppet Cambodian regime under Heng Samrin promised that by September all Vietnamese soldiers would be withdrawn. It seems that the promise was more or less kept. A year later secret negotiations began with China, and by the end of 1991 the relationship had been normalised.

The same could not be said of relations with America. In April 1991 America outlined a four-stage "road map": first, discussions on normalisation; second, the establishment of a UN peacekeeping force in Cambodia would be followed by a partial lifting of the American embargo on Vietnam and a greater lifting of the embargo on Cambodia; third, six months after the UN's arrival in Cambodia, both embargoes would end and America would stop its opposition to lending by the World Bank and other agencies; fourth, elections in Cambodia would be matched by a full normalisation of America's relations with Vietnam. In return, Vietnam would co-operate over the 2,293 Americans "missing in action" during the Vietnam war. The map worked: early in 1994 the American embargoes ended.

Subsequently, in 1995, Vietnam joined the regional community, the Association of South-East Asian Nations (ASEAN), whose origins lay in a common opposition to Vietnam.

The only remaining foreign policy issue was that of the "boat people". Since the fall of Saigon well over 1.5m Vietnamese had fled. Half had found sanctuary in America, but America's "compassion fatigue" had since stranded thousands in South-East Asia, notably Hong Kong. Most were classified as "economic migrants", liable, under a Geneva accord reached in July 1989, to forced repatriation. The first such repatriation, of 51 boat people in Hong Kong, took place in December 1989. An agreement covering all 55,700 of Hong Kong's boat people was reached in 1992.

Society: the north-south divide

The division of North and South has survived reunification: the southerners, not least because of the Chinese in Ho Chi Minh City, have a tradition of entrepreneurship; the northerners are more steeped in communist orthodoxy.

The economy: poor but promising

Vietnam is one of the world's poorest countries. The sense of crisis worsened in January 1991 when the Soviet Union, before its collapse, ended its aid and concessional trade and sent back its Vietnamese contract workers.

Paradoxically, the future is bright. Vietnam has coal, petroleum and other minerals and an agricultural sector ranging from rice to rubber and timber. Fine beaches promise a future tourist industry. An economic restructuring programme, *"doi moi"*, was begun in 1986; the following year one of Asia's most liberal foreign investment codes was enacted.

Total area	329,566 sq km	% agricultural area	25
Capital	Hanoi	Highest point metres	Fan Si Pan
Other cities	Ho Chi Minh, Hue		3,143
		Main rivers	Hong, Da, Mekong

The economy[a]

GDP $bn	17.6	GDP per head $	240.0
% av. ann. growth in		GDP per head in purchasing	
real GDP 1991–96	…	power parity $	…

Origins of GDP	% of total	Components of GDP	% of total
Agriculture	28	Private consumption	77
Industry	30	Public consumption	7
of which:		Investment	27
manufacturing	22	Exports	36
Services	42	Imports	47

Structure of manufacturing
			% of total
Agric. & food processing	…	Other	…
Textiles & clothing	…	Av. ann. increase in industrial	
Machinery & transport	…	output 1991–96	…

Inflation and exchange rates
Consumer price 1996 av. ann. incr.	6.5%	Dong per $ 1997 average	12,375.0
Av. ann. rate 1991–96	15.3%	Dong per $ end-1997	13,500.0

Balance of payments, reserves and debt
			$bn
Exports, goods & services	7.3	Net capital account	…
Imports, goods & services	9.5	Net direct & portfolio investment	…
Net income	-0.3	Other net investment	…
Net current transfers	0.5	Net errors & omissions	…
Current-account balance	-2.0	Net change in reserves	…
as % of GDP	-11.5	Level of reserves, end-Dec.	…
Foreign debt	26.5	Debt service	1.9
as % of GDP	114.6	as % of export earnings	5.2

Principal exports	% of total	Principal imports	% of total
Crude oil	18.5	Materials & fuel	56.1
Textiles & garments	15.9	Refined petroleum	9.7
Rice	11.8	Steel	4.7
Marine products	9.0	Machinery & equipment	33.2
Footwear	7.3	Consumer goods	10.7

Main export destinations[a]	% of total	Main origins of imports[a]	% of total
Japan	26.8	Singapore	17.5
Singapore	12.7	South Korea	15.4
Taiwan	8.1	Japan	11.2
China	6.6	Taiwan	11.1
Hong Kong	4.7	Thailand	5.4
South Korea	4.3	Hong Kong	5.1

Government
System Socialist republic. Political power rests in the hands of the Communist Party of Vietnam. The National Assembly (Quoc-Hoi) is elected for a 5-year term. It meets 3 times a year and appoints a prime minister and a cabinet. It also elects the president, who is head of state.
Main political parties Communist Party of Vietnam

Climate and topography
Tropical in south, monsoonal in north, with hot, rainy season (mid-May to mid-Sep) and warm, dry season (mid-Oct to mid-Mar). The land area is mostly mountainous rain forest, apart from river deltas in the north and south and a coastal plain.

People and society

Population m	73.0	% under 15	37.4
Pop. per sq km	226.0	% over 60	7.0
% urban	21.0	No. women per 100 men	103.0
% av. ann. growth 1980–95	2.1	Human Development Index	55.7
No. households m	...		

Life expectancy	yrs	Education	
Men	65	Spending as % of GDP	...
Women	70	Years of compulsory education	5
Crude birth rate	26	Adult literacy %	93.0
Crude death rate	7	Primary school enrolment %	111
Infant mortality		Secondary school enrolment %	35
per 1,000 live births	41	Tertiary education enrolment %	2

Workforce	% of total	Consumer goods ownership	
Services	15		per 1,000 people
Industry	14	Cars	33.0
Agriculture	71	Televisions	110.0
% of pop. over 15 in workforce	51	Mobile phones	0.2
		Personal computers	...

Ethnic groups	% of total	Religious groups	% of total
Vietnamese	88	Buddhist	55
Chinese	2	Christian	8
Thai	2		

Tourism		Health	
Tourist arrivals m	1.3	Spending as % of GDP	5.2
Tourist receipts $bn	0.1	People per doctor	2,279.0

a 1995.

=Part III=
APPENDICES

Glossary

ABRI (Indonesia)   Acronym for Indonesian armed forces.

Amok (Malay)   Running wild, a phenomenon that occasionally afflicts South-East Asians, culturally conditioned to hide their feelings even at times of stress.

ANZUS   Defence pact between Australia, New Zealand and the United States, signed in 1951. The pact was strained in 1984 when New Zealand's Labour government under David Lange banned visits by nuclear-powered or nuclear-armed ships.

APEC   Asia-Pacific Economic Co-operation, formed in 1989 at Australia's initiative as a trans-Pacific talking shop. Original members were Australia, New Zealand, the ASEAN states (at the time, six), South Korea, Japan, America and Canada. In 1991 they were joined by China, Hong Kong and Taiwan, inter-Chinese rivalries having been sidestepped, and then by Papua New Guinea, Chile and Mexico.

ASEAN   Association of South-East Asian Nations, formed in 1967 by Indonesia, Thailand, Malaysia, the Philippines and Singapore. Brunei joined on independence in 1984. Theoretically set up for economic co-ordination, in fact ASEAN's role was to oppose communist expansion from Vietnam. Times change: in 1995 Vietnam became a member; so too in 1997 did Laos and Myanmar (Cambodia's accession was delayed).

Bahasa (Malay)   The Malay word for "language", and by extension for the Malay language of Malaysia, Indonesia and Brunei. One of Singapore's official languages (and a requirement for its diplomats). Used as a qualification for citizenship in Brunei, so excluding most Chinese residents.

Barong (Philippines)   Filipino shirt for men. The tail is worn outside the trousers, originally at the command of Spanish colonisers to show the wearer was an inferior local. Nationalism reversed the snobbery, and the barong is now considered formal wear.

Bhumibol (Thai)   King Bhumibol Adulyadej (Rama IX) of Thailand's Chakkri dynasty. Born in 1927 and formally crowned king in 1950, four years after the mysterious death from a bullet wound of his elder brother. Also a saxophone-player and jazz-composer.

Buddha   Originally named Siddharta Gautama, Buddha – the enlightened one – lived from around 563 BC to 483 BC in north-east India. Buddhism is the philosophy of the "middle way": suffering is the result of one's desires, so to stop suffering there must be no desires, a state that ultimately leads to Nirvana (the "blowing out", the state of release when the individual is extinguished).

Bumiputra (Malay) Literally "son of the soil": Malaysia's aborigines and Malays, who as such benefit from affirmative economic and educational programmes.

Burakumin (Japan) Some 2m Japanese "untouchables", stigmatised by their work as tanners and butchers in the pre-Meiji era more than a century ago.

Cairns Group Some 14 unsubsidised agricultural exporters, led by Australia. Lobbies hard, but untriumphantly, against America's farm subsidies and the European Union's Common Agricultural Policy.

Cekong (Indonesia) Ethnic Chinese entrepreneurs who act as business agents for Indonesians.

Chaebol (Korea) Conglomerate, such as Hyundai.

Confucius China's most famous philosopher, lived 551–479 BC. He divided human relations into five categories: between ruler and subjects; between friends; between husband and wife; between parents and children; and between elder and younger brothers. Only between friends was there equality. The others involved obligation, which when kept led to social harmony. The Confucianist societies of East Asia therefore stress authority and obedience, although Mencius (371–289 BC), the "second sage" of Confucianism, upheld the right of the people to overthrow rulers intent only on power and profit.

Cultural Revolution (China) Launched by Mao Zedong in 1966 to renew the nation's revolutionary spirit. Urban youths were mobilised into the xenophobic Red Guards; they humiliated intellectuals and "class enemies", who were often sent to the countryside to work as peasants. Universities were closed. The madness ended with Mao's death in 1976 and the subsequent trial of the Gang of Four, led by Mao's wife, Chiang Ching.

Daoism See Taoism.

Doi moi (Vietnam) Vietnam's version of *perestroika*, an economic liberalisation begun in 1986.

Dwifungsi (Indonesia) Dual function; the part played by Indonesia's armed forces in defence and politics.

EAEG East Asian Economic Grouping (also called Caucus). A proposal in 1991 by Malaysia's prime minister, Dr Mahathir Mohamad, to unite ASEAN with Indochina, China, South Korea and Japan as a lobby to counter western supremacy. Many, including some invited to join, criticised the idea as an excuse for a trade bloc.

Endaka (Japan) Phenomenon of the strengthening yen, result of a meeting of finance ministers at New York's Plaza Hotel in 1985.

Fung shui (China) Literally, wind and water; geomancy,

or the balance of natural forces, extremely important to most Chinese, especially the businessmen of Hong Kong.

Guanxi (Chinese)   Connections, China's version of the Old School tie, or Old Boy network.

Juche (North Korea)   Self-reliance, a doctrine of Kim Il Sung that has impoverished North Korea.

Kampong (Malay)   The old-fashioned village in Indonesia and the Malay peninsula, except Singapore, where the kampongs were eliminated in favour of high-rise estates.

Karaoke (Japan)   Literally "empty orchestra"; entertainment where amateurs sing with pre-recorded backing music. Painfully popular in East Asia.

Karoshi (Japan)   Recently identified (but long common) syndrome of death through overwork.

Keiretsu   Cross-holdings by Japanese companies in one another's shares, leading to a loose form of conglomerate.

Kia su (Hokkien)   "Afraid to lose", a Singapore expression applied to swots afraid to fail their exams and more generally to the reluctance to show initiative for fear of embarrassing failure.

Kitsui, kitanai, kiken (Japan)   Hard, dirty and dangerous: description of the jobs increasingly done in Japan by illegal immigrants.

Kuomintang (Taiwan)   Nationalist Party, or KMT. Formed by Dr Sun Yat Sen, officially in 1919 but with roots in the earlier "Society for Regenerating China". On the communist victory in China in 1949, the KMT government of Chiang Kai-shek fled to Taiwan.

Macanese (Macau)   Eurasian inhabitants of Macau, Portugal's tiny colony on the South China coast.

Mai pen rai (Thai)   Never mind. A common, invariably useful expression in Thailand.

Merdeka (Malay)   Independence or freedom.

Pancasila (Indonesia)   Official and obligatory creed of Indonesia. First stipulated by Sukarno, its five elements are belief in one supreme god; belief in a just and civilised humanity; national unity; democracy; and social justice.

PAP (Singapore)   People's Action Party: founded by Lee Kuan Yew in 1954, it became Singapore's governing party three years later with self-government, and has ruled ever since. It started with a socialist ideology, now long abandoned.

PECC   Pacific Economic Co-operation Council: a non-governmental body set up in 1982 to link businessmen, government officials and academics from both developing and industrialised nations in the Pacific.

PPP (Pakistan)   Pakistan People's Party, founded in

December 1967 by Zulfikar Ali Bhutto, who took power in 1970 and was hanged in 1979. The PPP was subsequently led by Bhutto's daughter, Benazir.

Raj Rule, as in the British Raj in India.

Rohingyas (Myanmar) Muslims of Myanmar's Arakan province. Sometimes persecuted by Burman nationalists, leading the Rohingyas – as in 1991 – to seek refuge among fellow Muslims in Bangladesh.

SAARC South Asian Association for Regional Co-operation, launched in 1985. The world's most populous (and perhaps poorest) international body. Members are Bangladesh, Bhutan, India, the Maldives, Nepal, Pakistan and Sri Lanka – but India calls the tune.

Sarariman (Japan) Japanese version of salaryman, that is the fellow who risks *karoshi* in sustaining Japan's economic miracle.

Shinjinrui (Japan) Literally "new human race", or "new breed". Materialist, pleasure-seeking Japanese – therefore born after 1960 and frowned on by their parents.

Shinkansen (Japan) Bullet-train: speeds between Japan's cities and is rarely even a minute late.

Shunto (Japan) Regular spring wage offensive by Japan's trade unions. Often an opportunity for ritualised demonstrations.

Sultan Hereditary ruler, as in Brunei. Malaysia has nine, who take it in turns to be king.

Sumo (Japan) Style of Japanese wrestling, 1,200 years old, by grossly overweight men who yet possess balletic grace.

Suwannaphume (Thai) "Golden Land": term used by Thai prime minister, Chatichai Choonhaven, in 1989 to describe the vision of peace linking Indochina with ASEAN.

Taoism Religio-philosophical tradition (Tao is "the Way") developed in China 2,000 years ago. Life and death are simply different stages of the Absolute Tao. With its stress on individualism and spontaneity, it is in some ways the antithesis of Confucianism.

Three Noes (Taiwan) No contact, no negotiation, no compromise. Official Taiwan policy towards the communist "rebels" on the mainland. In practice, since 1987 there have been plenty of indirect contacts and negotiations.

Tunku (Malay) Malay prince. There are many in Malaysia. If they become sultans they rise above most of the law.

UMNO United Malays' National Organisation: founded in 1946 to strive for Malayan independence from Britain. The party has led all Malaysia's coalition governments, guarding

Malay political supremacy in the multi-ethnic nation.

UNTAC United Nations Transitional Authority in Cambodia, set up with 16,000 peace-keeping troops and a huge budget after Paris peace accord of October 1991, in order to prepare Cambodia for elections in May 1993.

Utang na loob (Tagalog) Philippine system of obligation: one favour demands another.

Yakuza (Japan) Gangster/criminal society (literally "good-for-nothing"). Japan's equivalent of the mafia originated in the 16th century, when unemployed samurai turned to crime. There are now over 2,000 gangs; they tend to be right-wing and ultra-nationalist, and they wield immense political power.

Zaibatsu (Japan) Big trading conglomerates, such as Mitsui, that were broken up by the competition-minded American occupation authorities at the end of the second world war.

Zaitek (Japan) Literally "financial technology" (as opposed to *haitek*, high technology): corporate, and personal, obsession in the 1980s with financial speculation.

Zen School of Buddhism developed in Japan in the 12th century. Zen masters teach pupils that enlightenment comes not from scriptures or ritual but by breaking beyond the boundaries of logical thought.

ZOPFAN Zone of Peace, Freedom and Neutrality, an idea originated by Malaysia in the early 1970s, but then pushed by Indonesia in the 1980s for South-East Asia.

Sources

The Asian Development Bank, *Asian Development Outlook.*

Asiaweek

CIA, *World Factbook*

The Economist Intelligence Unit, *Country Reports* and *Country Profiles.*
The Economist Intelligence Unit, *Country Risk Service.*

Encyclopedia Britannica

Europa Publications, *Europa – The Far East and Australasia.*
Europa Publications, *Europa World Year Book.*

FAO, *Production Yearbook.*

Heritage Foundation, *US & Asia Statistical Handbook.*

IISS, *The Military Balance.*

ILO, *Year Book of Labour Statistics.*

IMF, *International Financial Statistics.*
IMF, *National Government Statistics.*

OECD, *Development Co-operation in the 1990s.*

Statesman's Yearbook

UN, *World Population Prospects.*
UN Development Programme, *Human Development Report.*
UNESCO, *Statistical Yearbook.*

WHO, *World Health Statistics.*

World Bank, *World Debt Tables.*
World Bank, *World Development Indicators.*
World Bank, *World Development Report.*

Notes on data

Coverage

The country profiles cover 35 countries. The extent and quality of the statistics available vary from country to country. Every care has been taken to specify the broad definitions on which the data are based and to indicate cases where data quality or technical difficulties are such that interpretation of the figures is likely to be seriously affected. Nevertheless, figures from individual countries will often differ from standard international statistical definitions.

Statistical basis

The research for this section was carried out in early 1998 using the latest published sources. The data, therefore, unless otherwise indicated, refer to the year ending December 31st 1996. Exceptions are: purchasing power, origins and components of GDP, structure of manufacturing, population, life expectancy, education, workforce, consumer goods ownership and health data which, unless otherwise indicated, refer to 1995; ethnic and religious groups data refer to the latest year with available figures. Inflation and exchange rates are for the years indicated.

Figures may not add exactly to totals, or percentages to 100, because of rounding. Sums of money have generally been converted to US dollars at the official exchange rate ruling at the time to which the figures refer.

School enrolment ratios exceed 100% where pupils are included from outside the relevant age group.

UN data have been used for projections, based on medium-growth assumptions.

Definitions

Agricultural area   The area of arable land, land under permanent crops and pasture land expressed as a percentage of a country's total area.

Balance of payments   The record of a country's transactions with the rest of the world. The **current account** of the balance of payments consists of: exports of visible trade (goods) less imports of visible trade; "invisible" trade: receipts and payments for services such as banking, tourism and shipping plus dividend and interest payments and profit remittances; private transfer payments, such as remittances from those working abroad; official transfers, including payments to international organisations and some current expenditure aid flows (such as famine relief). Visible imports and exports are normally compiled on rather different definitions to those used in the trade statistics (shown in principal imports and exports) and therefore the statistics do not match. The **capital account** consists of long- and short-term transactions relating to a country's assets and liabilities (for example loans and borrowings). Adding the current to the capital account gives the overall balance. This is compensated by net monetary movements and changes in reserves. In practice methods of statistical recording are neither complete nor accurate and an errors and omissions item, sometimes quite large, will appear. Changes in reserves are shown without the practice of reversing the sign often followed in balance of payments presentations. They exclude monetary movements and therefore do not equal the overall balance.

Centrally planned economies
Statistics for the centrally planned economies are both scarce and unreliable.

Cif/fob When goods pass through customs and are recorded in trade statistics they are normally registered at their value at the point of passage through customs. Imports, which are valued at the point of entry to a country, will include the cost of "carriage, insurance and freight" (cif) from the exporting country to the importing one. The value of exports does not include these elements and is recorded "free on board" (fob). The value of imports will therefore automatically be greater than the equivalent amount of exports – in many cases by a factor of 10–12%. In most (but not all) countries the crude trade statistics record imports cif and exports fob; balance of payments statistics are generally adjusted so that imports are shown fob.

Cities The names of other cities in the statistical data refer to other major cities.

Crude birth rate The number of live births in a year per 1,000 population. The crude rate will automatically be high if a large proportion of the population is of childbearing age and low if this is not the case.

Crude death rate The number of deaths in one year per 1,000 population. Like the crude birth rate this is affected by the population's age structure. It will be high if there is a high proportion of old people in the population.

Debt, foreign Financial obligations owed by a country to the rest of the world and repayable in foreign currency. **Debt service** consists of interest payments on outstanding debt plus any principal repayments due. **The debt service ratio** is debt service expressed as a percentage of the country's earnings from exports of goods and services.

Enrolment ratio (gross) The number enrolled at a specific level of education, whether or not they belong to the age group relevant to that level, as a percentage of the total population in the relevant age group. The ratio can therefore be over 100% if children start an education stage early or stay in it late; conversely, a ratio below 100% can be consistent with full education if children of the appropriate age group have passed on early to the following stage.

GDP Gross Domestic Product. It is the sum of all output produced by economic activity within that country. Economic activity normally refers to goods and services that are exchanged for money or traded in a market system (activities such as housework, childcare by parents and household repairs or improvements carried out by occupiers are excluded). Subsistence farming and other activities that could potentially be exchanged for money are theoretically also included but national statistics vary in the extent to which they cover them.

GDP can be measured in three ways: by summing the output of all production (origins of GDP); by measuring all expenditure on a country's production and adding stockbuilding (components of GDP); or by measuring the income of businesses and individuals generated by the production of goods and services. The exports and imports figures shown in national accounts statistics are defined differently from visible and invisible exports and imports used in the balance of payments, notably by excluding interest, profits and dividends payments.

GDP can be measured either at "market prices", the prices at which goods and services are bought by consumers, or at "factor cost", the cost of producing an item excluding taxes and subsidies. In general the expenditure breakdown is shown at market prices and the production breakdown at factor cost. Data on total GDP generally refer to market prices. National income is obtained by deducting an estimate of depreciation of capital goods (capital consumption) from GDP.

The average annual increase in real GDP shows the growth in GDP excluding any increase due solely to the rise in prices.

Human Development Index   This index is an attempt by the United Nations Development Programme to assess levels of human development in various countries. It combines three measures: life expectancy, literacy and whether the average income, based on purchasing power parity (PPP) estimates (see below), is sufficient to meet basic needs. For each component a country's score is scaled according to where it falls between the minimum and maximum country scores; for income adequacy the maximum is taken as the official "poverty line" incomes in nine industrial countries. The scaled scores on the three measures are averaged to give the Human Development Index, shown here scaled from 0 to 100. Countries scoring less than 50 are classified as low human development, those from 50 to 80 as medium and those above 80 as high.

As with any statistical exercise of this sort the results are subject to caveats and the small number of indicators used places some limitations on its usefulness. The index should not be taken as a quality of life indicator since in particular it excludes any direct notion of freedom.

Inflation   The rate at which prices are increasing. The most common measure and the one shown here (but not the only one) is to take the increase in the consumer price index.

Level of reserves   Includes SDRs and foreign exchange, but excludes gold. The year referred to is 1996.

Life expectancy rates refer to the average length of time a baby born today can expect to live.

PPP   Purchasing Power Parity. Comparing GDP per head is an unsatisfactory way of comparing relative living standards since it does not take account of differences in prices of goods and services (the cost of living). PPP statistics adjust for cost of living differences by replacing normal exchange rates with rates designed to equalise the prices of a standard "basket" of goods and services. These are used to obtain PPP estimates of GDP per head.

Real terms   Figures adjusted to allow for inflation.

Abbreviations

bn	billion (one thousand million)
kg	kilogram
km	kilometre
GDP	Gross Domestic Product
m	million
PPP	Purchasing Power Parity
–	zero
...	not available